A COAT OF MANY COLOURS

By the same Author

*

MEMOIRS OF A SPECIAL CASE
THE WALLS OF JERUSALEM
A FEAST OF HISTORY

Under the pseudonym Jocelyn Davey
THE UNDOUBTED DEED
THE NAKED VILLAINY
A TOUCH OF STAGEFRIGHT
A KILLING IN HATS
A TREASURY ALARM

A COAT
OF MANY COLOURS

MEMOIRS OF A JEWISH
EXPERIENCE

Chaim Raphael

1979
CHATTO & WINDUS
LONDON

Published by
Chatto & Windus Ltd
40 William IV Street
London WC2N 4DF

★

Clarke, Irwin & Co Ltd
Toronto

British Library Cataloguing in Publication Data

Raphael, Chaim
    A coat of many colours.
    1. Jews – History – 1789–1945   2. Jews – History –
    1945–
    I. Title
    909'.04'924082   DS125
    ISBN 0-7011-2413-X

Set, printed and bound in Great Britain by
Cox & Wyman Ltd, London, Fakenham and Reading

For the *kinder* and *einiklach*

'It shall be health to thy navel
and marrow to thy bones.'
PROVERBS 3 :8

CONTENTS

FOREWORD

On One Foot? Never

If I say that I set out, in writing this book, to turn Jewish history upside-down, I am not being entirely frivolous. Being a Jew is usually presented as an experience which starts in the distant past with the Patriarchs and works its way through nearly 4,000 years of history to arrive at what one feels today. What I have done in this book is the opposite: to start with myself as a Jew and work outwards and backwards.

I could not tell, when I began, how far this approach would have some meaning for others. The subjects that I wanted to write about were in large degree personal to myself, ranging from the earliest memories of childhood to scholarly issues in which I became involved through accident or idiosyncrasy. I knew that I would be selective, concentrating on subjects which had appealed to me instead of offering a discussion organized in a formal pattern that tried to cover everything.

But I saw one overriding advantage in this method. I could write about the Jewish kinship as a living force. It has always seemed to me that being Jewish has furnished me with many special vantage-points. From childhood on, I saw connections to myself as a Jew that I was impelled to explore. It was never merely a search for facts of the past to fill out the picture of my origins. To express it this way sounds too static: I was responding always to a changing world and a changing self. In every situation, life was being enlarged through the interest one brought to it as a Jew.

What I have done in this book is to report on some of these explorations, moving from the experience of childhood to consider themes that took shape with lasting force to my recurrent delight – the Litvak strain in my family background, the Jewish worlds I came to live in, the books that spoke with a voice I had never heard before.

History has established a framework, but within it one is on one's own. One follows leads that seem significant, or just enjoyable, and they acquire their own momentum and depth. This, at any rate, has been my experience: and if I have recaptured the mood here, perhaps the reader will share it.

There is a clue to this approach in a saying attributed to the famous rabbi Hillel, who was a contemporary of Jesus. We are told that a heathen said to Hillel that he would be quite prepared to become a Jew if Hillel could teach him the entire Torah 'while standing on one foot'. Hillel's good-humoured answer is usually quoted in truncated form: 'what is hateful to you, do not unto your neighbour.' The full answer, as given in the Talmud, continues: 'This is the entire Torah. The rest is commentary. Go and study it.' The real weight of the reply lies, for me, in the last four words.

As I see it, Hillel was really saying, perhaps with a twinkle in his eye, that there are no short cuts to understanding what it means to be a Jew. It builds up in one's mind through 'study', by which one means not some dry, academic exercise but living reflectively with every form of Jewish experience that comes one's way. On the surface, Torah study aims at clarifying 'the Law'. More deeply, it means trying to interpret the words of the Torah to illuminate Jewish feeling and Jewish history. There will never be a finite meaning for this. In every age it grows richer and deeper.

The Jews, torn between pride and despair, have always tried to establish for themselves where the real meaning may lie: but the search presses on us today with a new intensity. As a Jew, one has been impelled by the events of our time into a recognition that the old kinship works on us now with a categorical imperative. To be casual about it, to belittle its implications, has become an act of moral indecency.

The canvas is wider today than it ever was, the themes more varied. But the assessment has to be personal. One lives out Hillel's injunction in one's own way.

Looking for a pattern, I had to recognize, as I wrote this book, how unpredictably my Jewish experience had taken shape. I seem to have jogged back and forth, absorbed in being Jewish, absorbed

in the world outside.   I expect that this is true of every Jew: but
if one sets the results out in a book, one has perhaps to look for a
pivot around which things have turned.

In my own case, I think of Oxford, not as the home of lost causes
but for the way it absorbs and transmutes all the heterogeneous
influences that are subjected to its mystery.   Exposed to this process, one has to be dull of heart to expect life to be predictable.
One lives for what is round the corner, alert for the accidents of
fate that are going to mould one's outlook.

Oxford worked this way for me, offering an enlargement to my
life as a Jew that had already begun at school.   In this happy
country of ours, many a Jewish boy is helped along this path
through the friendship of a Christian schoolmaster.   This is what
had happened to me, too, though in circumstances that were
inevitably tailored to my own background.

At the root of my Jewish experience was the intensely orthodox
home in which I had been reared.   My father was a *chazan*
(cantor).   Hand-in-hand with him, I went to synagogue services
three times a day on Sabbaths and Festivals in the little northern
town in which we lived.   Later, I was at a peculiar boarding-
establishment run by a choleric old rabbi, in which I was able to
combine the dubious delights of Talmud study with a grammar-
school education in classical English style.   The school headmaster was a saintly Christian clergyman and I have described in
an earlier book, *Memoirs of a Special Case*, how these two towering
figures of my schooldays struggled, in effect, for the mastery of my
soul.   Far from being riven by the struggle, I felt as if I had a foot
planted firmly in both worlds when I went up to Oxford.   From
then on, the accidents multiplied, all yielding experience, as I see
now, that would ultimately ask for expression in a book of this
kind.

It seemed natural at Oxford to study everything *except* the
Talmud, and the hotch-potch course of Philosophy, Politics and
Economics was ready-made for this mood.   Economics proved
later to have been a good basis for a career in the Civil Service, but

this wasn't how things were being planned at the time. The world outside was doing the planning, with the War as the focal point.

I had turned after graduation to a deepening of my Hebrew studies at Oxford, and begun to teach there. With the outbreak of war, I was switched, like many others, into Government work, and this took me after a while into the Treasury. In ordinary circumstances, my Jewish studies could have been stored up passively from then on as a kind of recreation, but there was no such thing as ordinary circumstances. The Jewish world was ablaze with interest, both tragic and satisfying. One could never be Jewish as a recreation. From Oxford days until now, it has been the central interest of my life.

But Oxford was more than a scholarly base for these alternations of work. Even the most routine of activities there was liable to lead one into worlds unrealized. In my first year as a student, the need to learn German for my exams had led me to accept a post in Germany as an English tutor in a Jewish home. As it happened, the contact with German Jewry which I established in this and subsequent visits drew me into special war jobs during 1939–41; but this was all far from the ken of an Oxford undergratuate twelve years earlier. In those days, Hitler was in the wings but not yet felt. What I saw instead on my visits to Germany was a rich culture bursting with 'modernity' in art, literature, architecture and music, far transcending in interest the parochialism of England and, even more, of English Jews. I had discovered a new world, and wrote about it excitedly to the headmaster. He wrote back suggesting, gently, that I curb my enthusiasm. There was a pagan element in the German spirit, he said, that had never been eradicated and that gave one a foreboding of evil.

How do people like this have such instinctive wisdom? Years later, I came across a letter written by Chaim Weizmann at the outbreak of the *First* World War expressing the same thought with the same prescience. Weizmann, who had an unfaltering respect for English values, was struggling at that point to wean the Zionist movement from its attachment to Germany. 'With feverish anxiety,' he wrote to a friend in New York, 'I am watching events which have for me a deeper hidden meaning. It is the struggle of the pagan Siegfried against the spirit of the Bible, and the Bible will win.' How my Christian headmaster would have agreed.

The magic of Oxford is that it greets you at one moment with apparent indifference and then embraces you, for no reason, with the most far-sighted generosity. I had been put off, when I returned there to pursue Hebrew studies, by an approach to the Bible which seemed cold and heartless. It was being treated 'scientifically' as if it were a dead literature, demanding dissection by 'Higher Criticism' in the spirit of medical students dissecting a cadaver. I came to terms with this after a while, as students do, and was suddenly offered a Fellowship which included among its provisions the obligation to spend six months in Palestine, looking at the Bible, so to speak, on the spot. How can one describe what this meant to a Jewish young man brought up on the memory of Zion? I lived in Jerusalem, attending lectures from time to time at the Hebrew University, and walking down from Mount Scopus before dusk by a route which would end in a stroll on the walls of the Old City. Much of what I wrote later had its roots in those quiet months of talk and reading. Jewish history opened up with new warmth; but if I was receptive also in academic terms, it was because of the grounding I had received in the cool atmosphere of Oxford.

Looking back on my Jewish experience, it is as if the wheel was always coming full circle, sometimes almost farcically, sometimes with a sense of recognition that was moving beyond expression.

For the first, I recall from Treasury days a meeting of the International Monetary Fund at Tokyo during which I had lunch with a number of American Jews living there who had decided to found a synagogue. To obtain a suitable rabbi, they had sent a young Japanese to study for a few years at a Jewish theological college in the U.S.A. He was now back in Tokyo, running the synagogue services with Japanese efficiency. They were all very happy with him, they told me.

For the second, I think of a poem called *The Jewish Graveyard in Malta* by Nigel Dennis, who is not Jewish in the ordinary sense but has a Jewish ancestor somewhere, like so many Christians.

Walking round the graveyard, he sees tombstones of Jews from all kinds of places who had happened to end their days in the island:

> *Oh, what a friendly place*
> *To be buried in! Orange marigolds warm*
> *Under a blue February sky; white narcissi*
> *In clumps beside the graves.*

He lists their names in eight successive lines – Elihu Salvu, born at Lodz, Poland, 1842, Simons of Vienna, Isaacs, a victim of the Hungarian War . . .

> *How far, how*
> *Strangely you have all travelled! How happy I feel*
> *To discover you here! The ground you are in is*
> *Never cold, as Lodz was; the wind here is never*
> *Sharp as it was in Vienna. You are all returned to*
> *The Middle Sea of your forefathers, the world of*
> *Stone, dust, and olive. Welcome a thousand times!*
> *Shalom! Shalom!*

1: ROOTS

The Zeppelin
The Raphaels of Vilkomir
The Ancient Memory

THE ZEPPELIN

IF it was a dark night on the way back from Hebrew class, the
Kaiser might be lurking round a corner in his spiked helmet
waiting to pounce on you. Bright moonlight could be even
worse. This was the kind of night, they said, on which a Zeppelin could come. We had never had one yet, in our little seaside
town on the north-east coast of England, but we had heard what
they had done to London. The Kaiser was bad enough, but he
was, after all, human. The Zeppelin was something *in the sky* –
like God. If it suddenly appeared, there could be no escape. It
would be like one of those terrible punishments in the Bible that
God was always threatening if the children of Israel were sinful.
I knew so many of these verses by heart, translating a chapter or
two of the Bible to my father at night, after supper. If we were
wicked enough, the way the children of Israel were always wicked
and rebellious in the Wilderness, this was the way God's voice
would be heard: a German Zeppelin would float into the sky,
some tremendous thunder and lightning would strike from it, and
we would perish.

There were so many sins that could bring this about. We
might eat pork, we might mix up meat and milk dishes, worst of
all we might break one of the laws of the Sabbath. Of course we
would never do this *deliberately*. We would be fully on guard
against sins as obvious as striking a match on the Sabbath or
carrying something through the streets. But we might commit
a sabbath sin accidentally, which could bring the same punishment. We might tear a piece of paper while turning the
pages of a book. More terrible still, it might be a *holy* book,
something with Hebrew writing on it. There were even
worse accidents possible, things almost too terrible to think of.
Suppose my father, holding up the Scroll of the Law after the
reading in synagogue, let it fall. One could hear God's voice
thundering *'Because ye have defiled my sanctuary and destroyed my
Holy Name . . .'* And in the same second one could hear the clap

of thunder and see the walls of our little synagogue crumbling into dust.

It seemed unreal at home, with Father listening to my translation approvingly, stroking his beautiful George V beard. In the background my brothers and sisters would be busy with their quarrelling and homework, while Mother bustled with the clearing up after supper. Home was safe; and even synagogue, where the awful warnings and curses were solemnly chanted, was normally a cheerful place, full of chatter and argument. It was only at night, and out alone, that terror sometimes came to the surface.

Apart from the Kaiser and the Zeppelin, everything else about the war was sheer delight. Each day brought excitement and adventure. I had never known any existence without the war, but I realized even then that it was the war I had to thank for so much of the fun of my life.

Most wonderful of all was half-day school. Two schools had amalgamated, because of the shortage of teachers. My group went only in the mornings, which left us free every afternoon without teachers, parents, Hebrew school or anything. Every day found us after dinner on the sand dunes, or climbing the cliffs. It wasn't just that we were free and happy; the war itself gave us endless games. The steep roads down to the beaches were barricaded with barbed-wire entanglements, to prevent a landing. There were huts and fences, and all kinds of useful material – barrels, tent-poles, corrugated sheets, tarpaulins.

There were trenches and piles of sand-bags, with anti-aircraft guns in their emplacements. Sometimes soldiers would be training on the beach; at other times we would stand by watching the Coast Guard at work; but mostly we would be on our own, using anything we liked for our games. The long stone pier at the end of the harbour had been shut off for civilians, but for us there were ways of climbing through or over the barriers, so that the enemy and the defenders could take up their positions, fighting battles that might last a whole afternoon, until a guard, or a policeman, would suddenly appear to send us all to flight.

Once some of us actually climbed from the pier on to a mine-sweeper which was moored there. Willie Fisher hid in one of the lifeboats and said he was going to stay there until the ship sailed. He climbed out quickly enough when we heard the sailors coming, but I believed for a moment that he might really have stowed away. For Willie, my best friend, was always doing really brave things – as when we fought the gypsy boys. The gypsies had an encampment in the fields behind the beach. We were frightened of the gypsies, but sometimes hid in the cornfields nearby to spy on them. One could watch them for hours, with their dark faces and bright red shirts and scarves, moving around quietly, secretly, in front of their caravan, their horse cropping quietly at one side, while at the open fire a young woman, strangely like my oldest sister, cooked their dinner. But what went on *inside* the caravan? That was the great mystery. I crawled nearer one day and was suddenly attacked by three young gypsy boys who began beating me on the head and back with sticks. I crouched on the ground, my head in my arms, the blows falling, when all at once there was a shout and Willie was there, pulling, punching. I was on my feet, and in a minute we were away and safe.

Willie and I sat together in the same double-desk at school. He was tall for his age, and fair. I was shortish, dark, and, as I know now from old photographs, had large brown eyes. We were a good pair at school because Willie was very poor at schoolwork, bored with every minute of it, while I could help him. I found everything easy and was Miss Freeman's favourite. Miss Freeman, our teacher, was in my eyes dazzlingly beautiful. She was rather plump with a creamy skin. She had large coils of hair piled on her head, and always wore a white blouse and dark skirt. When she stopped behind us at our desk to look at what we were writing, she would sigh at Willie's work and then, looking at mine, would run her hand softly through my hair. I could always feel her leaning on me from behind. It was a nice feeling. No-one ever touched me in this pleasant way at home. We never kissed there, as I saw other parents and children doing. My mother was far too busy with her seven children and with the visitors who were always dropping in for tea or meals. Home, though it was safe, was also a battleground. We watched each other with great care, jealous for the extras that might be secured; a book, a magazine, a second helping of *tzimmas*, a piece of cake. There were battles, alliances, triumphs and defeats. But at school, with Miss Freeman smiling lazily at me, it was different. Once I stole a rose from our garden and gave it to her. She put it in a glass of water on her desk. It was our secret.

I never said much at home about what went on at school. No-one would have cared. I was the fifth child and everything seemed to turn on what was happening to the others, especially my two big brothers. I listened avidly for what the older children said, and even more for what they didn't say. All had their secret lives, and parts of them gradually emerged as I listened; amazing things, grown-up things. Most particularly I listened silently – fearfully, sometimes – to the angry talk between my father and my brothers. His face in anger frightened me. They were always doing the wrong things. It made me anxious to ensure that my own guilty secrets didn't come out.

One secret I was afraid to reveal was that my best friend at school was Willie Fisher. I had good reason for keeping him away from our house, though sometimes I went to his. It was not just that he was non-Jewish. There was something far worse, making him supremely taboo: his father was a 'pork butcher'. A pork butcher sold all forms of pig products, sausages and black 'blood' puddings. Like many pork butchers in England, Willie's father was a German. His shop, just down the road from us, still had a sign on it with his name in the original spelling: FISCHER – PORK BUTCHER. Willie told me that in 1914, at the outbreak of the war with Germany, the people of our town had smashed the Fisher shop-windows and pelted the children with stones in the street. This kind of thing had happened all over England. Mr. Fisher had been interned, the family had had to go away, and had lived for a little while with an aunt in the country.

Later in the war Mr. Fisher, with two sons now in the British Army, had been released from internment and had gone to work on a farm close by. His wife and Willie had gone back to live above the shop, whose windows were now boarded up. Mrs. Fisher was always nice to me when I went there, but at the back of my mind I felt guilty. The word 'pork' on the sign outside seemed to be engraved in letters of fire.

The friends whose existence *could* be admitted were, naturally, the children of the Jewish congregation which my father served as *chazan*. My closest Jewish friend, partly because his house was very near, was Sammy Woolf, whose father Joe Woolf kept a pawnshop in the old part of the town by the port.

The Woolfs were very different from us. For one thing, they were rich. They were so rich, in fact, that they had electric light, which you could turn on with a switch at the door. In *our* house, gas mantles had to be carefully lit with a match or a taper from the fire. And whereas my mother did all the cooking and baking and a million other things, helped only by my sisters and fat old Mrs. Moxon who came for the rough cleaning, Mrs. Woolf had a real maid, a plump country girl called Elsie, who baked scones in the afternoon and took tea in to Mrs. Woolf on a tray. I haunted their kitchen, where Elsie stuffed me with scones and strawberry jam; there was always a delicious smell of flour and baking around her. Mrs. Woolf was friendly too, but rather stately. She was, after all, the wife of the President of the Congregation; and Mr. Woolf was, in addition, a Town Councillor, so that *non-Jews* would sometimes visit their house for formal teas on Sunday afternoons. Sammy would be taken in to be shown off on these occasions, while I hung around happily in the kitchen with Elsie. But he was very off-hand when I asked him about it. It never seemed to him at all odd that their house could at the same time be Jewish and yet open to non-Jewish visitations. To me, home was by definition a Jewish fortress. Non-Jewish people had no place there, any more than in synagogue.

But this was only part of the different life that the Woolfs led, and which made them so exciting. They had broken through all kinds of barriers. Their shop was kept open on *Shabbos*; their children went to the pictures on *Shabbos* (I never went at all); they had a maid; they had non-Jewish visitors; and they had electric light. The Councillor himself looked like a typical north-country Englishman – stout, with ruddy cheeks and a big drooping black moustache. But in many ways he was still a traditional Jew from the old country. He had been a *yeshivah bochur*, a Talmud student, in early life. He loved sitting down with my father to go through a page of the Talmud, with the rabbinical commentaries, while they waited for a *Minyan* (a quorum of ten) to begin prayers on *Shabbos* afternoon. It never seemed odd that he had just walked across to the synagogue from his shop. For *him*, the breaking of the Sabbath was overlooked. He was so obviously a complete Jew that it didn't matter.

I loved listening to the men talking in synagogue on *Shabbos* afternoons while they waited for dusk and the *Ma'ariv* service. If Councillor Woolf and my father were not running through a passage from the Midrash or the Talmud together, they would be joining in with the others in talk about the war, and most particularly about the fighting in Palestine. General Allenby's campaign to win back the Holy Land from the pagans was a situation they were completly at home with. It had happened before with Abraham, Isaac and Jacob, and then again with Joshua and King David. I knew the place-names myself from the weekly Bible readings, and listened eagerly. Sons of our congregation were actually in the British Army *with* Allenby, fighting like the old children of Israel. It was almost as if the Messiah was on his way. I can recall the style of conversation perfectly as Mr. Woolf and my father exchanged verses, with others joining in.

'It says in the *Newcastle Chronicle* that they've taken Beer Sheba.'

'I suppose they will still use the well that Isaac found there.'

My father would nod approvingly. 'Rashi says that all those wells that Isaac's servants dug *before* Beer Sheba – at Esek, and Sitnah and Rehovot – were really places for study, 'wells of the Torah', and that is why God appeared there to him and promised that his seed would inherit the land.'

'If you ask me,' Mr. Woolf says, 'Rashi made up half his stories. How did he know?'

'How did he know?' says my father.   'It's in the Bible.   Everything is in the Bible.'

'I had a letter today from my son,' one of the congregants says proudly.   'He met some Jews who actually live in Palestine, at a place called Gihonah.'

'There you are,' my father says.   'That must be Gihon, from the Book of Kings.   *"And King David said: Mount my son Solomon on my own mule and take him down to Gihon".'*

Mr. Woolf joins in: *'And let Zadok the priest and Nathan the prophet annoint him there king over Israel.'*

'What will happen when Allenby wins?' a congregant asks. 'Perhaps a new Jewish king will be annointed in Gihon like King Solomon.'

'Will all the Jews go back to the Holy Land?' says another. *'Next Year in Jerusalem?'*

My father is doubtful.   'We must wait for the Messiah,' he says, stroking his beard.   *'Then* we go back.'

'I will go anyhow to see Jerusalem,' Mr. Woolf says firmly. 'Ah, we have a *Minyan*.   What kept you so long, Goldberg? Let us say *Ma'ariv*.   I have to go back to the shop.'

I sit listening, open-mouthed.   For the moment the Kaiser – and even the Zeppelin – have ceased to threaten.

I rarely played with Sammy Woolf during the week because, being rich, he went to a smart fee-paying school.   But he came to *cheder* (Hebrew school) three nights a week, which gave us a chance, if we walked home together, to talk about Dolly, his only sister, a 'big girl', already turned sixteen, very pretty, and, as everybody agreed, a real devil.   Talking about Dolly was part of our endless conversation about girls and babies.   We exchanged such information as we were gathering, while at the same time we speculated about what the older members of our family were up to, especially in this regard.

Our talk, in north-country ('Geordie') sing-song, was an attempt to out-do each other in revelations.

'Dolly and your brother Simon are sweethearts,' Sammy told me once.

'Go on!'

'Why aye! I saw them behind the Moor Rock last Wednesday afternoon.'

'Ye couldna have! I was playing near the Rock with Willie Fisher and I didn't see anything.'

'Well *I* did, I saw them both.   They were kissing each other.'

'I thought it was Dannie she was keen on.' Dannie was my other big brother.

'Oh, she was.   But Dolly is always out with different boys.   I saw her on the sands with Tommy Thomson's big brother, George.'

'*Kissing* him!   He's a *goy!*'

'Oh Dolly's terrible.   My father beat her with a strap.'

'How do you know?'

'I heard her crying.   She told me she's going to run away to London.'

'Go on!'

It was quite true that my big brothers Dannie and Simon were rivals.   I could understand them quarrelling over Dolly: they quarrelled over everything.   The whole family was very argumentative, but with Dannie and Simon the quarrels, and the raised voice of my father, went over into anger, black anger.   It always sounded to me like the quarrels in the Bible – the rebellion of Korah, the anger of Moses, and the wrath of God.   And now if Dolly had jilted Dannie, who was her own age, for Simon, just over a year older, it could be frightening.   The quarrels always started this way.   Simon would do something quiet and clever to get Dannie down.   Dannie would respond with something wild. I always felt rivalry in the air between those two.

They never quarrelled over *me*. I was their slave, but they did such wonderful things for me.   Dannie would take me swimming and, by the force of his own example, would get me to plunge into the roaring waves from the beach, or dive in from the rocks. He was a most powerful swimmer, and absolutely fearless. Simon took me climbing for gulls' eggs in the cliffs, and once he took me into the shipyard at Jarrow, nearby, where he had begun to work as an apprentice engineer. He showed me the skeleton of the ship, with the great plates laid; all around us were the myriad crane arms, the clanging of rivets, and the hoot of grey warships going up and down the river. I was almost too excited to sleep that night. And now Simon had got Dolly away from Dannie. He must have tricked her away somehow. It was like Jacob and Esau, or like Laban's trick over Jacob with Rachel and Leah. Something terrible would happen. Dannie was so wild . . .

But it was Friday now, when one stopped worrying. Mother had been baking all Thursday as usual, and cooking all Friday. The huge pans and dishes were ready, fish (fresh from the sea that morning) for Friday night; *cholent* (a baked stew) to be kept warm for Saturday dinner after synagogue. The house was spotless. The men of the family, including me, were off to synagogue for the evening service. All except the baby would be sitting down for supper later, eight at table in all, unless Father also brought home a stranger from synagogue, as he often did.

Since a camp had been opened at Hartley Moor, a few miles away, there was almost always a Jewish soldier or two in synagogue on Friday evenings. When Father invited them, they accepted quickly, probably homesick for *gefillte* fish. To us it was like a raffle each week to see who we would get. It was especially exciting if it was an officer, with his brown leather shoulder-straps crossing over to the belt which held his revolver.

On this particular Friday we had been lucky in a way which none of us could have expected. A soldier had come back with us and was sitting patiently through the preliminary blessings as if he were an ordinary Jew. He was an officer; his badges and leather straps shone in the candlelight. But he was no ordinary

Jew, he had introduced himself in synagogue with a name that had dazzled us: Lieutenant Rothschild. *A Rothschild! In our house!* My father sang on: '*Shalom aleichem malechei hashareth . . .*' 'Peace unto you, ministering angels . . .' We looked at the soldier and looked at each other excitedly. *Lieutenant Rothschild* – the magic name for all Jews. The wine was blessed. The bread was cut. We sat down to eat.

My sisters, who did all the serving, bustled shyly around the visitor from another planet. For a Rothschild he seemed rather hungry. He wolfed the food down, praising it heartily, accepting a second and third helping with cheerful grace, talking with an important air, as he ate, of the Army, his service in the trenches in France, and of his own family. It seemed almost incredible that a Rothschild should be so like the rest of us. We listened eagerly for something that would be different, something rich, something almost royal, as befitting a Rothschild. It never seemed to occur to any of us, remote from the world in our little northern town, that perhaps there were Rothschilds who weren't Rothschilds. No one asked questions too pointedly. We listened open-mouthed. He had now settled back, with the meal over, loosening his belt for comfort, and still talking while the dishes were cleared away. At that moment there was a knock at the door. 'Come in,' my father called. The door opened, and Dolly Woolf stood there, plump, pretty and simpering. It was clear that she had heard about the Rothschild, and had come to see for herself.

Dannie and Simon both got up. Dolly smiled at them, with a sly look at the same time towards the soldier.

'Hallo, Dolly,' my mother said. 'Would you like some tea and cake?'

'Oh, let me help with the clearing up,' Dolly said, following my sisters into the kitchen. My eyes darted round, watching my brothers, watching Dolly, watching the Lieutenant. All these grown-ups; they gave each other strange looks. Someone would ask an ordinary question and get a short, angry reply for no reason that I could understand.

My younger sister was being pushed off to bed. I pleaded for and won a respite. My father had taken out a Bible to run through the chapters for the next day's reading in synagogue. I sat near him, watching.

Dolly was now sitting next to the Rothschild, sipping her tea, flickering her eyelashes. Dannie got up abruptly and went out, slamming the door. Simon had picked up a book and was reading.

Lieutenant Rothschild looked at his watch and rose. 'I must get back to Camp,' he said. 'Very strict in the Army, you know. Even officers have to be in on time.' He stood, adjusting his belt. Somehow he had become less heroic during the evening.

'I must go as well,' Dolly said gaily. 'Mother said I mustn't be late.' She turned to the Lieutenant. 'If you're going towards Hartley Moor, you pass our house.'

'Then I'll accompany you,' the Rothschild said, smiling.

He shook hands with us all and thanked my mother and father. The door closed behind him and Dolly, and a peace came over the room again. It had been strange. *Shabbos* had been disturbed, somehow. I was glad he had gone.

Saturday morning was normally a heavenly time. There was an early cup of tea and a piece of *Shabbos* cake available in the kitchen, and none of the rush of weekdays, with everybody in each other's way. On *Shabbos* we could sleep late. Still better, we could take our tea upstairs and read in bed.

But this morning, though it was *Shabbos* and a bright summer's day, there were clouds of anger in the house. I was woken up by the sound of my brothers quarrelling in the room they shared next door to mine, and then, above their voices, I heard my father shouting at them. Perhaps it was late and they were not ready for the early morning service that I was allowed to miss. I heard Mother's voice asking Father not to get angry; he replied roughly. What had gone wrong? Was it Lieutenant Rothschild? Dolly? I snuggled back into the warm downy bed, hoping to stay safe from the noise.

In the synagogue itself later, things became normal again. There was excited talk among the men at news in the paper of the capture of some town in Palestine. And inevitably there was the other side of the war, too, when Mr. Isaacs got up to say *Kaddish*, the memorial prayer, for his son. The news had come that week that Monty Isaacs, nineteen years old, had been killed in France. As Mr. Isaacs said the *Kaddish*, slowly, the tears streaming down his face, I heard weeping from the women in the gallery. These scenes had become usual to me. Every day there were rows of small photographs in the papers, pictures of young men, all looking alike, *Killed in Action* . . .

There was a *Barmitzvah* (confirmation) that morning in *shul* (synagogue) and a small reception afterwards in the Vestry. Dannie was not there, which surprised me. We all loved these parties, whisky and herring for the men, wine and sweet things for the women and children. But nothing was said, and we strolled home quietly. Mother always looked different in her *Shabbos* clothes. Father walked beside her like a prince, calm and dignified, neatly dressed, unruffled, majestic in his neatly trimmed beard.

My two older sisters stood at the door of our house, waiting, with an expression of anguish.

'It's Dannie', the older one said.

A cloud of anger came over my father's face. 'What is it?' he said roughly. Mother, suddenly frightened, pushed past Father and rushed into the house. Dannie, the wild one, was her favourite.

Inside the front door it was clear where to go. The door on the right to the front parlour was open. Inside this room, with its upright piano and upholstered furniture, reserved for special visitors, was a heavy sideboard with a cupboard which Father always kept locked. The lock had been broken open and on the top of the sideboard was a letter from Dannie.

A terrible thought swamped my mind. Dannie had written the letter on *Shabbos*! He had forced the lock on *Shabbos*!

Mother was wringing her hands. Father had picked up the paper and was reading it to her:

*I am going to Edinburgh to enlist in the Argyll and Sutherland High-
landers as a drummer-boy.   I was afraid to tell you.   I have had to borrow
the railway fare from the cupboard but I will send it back.   Don't worry.
I'll be all right.*

My father stood motionless, holding the paper.   I had burst
into tears, with my mother.   To have broken open the cupboard,
and on *Shabbos* . . . It was as if the earth had opened up.

Father stood there, and then, after a long silence, said gently to
Mother: 'Come, Rachel, the children are hungry.'   We went into
the dining-room and sat down, with Dannie's place empty.   My
father had washed his hands in the ritual way for the meal, and
now said grace, as he cut the bread: '*Blessed art thou, O Lord, who
bringest forth bread from the earth* . . .'

With dinner over, I went off on my own down to the beach to see
if Sammy Woolf or Willie Fisher or anyone I knew might be
there.   I was particularly hoping that Sammy hadn't gone to the
pictures.   He had told me that morning in synagogue that Dolly
had come home very late after seeing the Rothschild at our house,
and had got into trouble.   Her mother had called her some name
which neither of us understood.   We wanted to look it up, if we
only knew where.   But now it seemed unimportant.   I wanted
to tell him about Dannie, not about the cupboard, but that he had
gone off to enlist, and in a Highland Regiment, with a kilt.   But
Sammy wasn't there.   It felt lonely.   People were sitting on the
hot sand, soldiers and sailors among them, with uniforms un-
buttoned in the heat.   Some people were swimming.   But no-
one could swim as far out as Dannie.   Thinking of him, I turned
back from the beach.

It was too early for the afternoon service, and as I came near our
house, I went on past it towards the market-place, to wander
among the stalls.   It was always cheerful there on a Saturday
afternoon, and my troubles soon faded.   I had just settled down
to watch a Punch and Judy show when I saw Mrs. Fisher, Willie's
mother, in front of me, heavily laden with shopping bags.   She

had stopped for a minute to rest and mop her brow, and gave me a smile as she recognized me. In turning to smile, she dropped two of the bags, which burst, scattering fruit in all directions. I bent down instinctively to help her, and we laughed at the problem she now faced, her arms full with broken bags. 'Let me help you,' I said to her. 'Oh, thank you,' she said, putting the broken bags into my arms. I held out my arms for more. 'I can take the bread, too,' I said proudly. 'You're a good boy,' she said, handing it to me. 'I'm really exhausted. I'd never have got home without help.'

We struggled along together, up the hill away from the market. My arms began to ache, but I was very happy to help her. When we got to her shop, she took her parcels off me and gave me an apple for myself. I took it and strolled away cheerfully, thinking that I was now a little late for *Minchah*, the afternoon service. At that moment, as I thought of *Minchah*, the enormity of what I had been doing swept over me. Without realizing it, I had broken the Sabbath! I had carried things in the street, which was absolutely forbidden. I was as bad as Dannie. A horrible sinking fear came into my heart. I looked at the apple in my hand and threw it away fiercely.

All through the service, and at home later, I went over it all to myself. Something bad was happening to us, to all our family. Dannie had gone, my hero. Simon would go too, with his quiet, clever ways. Were we all sinful, rebelling against Father, like the children of Israel? I muttered my night prayer fervently as I fell asleep.

But in sleep, the fear returned. I was tossing, struggling to get free from something holding me back, when I woke to find myself being carried into the cellar of our house, held in a blanket in my father's arms, like Isaac being taken by his father Abraham to the sacrifice. I knew as I opened my eyes that a great bang had wakened me, and then I heard another – a gun, a whole range of guns booming away overhead.

'Shush,' my father said, 'don't be afraid.'

I struggled out of the blanket and looked around in the dim light. They were all there, mother and the baby, and the girls, all in night clothes, shivering in blankets.

I knew, even before my father spoke, that the worst had happened. 'It's a Zeppelin,' he said. 'Sleep now; don't worry; it will be all right.'

'No!' I cried, 'No! No!' I managed to break away and run up the stairs. It was all my fault. I had sinned. I couldn't stay hiding in the cellar, waiting to be crushed.

'Come back,' my mother cried. 'The Zeppelin . . .'

Father was running after me, but I had got upstairs and run to the window in the large room which looked out towards the sea. The curtains were open, and I stood there breathless at what the Heavens showed. The sky was criss-crossed in a dazzling pattern of searchlights, switching swiftly up and down and across. And suddenly, caught in a criss-cross of light, we saw it, the great silver shape sailing straight at us . . .

The guns barked out in a cannonade. The earth shook, but the Zeppelin came on, unharmed, untouchable.

The searchlights had lost her. They flickered around, the guns were silent.

And now, first quietly, and then more loudly, we heard the motors. We could *hear* the Zeppelin. It was over our heads.

The guns spoke again, and the searchlights roamed the sky; but there was nothing to see now in the flickering light. There was only the sound of the engines coming nearer in a roar. The guns boomed again. At any moment now the bombs . . .

In the sky above our heads, we saw a red flash, and then in the same second a sudden burst of flame. It grew as we watched into a roaring mass of flame – the whole sky was on fire – the Zeppelin!

I felt a wild exultation. My father ran down into the cellar to fetch the others, and I dashed to the front door. As I opened it, the noise grew suddenly louder, the crackle of flames and the cries of the people in the street:

'It's going down on the Town Hall . . .'

'No, on the cliffs . . .'

It was, in fact, tearing its way into some fields near the beach,

where the gypsy caravans often stood. The trees around had
begun to burn, and the whole sky before us was lit up in flame.
The family had all come upstairs from the cellar to see. They
were laughing and shouting outside with everybody else. My
father stood immobile, slightly apart, his head lifted, his beard
glistening in the fiery light.

People were rushing through the streets towards the Zeppelin.
I ran upstairs for my trousers, and dashed out too. The Zeppelin
was down: there was nothing more to be afraid of. All kinds of
thoughts burst into my head, to pop like balloons. I was moving
into a higher class at school and would lose Miss Freeman. I
might have to find a new friend, with Willie Fisher left behind.
It didn't matter. The Kaiser was finished. Dannie would come
back, in his kilt. Father would be smiling. We would all be
together again.

THE RAPHAELS OF VILKOMIR

I NEVER realized, when I was very young, how much I missed by not having a grandfather in the offing. Now that I am a grandfather myself, it is obvious to me that small children get great pleasure at anything that is revealed to them, through the stories of grandpa, about their family roots, the more generations back the better. Clearly, I must do what I can on this score for my own grandchildren, or, as we say in Yiddish, the *einiklach*.

I am, however, in a quandary. Not having known a grandfather myself, I had to go out looking for him. I will try here to tell the story of the search, though this is bound to take me further than a few nostalgic family tales. However, if it is a little grown-up for the *einiklach* at this stage, they'll get round to it one day. Above all, they will understand, I think, that I was not just looking for my grandfather, but for myself.

It has become fashionable to dig out ethnic roots, and the Jews have a certain advantage in this, with a clear line to ancestors living in an ancient homeland. Today the homeland has been restored, giving new life to the old connections. Between these two polar opposites of Jewish existence, there is a long and graphic story to draw on, offering endless points of identification for Jews everywhere.

Yet the individual Jew, looking for roots that will be meaningful, can run straight into a paradox. Even with a clear picture of recent descent, the background enfolding it is so perplexing that a simple assertion of where he comes from, and what he is, may prove difficult to frame. In thinking about his identity, he may take an extreme position either in exaggerating the force in him of his roots, which can cut him off from those around him, or in claiming that they don't exist – a form of psychic suicide. If he avoids the extremes, he may take refuge in ambivalence, with roots acknowledged but amorphous.

Ironically, these issues, which have been tangible throughout two thousand years of Diaspora experience, have taken new forms in the one place where problems of Jewish identity are supposed to have been solved – in Israel.   By bringing Jews of all kinds together, Israel has highlighted the inherent social complexity of Jewish existence.   One historic rift visible there now is the difference between Ashkenazi Jews, whose origins lie in Central and Eastern Europe, and Sephardi Jews, who spread from the Iberian peninsula over the whole of the Near East.   And there is another problem: if there are new kinds of Jews in Israel, what is their relationship to the millions of Jews outside, in the Diaspora?

One can approach this question of identity through a development usually thought of minor interest but very rewarding if examined.   This is the now widespread practice of name-changing in Israel, in which Jews bearing Russian, German and other surnames acquired during their history have replaced them by names which are uncompromisingly Hebrew.   There is no better way of plunging into the question of roots, and we shall see, when we look at it, how wide are its ramifications.   If I concentrate on it here, however, the reason is personal.   I ran into the issue head-on when I first went into the question of my own family roots.   The path I had to follow became as complicated as an argument in the Talmud: but that, after all, is a tribute to its Jewish validity.

The individual Jew, looking for immediate roots, starts with his or her own surname as a launching point.   If the name does not seem to lead anywhere, one can try grafting on one's place of origin.   In my own case, the most clear-cut fact I knew as a child was that my father was a Litvak (Lithuanian-Russian) who came from a small, intensely Jewish town called Vilkomir.   I therefore appear to be Chaim Raphael from Vilkomir.   It has a pleasant enough ring, but where does it lead if I go back?   At one level, it opens up a story of comic confusion, identifying me firmly with some historic and mistaken developments in Israel.   At another level, it led me to my grandfather Shepsi, and that was surely worthwhile.

.   .   .   .   .

Raphael is a not uncommon surname in England – sixty-seven entries in the London telephone book – and there is a very elegant clan interspersed among them. If asked, as I frequently am, whether I am related to this or that member of the Raphael elite, I always answer confidently 'No', assuming, as I must, that it would be too much of a coincidence. It is not that I think it impossible that, like me, their surname before 'Raphael' was 'Rabinovitch'. That kind of thing happens all the time. But it would really surprise me if any of these other Raphael's had had the same surname as mine *before* Rabinovitch, for that is where the real distinction emerges.

In my case, the pre-Rabinovitch status seemed, when I first looked into it, to suggest an interesting connection both with Marcel Proust and with the seventeenth-century false Messiah, Sabbatai Zevi. I cannot rule out the possibility that the other Raphaels carry the same prestigious intimations of immortality, but it would, I feel, be quite a coincidence.

I have learnt a good deal, over the course of years, about these other Raphaels. They started with an Ashkenazi Jew of rather vague identity, Raphael Raphael, who arrived in London from Holland soon after 1700. His descendants took up banking, which is not a bad base for building up a grandiose clan: but it also is helpful to go in for dynastic marriages. In 1828, the head of the family married a Mocatta, which took them into the intertwined Sephardi aristocracy of Mocattas and Lousadas. But the next move was equally exciting historically: for the son of this union, working in Hamburg for the bank, returned to his roots by bringing home to London as his wife the daughter of an outstanding *Ashkenazi* family, the Melchiors, whose fascinating but more earthy lineage included merchants, rabbis and cantors originating in the heartlands of Central and Eastern Europe.

Here was Jewish history showing its true dynamic. Over the past three hundred years, the Sephardi hidalgos of northern Europe were trail-blazers in opening up the roads to economic and social freedom for the Ashkenazi masses. In turn, the Ashkenazis, emerging eagerly from a highly inbred existence, had within them a potential vitality that was to fertilize Western culture with far greater power than the Sephardis could demonstrate. In Israel today, the polarity has taken a reverse form, with an Ashkenazi elite leading the way for the Sephardi masses of the Near East. It may well be that in due course a corresponding originality and creativity will develop among *them*. Not that this can be seen as a simple seesaw process. In all this to-ing and fro-ing there is plenty of confusion, as a blunder or two of my own will demonstrate.

The trouble for me was that I began to be aware of these stimulating angles to Jewish history many years too late. Forty years ago, I was wrestling with a problem – not a disagreeable one, but rather like the teasers of a crossword puzzle. The surname Rabinovitch, which had been mine from birth, was not, as I have indicated, the true name of my father's family, but the name that he had fallen upon, virtually by accident, when he entered England in 1895 as an immigrant from Russia. It was, nevertheless, a very warm, comfortable name, with an affectionate diminutive 'Rab' by which I was known to most of my friends. I would never have thought of dropping Rabinovitch had I not reacted to a strong Jewish issue on which I had, as is now clear, a premature (and false) intuition.

The year was 1936, and I had just returned from a first visit to a country then called Palestine. The effect on me had been overpowering, not in the sense of leading me to want to settle there, but as an intense invigoration of my Hebrew roots. With the Bible and its language suddenly brought to life by Jews living in the ancestral homeland, one seemed to be taken back at a bound to one's true origin. Without any clear logic, and with woeful lack of historical insight, I was seized by the idea that I could symbolize this by dropping the 'Russian' name which I had inherited so accidentally and taking instead a name that would be purely and unmistakably Hebrew. As we know, it was a move which was to become extremely common eleven years later after the foundation of the State of Israel. With hindsight, I now regard almost every aspect of this name-changing process as mistaken, and will explain why, a little later. But in 1936, acting on my own, it seemed inspired.

My forename Chaim was already good Hebrew, as in the toast: *le-chaim* – 'To life!'. For a surname, I sought something that would have equal Hebrew validity, and would begin with RA – to echo my nickname. Someone suggested 'Raphael', and it seemed excellent – ready-made for me.

Never was ignorance more blissfully compounded with confusion – and at both ends, one might say, of the social spectrum. At the top end, I had no idea, at the time, of the existence of the great English Raphael clan, into whose ranks I might be thought to be inserting myself. At the other end, I was equally ignorant of the fact that in Palestine then (as in Israel now) the surname 'Raphael' has an overwhelmingly *Sephardi* connotation. And, in that country, 'Sephardi' suggests not the Jewish aristocrats with whom the clan had become entwined, but the very humble masses of Near Eastern – 'oriental' – Jewry, as plebeian as my own forbears in Eastern Europe but utterly different from them in background, character and feeling. Far from uniting myself innocently with the Bible, I was sowing confusion in every direction as to my origins. But at the time, it all seemed simple and harmless: and that is why there are today sixty-seven, and not sixty-six, Raphael entries in the London telephone book.

Of course my father – peace unto him! – was really to blame, in calmly accepting the name that was attached to him when he arrived in England, instead of sticking to the unusual but perfectly acceptable name 'Pruss' which his family bore in their hometown of Vilkomir, and which his three elder brothers carried with them when they emigrated to the United States. My father, though he could be genial on occasion, was rather a remote figure to his children. Although stories about the family were passed on from older to younger children, I was never given a coherent explanation of how we had lost our real name, thus separating us so unnecessarily from our innumerable Pruss cousins in America.

Two stories were somehow mixed up in the talk I heard as a child. One was that my father had been told by some knowing fellow-passenger on the boat that if he wanted to be properly accepted in England, he should drop Pruss (so foreign-sounding) at the first opportunity and take an *English* name – such as Rabinovitch, which many English Jews managed with very nicely. Overriding (and perhaps embracing) this was an explanation relating to travel documents.   Many would-be emigrants from Russia had to buy or borrow somebody else's papers in order to get away.   My father had a special, if slightly bizarre, reason for subterfuge – his knowledge of music as a *chazan*.   As a boy, he had studied music rather seriously, and acquired a superb music handwriting.   This had led him to become attached to an Army bandmaster – presumably to copy out parts.   Even a low-grade military involvement of this kind could throw up a bar to emigration under one's own name, hence the travel document which labelled him 'Rabinovitch'.   With a little *savoir-faire* he could have reasserted his Pruss identity after passing the English immigration official, but he never did.   And perhaps this is where his fellow-passenger's advice came in.   What a bit of luck to be travelling with a name so suitable for England! *Rabinovitch*: it was perfect.   Why not keep it?

All children are fascinated by their names, and I was always trying to find out more, especially as both my grandfathers stayed on in Russia and were therefore mysterious figures from a world – *der Haim* – that was shadowy but full of imagined magic.   On Mother's side I had learnt little that seemed interesting.   In any case, there was a predisposition to think that the lineage that mattered was through Father.   If I could give body to Grandfather Pruss, I would be surer of who I was myself.

It is strange to me now that I never badgered my father with questions about this.   Perhaps I was too afraid of him.   All I had was an impression that his father, too, was stern and orthodox, his life given over completely to the rota of the synagogue.   I accepted this as perfectly natural: yet I was always trying hard, as I realize now, to find out more.

My first clue – or so I thought – came through a teacher at school who explained to us one day that names which we regard as fixed are often variations, in major or minor degree, of something quite different.   He gave us instances of place-names to which this applied, and went on to extend the principle to *personal* names, encouraging us to guess at, or invent, derivations. I started thinking immediately, of course, about the great mystery name of Pruss, and soon arrived at the idea that it might really be 'Preuss' (Prussian) – which may indeed be the source. But this in itself had not much magic until sometime later, when a Jewish schoolfriend told me proudly that Marcel Proust, whose name hovered in the air as the epitome of French distinction, was in fact not so much a Frenchman as a Jew. *Proust!* The name must surely have also come from Preuss – a cousin, no matter how far removed, of Grandfather's! I was well on my way to building on this when I learnt to my chagrin that Marcel was Jewish only on his mother's side. His father's family was long-established French provincial Catholic. I was never going to find Grandfather this way. But it was a pleasant dream while it lasted.

Much more fruitfully – to begin with, anyhow – I tried pursuing him through an unusual *first* name that he bore: 'Sabbatai'. I had heard this name from earliest childhood because in synagogue a man is called to the Reading of the Law by his own and his father's first (i.e. Hebrew) names. When my father, not himself officiating, was called – always a moment of high drama to a small child – the synagogue would resound to what was to me a very personal cry: 'Arise, David son of Sabbatai!' It was a name very different from the common Jewish names around me, but at that stage nothing more. The magic began when I first read a book on Jewish history and discovered that in the seventeenth century the whole of Jewry – indeed the whole of the western world – had been convulsed by the appearance of a Messiah bearing this same first name: Sabbatai Zevi. My grandfather, it seemed to me, must have been called after him, and this would be no accident. For, as I pursued my reading, I learnt that though this Messiah had become an apostate to the Moslem faith, thus shattering all the Jewish dreams that had been built around him, some of his followers had kept their belief in him intact in secret societies that continued to flourish in Eastern Europe until modern times. To these latter-day Sabbateans, the fact that the Founder had sinned in apostasy was, if anything, the final proof that Redemption would still arrive through him; for the ancient hope had always specified that the Messiah would come only when traditional Jewish moralities were brought into complete ruin. The Sabbateans held Evil to be as necessary as Good. Sabbatai himself, at the height of his fame, had based his preaching on terrifying heresies of this kind, and had been party (in fact or rumour) to every kind of sexual aberration. The later Sabbateans kept this side of him alive in secret rituals and sexual orgies that led to their repeated excommunication. Yet they stayed in existence. To have called a child by this legendary name must surely have been the act of a secret adherent. Was there a streak of this in my lineage?

Alas! I soon discovered that 'Sabbatai' – and its familiar form 'Shepsi' in Yiddish – had been an extremely common first name in Russian Jewry, with no orgy significance of any kind. When Grandfather Pruss finally came to life for me, it was to be in quite a different way. Yet it was a healthy instinct to have sought him in whatever form, and to have mourned the break in lineage that my father's change of name implied. I had compounded it myself with a further change, which in time I came also to regret. For though my motive, ostensibly, was to reach back into my Hebrew past, there is something phoney – even shoddy – about all such manipulations of identity. It is human, it may even be necessary, sometimes. But it is also, in the deepest sense, self-defeating.

The Jews, of course, have always been caught in this peculiar paradox. There was no problem where they lived cut off in their own communities, but whenever the barriers began to fall, the problem of identity raised its head, symbolized for all of them by the surname they bore or chose to adopt. It has reached an extreme form in Israel today, where a large part of the entire nation, by a conscious act of will, has severed itself from the immediate past by discarding all Russian and German sounding names, and returning to, or concocting, Hebrew names. Here, one might think, the motivation is so open and clear that it can carry no psychological disadvantages in its train. Yet even as

part of a national movement, with all the confidence that this
engenders, there is an underlying confusion of identity, just as
potent as in the more modest case of Chaim Raphael from
Vilkomir.

On the surface what has happened in Israel seems direct and
healthy, in contrast to the process in the *Galuth* (exile), where the
unending name-changing had many motives that are usually
thought less admirable – snobbishness, cowardice, convenience,
safety, fashion. But the contrast may not be as marked as this.
In Israel also, the newly adopted names may carry some elements
of concealment, false pride and subterfuge. On the bandwagon
of Hebraization, one ceases to be different from one's neighbours –
a common element in *Galuth* name-changing. From another
angle, one may be harking after distinction. One can pick a
name that somehow implies *yichuss* (proud lineage), one can drop
a name associated with inferior class-status (e.g. oriental origin).
These are human foibles, and if one mentions them in relation to
Israel, it is to establish the fact that on names (as on some other
things) the Jews of Israel are sometimes guilty of typical *Galuth*
failings that they claim to have left behind.

Trying to be as kind as one can about name-changing, one has
to admit that there can be a sense of renewal in it. The real test is
whether the new name becomes natural, if not for the changes, at
least for his children. It cannot work properly if it is only a
desperate attempt to conceal the past. One helpful ingredient
in making it work is to recognize that a process of this kind is likely
to carry some comic overtones, especially at first. The one crime
is to be too pompous about it.

Certainly in England, name-changing to sound more English
than the English themselves has always brought with it a good
many jokes, as well as ironies. Among the ironies there was the
moment, at the outbreak of the First World War with Germany
in 1914, when the process, which had been going on discreetly for
generations, was suddenly given public blessing by the example of
the Royal Family. The noble English Battenbergs, cousins of the
King, were thought to sound too German and became 'Mount-
batten'. With no delay whatever, the Jews leapt on this golden

opportunity to be equally patriotic in burying their German links. Hermanns were dropped right and left, Loewenstein was turned into Layton, Rosenheim became Rose, Schloss became Castle and also (through taking a mother's name) Waley – the famous translator of Chinese and Japanese poetry. The determination not to sound German was almost Israeli in its fervour, and often just as *gauche* in execution, as when the bearer of a really distinguished name in the art world changed overnight from a euphonious Rothenstein into an awkward Rutherston.

Should one really just enjoy all these ironies? While the Jews of England were desperately burying German names, the Jews of Germany were trying with equal fervour to establish them. It had been going on there for very much longer, of course, and one can see the process acted out with all its black humour in the story of one family – the progenitors of the musician Felix Mendelssohn Bartholdy. At the first stage, in the middle of the eighteenth century, Felix's grandfather, the great Moses Mendelssohn, had assumed this surname with the aim of expressing the new harmony that could exist in being both a Jew and a German. As a young man, he had moved to Berlin from Dessau, where his father Mendel ran a *cheder* (Hebrew school), and quickly absorbed German culture. When he came to publish his first major essay, he looked for a signature that would express his rising status. Jews in those days usually took their place of origin as a family name, though in some cases they were identified through their mother, as in 'Deiche's children', which has yielded the proud surname now spelt 'Daiches'. A signature in either of these forms must have seemed too Yiddish for Moses. Instead, he chose a sonorous patronymic, and became Mendelssohn.

Nothing, alas, is ever resolved as easily as this. In the next generation, his son Abraham, who had become a banker, was baptised into Christianity; and soon Abraham was ready to accept the argument of an oily brother-in-law that 'for the sake of the children' he should put a more Christian-sounding name on top of Mendelssohn. The brother-in-law, born Salomon, had taken the name Bartholdy from a house he owned in Rome. Abraham agreed to soft-pedal his origin this way and emerged, rather timidly at first, as a hyphenated Mendelssohn-Bartholdy. So far, it was a familiar process: the twist came with his son Felix, a musical prodigy as a child and now ready to move into higher things. Before his first major concert, Abraham had cards engraved for his son in the form: *Felix M. Bartholdy*. But Felix, though a sincere Christian, refused to use them, insisting that his name was Mendelssohn. Abraham now became desperate. His son *had* to drop the name Mendelssohn:

> A Christian Mendelssohn is an impossibility. There can be no more a Christian Mendelssohn than a Jewish Confucius. If Mendelssohn is your name, you are *ipso facto* a Jew.

With great reluctance, Felix agreed to use both names, at least in Germany. In England – scene of his greatest musical *and social* triumphs – he was known, and still is, as Felix Mendelssohn. The Bartholdy cover proved useless in Germany, even against the anti-semitism of his own time. Under the Nazis, his music was totally forbidden.

The pressures were far less strong in England; but if the process of name-changing took much longer there to get into full swing, it still left ample opportunity for irony to raise its head more than once in the story. The Swaythling family is a good case in point. The noble barony of Lord Swaythling descends from a bullion merchant who started first as 'Moses Samuel', moved on to become '*Montagu* Samuel', and then, with a neat reversal, 'Samuel Montagu'. There is a story that on the day on which this last change was announced in the *London Gazette*, the bearer of the new name was greeted, as he arrived in the City, by a large banner stretching across the street which read: 'And the Lord said unto Moses: MONTAGU!'

As it happens, this was not a case of fleeing from being Jewish. The first Lord Swaythling was, throughout his life, a passionate and 'public' Jew. Indeed, his family name 'Samuel', which had apparently been so carefully buried, survived to become of the utmost distinction in British life, as borne by his nephew Herbert, the first Viscount Samuel. However, there are no loose ends in history. The Moses-Montagu syndrome was to make itself evident again when Swaythling's son Edwin Montagu, who was a top political figure, did his best, as a member of the British Cabinet of 1917, to prevent the Balfour Declaration from being issued. He argued that the idea of Jews having a special link with Palestine would hurt the status of 'British Jews'. Luckily for Jewish history, his cousin Herbert Samuel – also a member of this Cabinet – fought on the other side, and ultimately took on the job of making the Jewish National Home a reality by becoming the first High Commissioner of Palestine. The two cousins expressed perfectly between them the ambivalence of Jewish life in the *Galuth*.

Of all the changes, the most objectionable are, perhaps, those of the pussy-footing type, where the character is trying to pretend that nothing has really happened (as when 'Levine' becomes 'Le Vien'), or when a minute change miraculously turns something essentially Jewish into something essentially English, for which the classic example must surely be 'Katz' into 'Keats'. Speaking for myself, my hackles rise less when the change is abrupt and ruthless, as it is so often with writers ('Emile Herzog' into 'André Maurois'), or in the world of the theatre, and especially the movies. It is entirely acceptable, for example, that a contortionist called 'Erich Weiss' became 'Harry Houdini'. Hollywood being above all a fantasy place, it fits in perfectly to learn that the Warner Brothers were originally called 'Eichelbaum'. Good for them, and for all the others. There is a touch of supreme bravado in turning 'Avrom Goldbogen' into 'Mike Todd'.

Any change with this kind of authority or panache is acceptable, provided one is prepared to laugh at it at the same time. And let no one think that it is easy to pick a name in this way out of the blue. The right degree of *chutzpah* has to be calculated to a T. A *New Yorker* cartoon made this point perfectly in showing a lawyer giving advice to a rather pimply young man sitting on the other side of his desk: 'There is no difficulty that I can foresee, Mr. Goldstein, in changing your name to Ashley Pointdexter, but "Ashley Pointdexter 3rd" is perhaps pushing things a little hard.'

The latent humour embedded in Jewish *Galuth* names depends on their reflection of the comedy always inherent in human adjustment – the alien landing on a foreign shore, the country bumpkin coming to town. It is a universal theme, but the Jews have symbolized it particularly and are entitled to milk it for laughs, given all the tears that have been there too. Often, of course, the fun arises in the contrast that emerges very pointedly – but also naturally – between forename and surname. One has a suspicion that in Israel today something more than the old name humour has been lost by flattening out the two halves of a *Galuth* name into something solidly (and often artificially) Hebrew.

Even as comedy one regrets the loss. There is something beautifully apt and wry in the split personality names evoked so effortlessly in the writings of S. J. Perelman. Randy Kalbfuss, Howard Lebkuchan and Ivy Nudnick ('sauciest co-ed in the class') are up in his gallery of immortals with Manuel Dexterides, the Greek shipping-owner. The Israelies decided to turn their back on all this. The *Galuth*, and all that it had brought with it, was to be wiped out. Jewish history, which had been interrupted in A.D. 70 with the destruction of Jerusalem by the Romans, would now be resumed where it had left off, or rather would go back to a still earlier period, the original Old Testament days when the Hebrews lived proudly and independently in their own land. The symbol of this would lie in the adoption of pure Hebrew names – as pure, in fact, as Raphael.

The trouble is that history doesn't work this way. The *Galuth* world is vividly present everywhere in Israel, and not simply as a bad memory that has to be obliterated. The marvellous achievements of Israel are based not on the mystic heritage of the Patriarchs but on the skill of generations of *Galuth* folk – the Goldsteins and the Rabinovitchs – who grew out of their own time and place and took with them the qualities that had developed. It is true that their *ideology* envisaged something entirely new, harking back for authority to an ancient past: but in expression it was a continuation of the essential character of *Galuth* existence – the warmth and kinship of Jewish life, infiltrated at every level with the ideas and experience of the non-Jewish world around it. In this unique amalgam, it was as modern Jews, not ancient Hebrews, that they turned and still turn with such enthusiasm to the European ideals of political liberty, humanism, socialism, and every form of economic and artistic experiment. The flirtation with an archaic Hebraism has proved abortive; and to this extent the earlier passion to Hebraize all surnames is out of tune with the full acceptance, evident everywhere in Israel today, of the unique genius and influence of the *Galuth* character.

This is not to say that the abiding presence of the Bible in everyday Israeli life is in any way weakened, and one evidence of this is the way in which the Bible text is combed assiduously for the most obscure *forenames* that can be resurrected. What we are now being spared, however, is the pressure that originally forced anyone at all active in public life (and, by osmosis, masses of private citizens) to abandon a lineage expressed in a *Galuth* surname.

It had begun in its *official* form, with an Order of the Day issued in 1948 by David Ben-Gurion, who had adopted this resounding surname ('the lion's whelp') nearly fifty years earlier in exchange for 'David Gruen'. At the height of the battles for independence, this warrior Prime Minister called on all leaders to adopt Hebrew names immediately, so that history, recounting the tale, would see the heroes in full Hebrew guise. But if this was a natural sentiment during the excitement of war, name-changing in the years which followed began to take on some of the fashionable quality of Jewish name-changing in the *Galuth*. What persuaded the outstanding Bible scholar Torczyner – he deciphered the Lachish Letters in 1936 – to become an unnatural 'Tur-Sinai'? Why did the famous archaeologist Maisler give up this very old and distinguished Jewish surname and turn into 'Mazar'? And is there any validity in adopted names like 'Oz' (strength), 'Ishon' (apple of the eye), or 'Duvdevan' (cherry, presumably for Kirsch), not to mention the now innumerable and unmemorable varieties of Ben-this and Bar-that.

Perhaps, in perspective, nothing that has happened will be too

serious. One simply feels it a pity to have lost some special
memories of the Diaspora, as when a professor born of an ancient
academic family in Italy turned the delicious 'Bonaventura' into
'Asheri'. Those that stayed with their *Galuth* names seem now
to have asserted something of special significance. Can one
imagine Chaim Weizmann, the greatest leader of them all, taking
on a synthetic front through a change of name?

The pen-names that writers take reflect something different: it is
part of their act of imagination – a name to match the world they
are creating for us. Yet even here, name-changing can go
slightly awry. I have no complaint of the famed pen-name
'Sholem Aleichem' (though naturally I miss his original name,
Rabinovitch). But there is something disappointing in the fact
that the outstanding writer of our time, the Nobel prize-winner
Samuel Joseph Agnon, took this surname – an echo of the title of
his first book – for himself completely, to replace his original and
expressive name 'Czackes' or, as we Litvaks pronounce it,
'Tzatzkess'. Certainly it would have been an awkward name to
spell in Hebrew. What we have lost, however, is a living evocation, through the earlier name, of the world he wrote about.
There was a case here for keeping the link. With no other writer
does one feel so clearly the timeless quality of Jewish existence, far
above fashions in names or feelings. If I press the point, there is a
reason. It was through Agnon, as I will tell, that I came finally
to recover my grandfather Shepsi: and Shepsi would certainly
have been quite at ease with 'Tzatzkess'.

If one's origin lies in the lost world of Eastern Europe, as it does
for so many Jews of today, it is through Agnon's imagination that
one comes to understand it. Agnon wrote not as a social realist
but as a poet. There is no false sentiment, no bravado, no cute-
ness, no *schmaltz*. His characters are, at one level simple earthy
people, saints and sinners; yet at another level they reflect qualities
they could not themselves define – an absorption in the mystery of
Jewish existence, the endless dialectic between things spiritual and
material, the knife-edge balance between subservience to God and

defiance. In my own case I began to feel, when I first discovered Agnon, that it was in reading his stories of these people, rather than by inventing derivations of my family name, that I was finding my way back to the grandfather I had never known.

I had read much else, of course, about that far-off world, and in particular had sought in books to find out something about the one firm element in my family's history – the town of Vilkomir that had been mentioned so often in my childhood as our place of origin. At first I seemed up against a psychological barrier on this. In the reference books of today the town no longer exists. When Lithuania was created after the First World War, Vilkomir was re-named Ukmerge. Everything that was warm and mysterious seemed to disappear in a change of this kind.

And then one day, some years ago, the curtain began to lift. In conversation with a very old Yiddish-speaking lady, I discovered that she too had come from Vilkomir. She had grown up there, in fact. Had she ever heard of my father David as a young *chazan* there, or of his father Shepsi? 'Shepsi?' she cried. 'Of course! Shepsi the Shammus!' A *shammus* is a beadle, the man-of-all-jobs in a *shul* (synagogue). Her family had been members of his *shul*. She remembered my father as a very young man for his beautiful singing voice and his fair colouring. But it was Shepsi who had been most vivid to her as a child. He had been a tall burly man with a great red beard. She could see him now in her mind's eye, standing on a little hill in the quarter of Vilkomir they lived in ('*untern Vasser*') calling everyone to prayer at the set times, morning, afternoon and evening: '*In shul arein! In shul arein!*'

At last I was finding him, and as a *shammus* – the most solid, familiar character in the whole of that mysterious world. I remember Agnon, in *Days of Awe*, describing the special holiness of *Rosh Hashonah* (New Year) precisely in terms of the *shammus*'s call to prayers:

One rose earlier for morning prayers on *Rosh Hashonah* than on any other day. In some places, the *shammus* calls people to prayers while it is still night, so that all may be in *shul* by sunrise . . .

This was my grandfather: '*In shul arein! In shul arein!*'

And there is another *shammus* that I know from Agnon, the widower Mechel in *The Bridal Canopy* who, at a memorable Seder *à deux* on Passover Eve, finds love with the rich widow Sara-Leah. Mechel is no dreamy, accident-prone, quixotic character like Sholem Aleichem's Tevye. He is a proud, stubborn man, utterly independent in the menial duties which Fate has allotted him. His loneliness that night, as he locks up the *shul* and sets out to walk back to his empty house, is deliberate. With festivity in the air around him, he has refused all invitations to the Seder. A man can exist alone. The *shul* that Mechel guards, the prayers and the daily study-sessions which centre around it, are self-sufficient: they come together as an absolute of life – a Jew's bargain with his Creator. We are not taken through Mechel's philosophy, but we see it emerging in Agnon's exploration of what kinship means to a Jew. The kinship of Jews with God is expressed in the routine of the synagogue or *Beit Midrash* (study house) – a mixture of fear and familiarity. The kinship of all Jews with each other can be symbolized happily in the fellowship of the Seder. But there is a third type of kinship, in which two individual souls – a man and a woman – approach each other at the deepest level in a joint celebration of their joy at being Jewish. This is what grows in Mechel's mind as he accepts Sara-Leah's invitation and sits down at her table for a calm but increasingly joyous recital of the Seder service. Two human beings are reborn to life that night. In the morning, the sound of a man singing can be heard again in Sara-Leah's house as she busies herself with the daily routine.

I was content, now, with the image of Shepsi that was growing in my mind; but suddenly – within a few weeks, in fact – I made the second discovery and the story was complete.

My father's elder brothers, well-settled in the United States, had sent us many letters in the old days, or rather our Pruss cousins had – exciting-looking letters on large sheets of crisp, expensive writing-paper. Over the years, the flow had dwindled. Only one cousin wrote now, and at long intervals, mostly to tell us of marriages and deaths in the family. A letter from this cousin

arrived one day to say that another cousin – a very old lady, the
eldest daughter of the eldest brother – was on her way to England
as part of a package Zionist tour to Israel. I was told of the hotel
and the date, and went to see her.

We exchanged pleasantries, and then I began to ask if she
remembered anything from her childhood about our grandfather
in Vilkomir. It was an effort for her to think back, but she tried.
Before the War – World War I, of course – they had received
letters from time to time. Our grandmother had died. Grandfather had remarried, and his second wife had died. He himself,
now of venerable age, had survived.

When the War broke out, all letters had stopped. And then,
shortly after the War – around 1920, it seemed – they had a message
about him through a new immigrant from Vilkomir. The
Germans had invaded Lithuania. There had been starvation,
burning of villages, pogroms, with the Russians as violent and
murderous as the Germans. What difference did it make whose
soldiers were on the rampage? Whatever happened at a time of
violence, it was the Jews who suffered.

One day, a troop of horsemen had ridden into the town –
plundering, beating, ravaging. Grandfather was standing on the
little hill outside his *shul*. They had ridden him down, and that
was how he had died – trampled to death by a 'Cossack'.

I had been waiting for something like this to complete the story.
It was not the martyrdom of Hitler's day, but it was enough. In
every generation, the Jews of that world saw the Four Horsemen
galloping towards them. Always it seemed the end, yet something survived.

Again I thought of Agnon. In one of his most mysterious
books, *A Guest for the Night*, a writer now living in Israel returns
to his little hometown of Szibucz in Galicia. Only a remnant of
Jews are left from the Holocaust, and they are all planning to leave
for Israel and other places. He goes to his old *Beit Midrash* – the
prayer and study-centre which in childhood had seemed huge, the
rock of existence. It is a small crumbling building which is now
going to be abandoned. 'You can have the keys, if you like', they
tell him. He takes them and begins to spend his days in the

deserted building, listening to the stories of people who drop in, and letting his mind wander over a past of history and folklore. Slowly, a tapestry of life is rewoven. Someone brings wood for the stove. He finds some oil for the Eternal Lamp, 'which lit a tablet on the wall on which the names of the sacred communities killed in the pogroms of 1648 are engraved'.

The world had seemed to end then, but faith had been too strong. The story of Szibucz was over, but its people went on. He recalls what the Midrash says: when the Messiah comes, the Jews of all history will roll underground to come to eternal life in the Holy Land; but those who are martyred for the sanctity of God's name do not suffer this terrifying journey. As they die in *Galuth*, they are reborn instantly in Israel.

THE ANCIENT MEMORY

I WILL write later in this book about the studies I was led into when I began to explore Jewish history in general and not merely my own. But there is one area of exploration that has its roots immutably in the emerging child, however wide its later ramifications.

There is an ancient memory in Jewish experience that was for many centuries more pervasive, and more intimately felt, than anything else of the past. Unlike the Revelation at Sinai, which took the Jew into the far reaches of myth and poetry, this was a tangible event in history, the destruction of Jerusalem by the Romans in A.D. 70, known quite simply as 'the Destruction'. Every prayer and ceremony referred to it. As a child, the Destruction and the dream of a Restoration filled my mind.

The memory persisted as an underlying theme when I began, in the mid-1930s, to get involved in Jewish studies and spent six months in Jerusalem at the Hebrew University. It occurred to me, on returning to Oxford, that here was a subject I should write about. One could study the Destruction factually, mostly in the writings of Josephus. One could study it in a different way from the inside, in the writings of the rabbis of the time.

But the real purpose of a book of this kind would be one's preoccupation with the Destruction as a living factor in Jewish experience. The rabbis of the first Christian centuries had produced a work in this spirit, the *Midrash* (commentary) on *Lamentations*. If I translated and edited this text and let it speak to me, an English Jew of the twentieth century, with all the personal overtones that history adds year by year, I might be able to communicate something of the abiding feeling that all of us are heirs to.

In the event, history was preparing to take the Jews by the throat at this precise time, giving the subject of the book an unforeseen symbolism, but also throwing a shadow over a work couched so heavily in academic terms. By 1939, when the book was ready, I hesitated to publish it. 'Study' had become an irrelevance against the reality of Germany. The horror revealed in the war years was the final bar. One was baffled, speechless.

The years passed, and values – old and new – began to reassert themselves. Living with a new Destruction had given depth to the enlargement I had experienced in pursuing the story of the old one. In academic terms, startling discoveries in the postwar years had transformed one's knowledge of the ancient past. At the level of feeling, two totally opposite experiences had surfaced, one inexpressibly tragic, the other resonant with happiness – the birth of Israel. The book began to grow again in my mind with these new dimensions.

I had been engaged since the war in Government work, but the ancient memory still obsessed me. '*O joy! that in our embers/Is something that doth live.*' For Wordsworth this was inspiriting, but not enough. It was the 'obstinate questionings', he said, which gave life meaning: and there is a resilience in this which I wanted to express. If I needed a testing-point, it came when I had finally re-written the book in this new spirit, and had it ready for publication.

There had been a long gap of time, and if I say that I finally sent it to my publisher at the end of May 1967, I am half-way to revealing the new drama that had now caught up with it. For a time, we had thought that Jewish independence had been secured with Israel, but now the enemies were again at the gate. The nightmare of a new Destruction froze every Jewish heart.

We waited: and there was a six-day deliverance which had the air of a miracle. In its afterglow, my mind turned not only to the book but to all the experience that lay behind it. What a long road it had been from the childhood days of sitting with my father, listening to tales of the Destruction. As I thought of it now, it brought back not merely the outward dramas we had all lived through, but years of enrichment as I was led, through teachers and friends, to explore the world I had inherited.

This is the path that I want to retrace. How else can I evoke the feelings that finally surfaced for all of us in June 1967?

．　．　．　．　．

The book I had written was for those who know that the history of one's own people is never a mere collection of facts. Facts are available to anyone: but history from within evokes different associations. Sometimes a single word is etched in the mind, as 'Flodden' is for the Scots.

For Jews, the loss of Jerusalem and its Temple to the Romans in A.D. 70 was not simply a searing memory, for more than their own sorrow was at stake. It was not just the Jewish people whose sense of exile now began. God Himself had been driven into exile. The world was out of joint. The Destruction was the symbol of it.

Hundreds of years earlier, when the *first* Temple had been destroyed by Nebuchadnezzar (586 B.C.), a beautiful elegy had emerged – the Book of Lamentations, ascribed to the prophet Jeremiah. Meeting in the shadow of the new sorrow, it was to *Lamentations* that the rabbis now turned, applying every word, by way of poetic parallel, to their own tragedy. 'Midrash' means, literally, exegesis, and thus it was that endless rabbinic commentary was built up, generation after generation, around the book that spoke most intimately to them of the Destruction.

For centuries the talk was transmitted orally, but its power survived when it was finally edited into an independent work, probably in the sixth century. To read it is to hear echoes of what the Destruction felt like from within, not merely when the stories were first told by the rabbis but in all the centuries that followed.

Not that it is solely a book of anguish. Even for the old rabbis, much more was likely to emerge as a reflection of their world. Wit, reason and the simple desire for entertainment – in the terms of their age – break through. They might have lost their Temple and their independence, but life went on. These people tilled the soil, engaged in business, and travelled all over the Mediterranean countries where their fellow-Jews lived in large communities. They feasted, fasted, quarrelled, and rejoiced among themselves, and struggled as all communities do with the problems of rich and poor, envy and pride.

But above all, they loved to meet and talk, and though the teacher always opened a discourse with a Biblical text, any kind of

story was liable to get dragged in.   There are travellers' tales, as
tall as they come, echoed in the *Thousand and One Nights*, tales of
deduction by a rabbinic Sherlock Holmes, dream interpretations
half on their way to Freud.   If memory could be searing, it could
also recall the good old days when, as one always tends to feel,
everything was better than now.   If the fighting was recalled,
everyone had a blitz story, and the the synagogue was the place to
find a listener.

Most of the talk turned inward – to the Torah and the Jewish
fate; but this led them inevitably to consider also the world around
them, so that the Midrash is full of detailed comment – descrip-
tion, argument or diatribe – on the strange ideas and practices of
those peoples who were free from the blessings and curses of the
Jewish destiny.   It is absorbing to see in the rabbinic writings the
reflection of the classical and the early Christian world, distorted
in one sense, enhanced in another by the special viewpoint.   In
comparison with any classical text of the time, the Midrash is
exaggerated and inchoate; but it is also lively and imaginative,
bursting with variety, and an endless subject – as later scholars and
poets found – for further study and exposition.

The Midrash on *Lamentations* was, then, my starting-point.   In
academic terms, the immediate task was to establish the rabbinic
background, but it was impossible to write without being aware
that the subject had not come to an end then.   All of us, involved in Jewish life throughout the centuries, have constantly
enlarged this Midrash on our history, expressing it in terms of our
age.

For centuries after the Destruction itself, the feeling never
changed: but if the same source was drawn on, the writers themselves had different horizons.   The Psalmist who had wept by the
waters of Babylon when he remembered Zion, had expressed his
feeling with infinite simplicity: *How can we sing the Lord's song in a
strange land*?   Sixteen hundred years later, the poet Judah Halevi,
living in Moorish Spain in the twelfth century, felt an almost
identical longing, and expressed it in a Hebrew just as pure: but he

was a man of another time. The rhythms of his poignant *Ode to Zion*, like those of his very personal love poems, are in Arabic verse forms learnt from his Moorish contemporaries. He practised medicine in Toledo, presumably writing his poetry (like Dannie Abse today) in time off from his patients.

If we leap from that golden age to yesterday's turbulent world of Czarist Russia, we find the memory of the Destruction still expressed in the most elegant Hebrew; but by now, as in the hands of the poet Chaim Nachman Bialik, it carries with it the vehemence of the world outside. Bialik's epic poem on the Destruction of his own day, the Kishinev massacre of 1903, moves far beyond the traditional acceptance of God's will. Overcome with grief, he bursts into a revolutionary anger as he listens to the survivor's dirge in the synagogue:

> They beat their breasts and confess their sins, crying: We have sinned, we have betrayed . . . But their words belie their hearts. Can a broken vessel sin? Can a shattered pot transgress? Why do they *pray* to Me? Tell them to thunder *against* Me! Let them raise their fists against Me and claim recompense for their shame – the shame of all their generations from time immemorial.

The balance changes with each generation. In our own time, with Bialik's cry realized and the bonds of the past apparently loosened, the Midrash nevertheless continues to reassert itself. Writers of Jewish origin have something to say of the history that lies behind them as if this is part of their personal celebration of existence. Would the old rabbis, transported to the twentieth century, recognize their kin? Easily, perhaps, in an American writer like Malamud – Rabbi Bernard the Meek. They could be at home anywhere in his books, but especially in *The Assistant*, built, as it is, entirely around the rabbinic concept of the *Ger Zedek* – the non-Jew who feels the need to take on the burden, King Christian of Denmark putting on the yellow armband to defy the Nazis. And what of Saul Bellow and his rabbi *manqué*, Moses Elkanah Herzog? Is anything more in the tradition of the prophets, the Midrash, and the medieval *maggid* than the wild letters that Herzog is always writing:

Has the filthy moment come when moral feeling dies, conscience disintegrates, and respect for liberty, law, public decency, all the rest, collapses in cowardice, decadence, blood? ... The subject is too great, too deep for such weakness, cowardice – too deep, too great, Shapiro. It torments me to insanity that you should be so misled. A merely aesthetic critique of modern history! After the wars and mass killings! You are too intelligent for this. You inherited rich blood. Your father peddled apples.

An American Midrash. Back among the early fathers, Rabbi Elishah ben Abuya, the atheist who never really left home, would have approved. From the British shore the voice is different. In a recent poem, an English Jew, Nathaniel Tarn, speaks through Rabbi Simon ben Yohai, the mystic of the second century:

> On the thrones round the sky's house of study
> the wise blind themselves with God, come down no more,
> while Zion's rooster crows for me, the Jordan-winged.

It seems that everyone may have his or her own Midrash on Zion, in which thoughts, feelings, memories are dealt with – sometimes put down in writing. There is no need to search for historic parallels, they exist everywhere: it is simply a matter of what one responds to. I worked briefly, in 1940, in an internment camp for German-Jewish refugees in England. Entering a hut there, one day, I found a group of Orthodox Jews, abstracted from the confusion around them, while they chanted, to the ancient mournful tune, the Book of *Lamentations*. I had forgotten – it had never occurred to me – that it was the Fast of Ab, the anniversary of the Destruction. They took no notice of me when I walked in: I was a British official, as remote to them as Joseph to his brethren. When I made myself known as their brother, in Joseph's words, they invited me to stay. A small group, led by a rabbi, had formed a study class; they were planning to spend the afternoon reading the Midrash on *Lamentations*. They would start at the beginning and plough on – endless tales of sorrow lit by the certainty of hope.

Around them, nothing could have looked more desperate. Hitler was triumphant everywhere; his bombers were over

England daily, his Afrika Korps was pointed towards Palestine.
But as they read the Midrash they would accept quite simply that
there would be a Return – when Israel had suffered enough, or
when God was ready. Was Germany the final horror, too
much even for the God who had tolerated the massacres of
Masada, York, and Kishinev? Perhaps, for this time there
was redemption. Within eight years of this particular Fast of
Ab the Return was accomplished – the State of Israel was re-
established, and many of these same Jews are no doubt living
there. Is the story over? By no means. What does it signify?
I don't know. One responds to it in the way one responds to
tragedy in the theatre. Forces are around in the air; in one's
own brief span of life, one catches the tune without knowing
the words.

Every nation has its Midrash – the feeling that history has
lighted on it in a mysterious way from time to time, and that
words from the past have a recurrent magic. I think of the film
Henry V, made in England during the war. For Shakespeare's
audience in 1599, when he wrote the play, Henry's great speech –
We few, we happy few – spoke not so much of Agincourt, nearly
two hundred years earlier, as of their ten-year-old victory over
the Spanish Armada and their new feeling as a nation. When we in
turn heard the words, in the cinema in 1944 with the buzz-bombs
overhead, another fleet had just sailed for the coast of France. No
one needed to explain – or could explain – what it all meant. We
sat in the dark, at some moments in tears.

The Midrash on *Lamentations* was clearly following me around.
It seemed a further illustration of the way a subject grows in one
of its own volition if one is open to receive it.

In working on the Midrash I had no expectation, even when I
was amassing long scholarly footnotes, that I was going to make
some original discoveries. For that, I would have needed a
rabbinic expertise that was beyond me. Yet I did feel a special
involvement, going back to the schoolboy experience of learning
that there were direct links between the general history emerging

at school and the Jewish world which had enveloped me since infancy.

The most graphic example surfaced, in fact, in relation to the Destruction. As a child, I had been told stories from the Midrash about an Emperor called Hadrian who had slaughtered our ancestors. How startled I was to discover one day that this same man, before going to Palestine, had built a wall – 'Hadrian's Wall' – in England, still standing only a few miles from our house, as part of his war against the Picts. I began to wonder where the Jewish story fitted in with what was told to us at school. Every time I lifted the curtain a little, the light flowed in.

Rummaging about in the school library one day, I came across a musty old book, apparently by a classical writer called Flavius Josephus, called *The Antiquities of the Jews*. It was William Whiston's translation (1890), which has no explanatory Introduction, and it was therefore a long time before I realized that Josephus was not a 'classical' writer, but a Jew like me! I vividly recall how moved I was when, at the age of eighteen, I summoned up enough courage to go through the door of a Catholic church for the first time and heard the priest, to my amazement, reciting an exact Latin translation of our Hebrew prayers.

Things began to fall into place when I read some standard books on Jewish history, but the greatest illumination came when I finally caught up with the marvellous comparative studies which – all unknown to my father, and *his* father – had developed during the nineteenth century, mainly in Germany, in Jewish history and literature. Working on the Midrash, I plunged into some of the books written by these Jewish scholars, astonished at the width of their learning. Though without any great erudition of my own, I was able at least to enjoy some of the fruits of this scholarship. I saw in it, as in the Midrash itself, a succession of *tradents*, handing on to each other, arguing, supporting, denouncing. I even sat for a short while at the feet of some of the direct participants in this great tradition – two in particular who had come to live in England in the early years of the century, Adolf Büchler and Arthur Marmorstein. My most moving memory of these men is not their scholarship, but their piety. As with the rabbis of old, study was itself holy, to be approached with the same *kavanah* (devotion) as an act of prayer.

It is one of the marvels of our time that this instinctive respect for the Jewish tradition has been justified so strongly in recent decades by the momentous discoveries of archaeology. So much of what these scholars felt in their bones has been shown to be true.

They had never doubted that the Jewish tradition would be justified by outside learning. To their expertise in the rabbinic writings of ancient and mediaeval times, they had added a boundless interest in all kinds of 'non-Jewish' study – the Church Fathers, law, the natural sciences of the times, philosophy, folklore, and anything else that might be relevant.

In form, it was all heavily Germanic: but even at an early stage I was able to feel an essential difference between these 'interior' Jewish studies and the other kind of German scholarship – that ponderous, inhuman, and in one sense destructive criticism written by the great non-Jewish scholars of the late nineteenth century. On the Bible itself, books and passages in them had been ruthlessly ascribed to different authors and periods, obscure words had been daringly changed as 'corruptions'. What made things worse was that this was accompanied by disdain, and even contempt, for the 'unscientific' tradition of the rabbis, for whom every word of every text, biblical or talmudic, was sacrosanct. The rabbis were seen as the Pharisees who believed in the letter rather than the spirit. As a Jew, one felt that there was something wrong in all this.

The trouble was that in my student days there seemed no way, short of blind faith, to justify this feeling. There were no manuscripts of the Bible going back to ancient times, and little else even of the early post-Biblical years to show whether the Jewish tradition of the text, which assumed preservation rather than corruption, had genuine validity. While the later rabbinic interpretations seemed echoed in other surviving books, nothing tangible had emerged to give these interpretations some ancient origin, so that comparative studies could be built on a firm foundation. Everything was, so to speak, theoretical. The *Halakhah* – a vast compendium of laws discussed in the Talmud – seemed too full of abstract hairsplitting of Biblical verses to have any relation to practical life. The *Haggadah* (story-telling covering history and myth) was equally vague. One never knew to what extent the rabbis based it on the past or had made it up out of their own heads. Even the *characters* in rabbinic stories, such as the rebel leader known alternatively as 'Bar Kozibah' or 'Bar Kokhbah', seemed half legendary. There was no other mention of him except in later writings of the Church historians. Like so much else in the rabbinic tradition, there seemed nothing firm to hold on to except a certain ring of truth.

And then, in 1947, came the discovery of the Dead Sea Scrolls, and the unearthing of much else in the soil and rocks of the Holy Land, which gave body to one's feelings both by the sight of the documents themselves and by the fact that their contents answered so many uncertainties. Much of what had been felt to be true was now *shown* to be true. And for good measure, the discoveries came in a succession of surprises each more startling than the other.

First, there were what can now be called the 'original' Dead Sea Scrolls, emerging from the area of Qumran almost on the shore of the Dead Sea, not far from Jericho. Among them were Bible manuscripts going back to Temple times, written with loving care in the familiar square script, the text sometimes exactly in line with the preserved tradition, in other cases throwing light on the pre-Destruction translation into Greek. There were Hebrew originals – or portions of them – of books known only in translation. There were Bible commentaries going back to the century before the Destruction and earlier, interpreting the verses in Midrashic style by relation to the events of the day. In the search for more scrolls, the settlement – or 'monastery' – of Qumran itself was unearthed, throwing a vivid light on how a sect of Jews (probably the Essenes) lived, worked, and prayed before their home was destroyed by the Romans, in A.D. 68, during the advance on Jerusalem.

Even the timing of this first series of discoveries had a provi-
dential air about it.   Qumran is on the west bank of the river
Jordan, but within the Jordan State as determined in 1948.   By
luck or Providence, the scrolls from there began to emerge before
the 1948 division of territory took place, so that the Israelis were
able to get legal possession of some of the most important of these
scrolls.   This would certainly have been more difficult, if not impossible, if they had come to light a year later.   And it was somehow satisfying that it was a Jewish scholar, Professor Sukenik of
the Hebrew University of Jerusalem, who was the first to feel
certain about the true age of these writings, and to guess at their
Essene origin.

Next to be mentioned came something, on the Israeli side of the
border, even more closely related to the Destruction: the opening
up of the ancient fortress of Masada, scene of the Zealots' last stand
against the Romans in A.D. 73.   Masada had lain untouched and
almost unapproachable at the top of the cliff towering over the
Dead Sea since its defenders, three years after the Destruction of
the Temple, had taken their own lives in a mass suicide – nobly
described by Josephus – rather than fall into the hands of the
enemy.   But now a series of excavations, completed in 1965,
revealed in profuse detail the events and conditions of the time.
As if to underline the inner unity of this whole subject, this excava-
tion was led by Yigael Yadin, a son of Sukenik and a military
leader of Israel's 1948 War of Independence.   Yadin and a great
band of Jewish and non-Jewish volunteers from many countries of
the world did more at Masada than document the Destruction
period.   The whole history of the fortress, going back to the days
of Herod, was uncovered.   But it was the evidence of the last
defense which now rivets our interest.   They found Biblical
scrolls and other writings, holy and secular, contracts, personal
letters, pottery, food, clothing, weapons and, most touching of
all, the skeletal remains of some of the defenders.   One was of a
woman, with dark-brown plaits still attached to her scalp,
her sandals close by.   A *miqveh* (ritual bath) was found, the
only one extant from the time of the Temple.   Two of the
Biblical scrolls – portions of *Deuteronomy* and *Ezekiel* – were found

beneath the floor of an assembly hall, probably a synagogue, and
if so the oldest ever discovered. For any Jew with feeling for his
past, the personal link through Masada, as with the earlier discoveries at Qumran, was overwhelming.

But more has to be told, for the discoveries mentioned so far
deal mainly with Temple times and the Destruction period.
Equally startling for history – and much more revealing for the
background which came to be enshrined later in the writings of
the rabbis – the Judaean desert had begun to yield up at the same
time documents from a period sixty or seventy years *after* the
Destruction, and in particular from the three brief years – A.D. 132
to 135 – covering the revolt of the man we have always called Bar
Kokhbah.

Here again Providence – and tough work by the modern
Israelis – saw to it that a period of history which belonged to them
in legend was not to be illuminated solely by non-Jewish hands.
At first this had not been the case. Fragments had begun to
emerge on the Jordan side of the frontier in the early 1950s that
were sensational for Jews because they included letters from the
legendary Bar Kokhbah himself. For some time, the facts were
shrouded in mystery and rumour; but as material began to be
published from the Jordan side, it became clear that what was
emerging derived not only from exploration by reputable scholars in caves on their side, but also from forays by the Bedouin into
caves on the Israel side. Israeli scholars had already explored this
area, but their efforts had yielded little; now it was tackled differently. In the spring of 1960, and again a year later, the Israelis
mounted an intense search into four areas, each under a separate
leader, one of whom was Yadin, and with the powerful help of
the Israeli army. Fortune smiled on their work, and once again
particularly on Yadin. For, in one of the caves in the section
that he was in charge of, the Israelis, with enormous relief, unearthed caches of documents from the key period, including fifteen
letters from Bar Kokhbah himself or his headquarters, at least as
interesting as those in Jordanian hands.

With pride thus satisfied, the Jewish reader can now look as a
whole at these discoveries from the second century, to consider

what they mean to our personal contact with history.   We think
first of Bar Kokhbah himself.   His name, we see, was really Bar
Kosiba, though we shall presumably always keep the messianic-
sounding 'Bar Kokhbah'.   Everything in the letters is in line with
the very brief and scattered references to him that surfaced later in
rabbinic writings, both on his personal character and on incidents
in the rebellion.

But contrary to what might have been expected, the personal
echo of the legendary hero is by no means the most interesting
aspect of the discoveries.   The other documents – from both sides
of the frontier – deal not with heroics but with the humdrum day-
to-day business of people of the time.   Looking at them, one
sees eighteen centuries of abstract Talmudic discussion suddenly
verified in practical form.   Here are actual records of marriages
and divorces, with personal and property arrangements set out in
the exact form formalized by the rabbis of later centuries.   There
are contracts, equally graphic, for the ordinary purchase and sale
of property and for the leasing of land, with details of tithing and
taxing.   The documents are written, witnessed, and physically
set out in the precise form regularized in all later rabbinic ordinance.

The tradition, so long theoretical, comes to life in two ways.
First, these documents illuminate what has been received.
Second, since they exist often in only fragmentary form, they are
themselves only fully understood by virtue of the great corpus of
tradition to which the scholars turn for help.   The 'narrow'
Jewish tradition is suddenly of the widest significance, drawn on
by Jewish and non-Jewish scholars alike, but more intimately and
instinctively, as one would expect, by the former, who feel the
subject in their bones.

What comes to life also is the character of that brief and poignant period – A.D. 132–5 – in which the Jews of that small area of
Palestine tried to pretend to themselves that they could exist under
their own ruler, going about their daily lives and holding the
Romans at bay.   One of the scholars from the Jordan side, Father
J. T. Milik, who has presented many of these documents, has used
them to paint a vivid picture of the administration that the rebel

leader maintained. The rabbis, he says, looked back with nostalgia to many aspects of this era: 'The Midrash on *Lamentations* is
the requiem for this period of prosperity.'

But if the rabbis longed for the old prosperity, the Midrash
shows also how bitterly they remembered the toughness which
had put the rebel into this brief period of power. Their tradition
tells of his ruthless system for testing the bravery of his soldiers,
and how he did not flinch from putting his own uncle to death for
supposed treachery. They recall, too, the blasphemy of his devil-
may-care prayer on entering battle: 'All we ask, God, is: do not
help the enemy. Us you need not help.' He always seems
larger than life in the Midrash; and now we can hear him speaking
in the same style in a letter to the leader in charge of one of his
military posts: 'From Simon ben Kosiba to Joshua ben Galgula
and the men of the fort: Greeting! I call heaven to witness against
me that unless you destroy the Galileans who are with you, I shall
put you in fetters as I did to Ben Aphlul.'

It is hard to resist telling the story in terms of the thrill with which
one sees individual discoveries linking the present to the ancient
past. Yigael Yadin found himself in this stance when he revealed
his find of Bar Kokhbah letters to a gathering of archaeologists at
the home of the President of Israel. 'A screen had been erected,'
he writes, 'and when my turn came to report, I projected part of
a document and read aloud the first line of writing upon it: *Simon
Bar Kosiba, President over Israel.* Turning to the Head of State, I
said: "Your Excellency, I am honoured to be able to tell you that
we have discovered fifteen despatches written or dictated by the
last President of ancient Israel 1800 years ago".'

The discoveries affecting the Bible itself have the same kind of
direct personal interest for the Jews of Israel, and for Jews everywhere. The material unearthed at Near Eastern sites has been
enormously rich in recent decades. In my own student days,
Bible studies began to be enlarged to an unpredictable extent by
the discovery of vast archives and literature at Ras Shamra (from
1928), Nuzi (1931) and Mari (1933). Since the war, this has con-

tinued with major revelations at Jericho, Hazor, and, as recently as 1976, at Ebla.

But though the discoveries are reported, naturally enough, in newspaper headlines, the meaning has to be assessed in a longer perspective.   One gets on to the wrong foot by talking of them as proving that the Bible is true, for the truth of the Bible is not established by archaeology.   It lies, as it has always done, in the power of its teachings.   What the discoveries do is to illuminate the historical background in which these teachings first found expression.   And the same has to be said of the way the rabbis, who were to dominate Judaism for the ensuing 2,000 years, can now be seen in their original setting.

The discoveries do not confirm everything in the tradition. Their real bonus is that they restore an open mind.   With archaeology and other linked sciences filling the gaps in under-standing, the received view of the past can no longer be dismissed as simply archaic.   One can now assume 'scientifically' that what has come down through the generations carries with it echoes and memories that are always to be taken into account.

Bearing this in mind as I worked on my book, I often wondered how far the light that was being shed increasingly on the rabbinic period – crucial to Jews and Christians alike – would affect the ability of the scholars to break away from preconceptions, a disposition to work things out in ways which fit in with their respective religious faiths or with other *idées fixes* nourished by chauvinism, romanticism, or simple narrow-mindedness.

I had already detected this in the attitude of German Christian scholars to the Jewish tradition.   How understandable this was for people whose acquaintance with the 'Scribes and Pharisees' started at an impressionable age with what is said in the Gospels, and in such unforgettable language – 'generations of vipers (who) being evil, speak good things' . . . 'blind leaders of the blind'. How natural for them, without any more direct contact with the life and teachings of the Pharisees, to see the teachings of Jesus as a revolutionary break with his Jewish origin.   The condemnation and crucifixion of Jesus must have arisen from his rejection of their hypocritical adherence to the letter, rather than the spirit, of the Law: and if this was Pharisaism in its original form, how evil must be the Jewish tradition which derived from it.

From the other side, Jewish scholars, well aware of the anti-Jewish feelings which this view of Pharisaism encouraged, attempted to rebut it in their work with an equally strong gut reaction. They knew from the inside how utterly false it was to present the Pharisees in this villainous pose. It was never difficult for them to produce numerous quotations from the rabbinic writings to prove how the Pharisees themselves had denounced hypocrisy and tried to instigate the highest standards of personal morality. But how natural it was for them, in turn, to blot out any serious consideration of Christian teaching as related validly to the Judaism of the time. What they saw in the foreground of Christianity was its baleful role as the source of persecution.

In the wake of the new discoveries and of studies based on them, much of this sharp dichotomy has been blunted. Many Christian scholars have turned increasingly to rabbinic writings to help them to understand the period, and have re-interpreted Pharisaism. Jewish scholars, exploring the new material, have become more familiar with the sectarian background to Judaism of the time, which reveals an eschatological tone very different from the rational emphasis projected later in rabbinic literature. If inherited instincts are still strong, there is certainly a wide common ground now in which the argument takes place: and for me this is a striking change from the atmosphere prevalent when I first turned to writing my book.

I see it, in some ways, as a tribute to the pioneer scholars I spoke of earlier, who first opened up rabbinic studies to the influence of the learning of the wider world. The two I had known myself, Büchler and Marmorstein, were very much in my mind when I thought of the new discoveries. How happy they would have been had they lived to see with their own eyes, touch with their own hands, a Biblical scroll dating back to the time of their beloved rabbis, and even much earlier.

I like remembering all these old scholars. One could call a roll of their names, starting with Zunz, a friend of Heine, and working one's way through the giants – Geiger, Krochmal, Steinschneider, Bacher, Krauss, Ginzberg and the rest who form a living chain with the two I had known. There are hundreds of names in what was, in effect, a renaissance of Jewish study. They led hard lives, most of them, and like all scholars were in constant dispute; but between them they laid an essential foundation for what came later.

I had re-lived the Destruction working in their shadow. Now, with my book ready for publication, I had something, however modest, to offer in return.

It seemed to me that I had a perfect title for the book: *The Walls of Jerusalem*. The memory of Zion Lost was its theme, offset, with the re-birth of Israel, by Zion Restored. At this point, in May 1967, there was only one sadness. In a flagrant breach of the 1948 Truce, the Jordanians had excluded the Jews for the ensuing nineteen years from entering the Old City of Jerusalem. Could one dream of the city united and free? I thought of Nehemiah: *Come, let us build up the wall of Jerusalem,* and took this as the book's epigraph.

But now, as we all know, the sky suddenly darkened. The enemies surrounding the State were openly preparing for an attack which, in their own words, was to drive the people of Israel into the sea. The diplomats of the outside world did nothing. On the eve of Monday 5 June, Israel stood alone, apparently doomed. With unbounded courage, they decided to stake everything on a bid for preserving their existence.

Within one day the miracle became apparent. Surrounded still, and with Jordan joining in the attack, the Israelis were – incredibly – moving towards victory. On the third day, Wednesday 7 June, they entered the Old City. On the sixth day they captured the long-threatening Golan Heights and the story was complete.

But it was the victory in Jerusalem which overshadowed everything. For the first time since the Destruction, the ancient Jewish capital was in Jewish hands. The millennial dream had

been realized.   In gratitude – and in tears – the Israelis poured into
the Old City to pray again at the wall of the Temple.

My publisher in New York telephoned me in some excitement.
The manuscript of my book, he told me, had arrived on his desk
on the 7th of June, just as the messages of liberation were coming
in.   I thought of the long years in which the subject had grown
within me, to reach fulfilment on this very day.   How could
one's feelings be expressed?   Only, perhaps, in the words of
Isaiah: *The Lord has comforted His people: He has redeemed Jerusalem.*

II: THE LITVAK CONNECTION

The Gaon of Vilna
A Jew from Pinsk

THE GAON OF VILNA

I HAVE already identified myself as a 'Litvak' in terms of my father having been born in Lithuania, but this is only the starting-point for talking of the Litvak connection. Being a Litvak goes far beyond a continuing relation to the place itself. It is a state of mind.

Litvaks are prepared to joke about it but also take it very seriously. We have got it into our heads, somehow, that qualities hammered out in that setting many years ago have been uniquely significant to Jewish life. Symbolizing this, we have ready at hand the memory of a towering figure who is the Litvak's patron saint – the Gaon of Vilna.

Wherever we Litvaks happen to meet, we are ready to offer each other a self-indulgent picture of the qualities inherent in our tradition. The Litvak likes to think of himself – especially *vis-à-vis* his traditional enemy the 'Polack' or Polish Jew – as endowed by Providence with a true sense of values. The Polack, he will argue, is artistic but harum-scarum: the Litvak is a realist. He is responsive, as every Jew is, to the power of mystery in life, yet fights with every breath to assert his intellectual independence as a human being.

Hamlet, in this sense, was an honorary Litvak – a rationalist full of obstinate questionings, yet imaginative enough to have his inner feelings conveyed to him in the shape of a ghost from the past. It is exactly in this spirit that Litvaks turn to the man whose legendary presence has haunted them now for two centuries – Rabbi Elijah ben Solomon (1720–97), the Gaon of Vilna. Vilna, ancient capital of Lithuania, was the Litvak's Jerusalem. 'Gaon' – which has the force of Excellency – was the accolade they gave to their hero.

It was not at the time, and has never been since, merely a tribute to scholarship, though in this regard Elijah Vilna (his 'secular' name) was undoubtedly outstanding in a recognized pattern – descendant of a long line of rabbis, a talmudic prodigy at six, master in every field of Jewish study. Perhaps his contemporaries recognized – as we certainly can in retrospect – that there was a peculiar radiance in his intellect through which a rabbinic tradition that had been running to seed for centuries was clarified, shorn of excrescence, almost revolutionized, through a return to first principles. Looked at this way the Gaon has become, for the instinctive Litvaks of this world, a symbol of what they feel far beyond the confines of Talmud study.

Litvak/Polack is one polarization, but not to be taken too seriously. More significantly, a Litvak is liable to be a *Mitnagged* – an 'opposer', a spurner not merely of Polish Hasidism, in connection with which the term arose, but of all slavish mass-movements involving blind adherence and the abnegation of reason. It is as the arch-Mitnagged that history presents the Gaon. Hasidism, a folk pietism strongly anti-intellectual in its early form, had begun to penetrate Vilna. The Gaon opposed it firmly, which encourages me, in what I shall write here, to break a lance with the Hasidic-chic of our own day.

But I have a broader aim in discussing him. The abiding question for all of us is how the mediaeval Jewish masses began to join – and help to fashion – the modern world. If I am concerned in this book with my own Jewish consciousness, it is only to un-cover the background on which all of us have drawn – Litvak, Polack, Hasid and Mitnagged alike. The Gaon, one soon dis-covers, straddles it all.

Jewish life, in the Gaon's day, was poised, as we can now see, for deep and startling change. Nothing, it must be said immediately, was to alter the special role of Vilna as the capital – the holy of holies – of Jewish life and thought in their area of settlement in Russia – 'the Pale'. If anything, this role was intensified. In the Gaon's time there were about 7,000 Jews living in Vilna, perhaps a third of the population: a century later, at 64,000, they were nearer half. Inevitably the social inwardness continued, but in new forms. In the Gaon's day, the *kahal* (community) had some-thing like self-government, with many regulatory powers granted by the authorities affecting residence, occupations, taxes, fines and even imprisonment. Infighting among the Jews centred on this. Later, with political and economic conditions less restrictive, Jewish quarrels were more ideological. Zionists battled with labour *Bundists*; the extremely orthodox *Agudah* denounced the hardly less pious *Mizrahi*. In time, the same intellectual intensity was transferred to another dominantly Jewish setting – New York.

The terms in which the endless arguments took place can all be seen emerging in the Gaon's day. One recognizes the conflicting elements in the story – the deep (almost metaphysical) sense of being 'different', the bonds of tradition, the pull of German *Haskalah* (Enlightenment) towards modernization, the apparently opposite force in the eruption of Hasidism. If the Gaon straddles it all, it is because the issues debated so fiercely were never, in fact, black-and-white. As the opponent of Hasidism he might seem to have been uninterested in the mystical elements in Jewish tradition – a blatant misunderstanding of his position, as we shall see. From another vantage point, it becomes clear, when one looks at the Gaon's Vilna, that there was no clear-cut rejection of the modernization process that was being expressed in German *Haskalah*.

It is true that the trimming ideas of German Jews were alien to Vilna. Yet while the Litvaks resisted the *tone* of German 'modernity' they drew on its substance, creating a *Haskalah* in their own style, rooted in affirmation. Somehow these Jews were able to build a relationship with the nineteenth century that left their Jewish background intact, yet open to every fertilizing influence from outside. There was never a moment when a neat balance was struck, but some kind of harmony – restless but stimulating – was there in the making.

It is when one gets down into the elements within this generalization that one begins to see how the Gaon set the style for what became the Litvak tradition. To spell this out, it is necessary to understand his work in its own terms, looking first at the canons of scholarship that he established, and then at the principles manifest in his attitude to mysticism generally and Hasidism in particular. I find a sturdy individualism in all this, very appealing to a modern Litvak. Most startling in this connection is the role of the *Yeshivah* (talmud-school) founded after his death to give expression to his ideas. Nothing seems narrower in approach than an old-style *Yeshivah*; but this one took root in a new style to become a forcing-house of thought in university terms, perfectly tuned to the social background as a tool of emancipation.

I will be brief in discussing the *content* of the Gaon's writings since what I am concerned with here is the *attitude* which he brought to bear on his work. Nothing of what he wrote was published in his lifetime, but notes on a great range of subjects – Bible, Talmud, Midrash, Zohar – were collected and published later by disciples. The Introductions to these books include a good deal of first- and second-hand information about his life, and even more about his personal ideas, sometimes highly evocative. Most important in this regard are the memories of his main disciple, Rabbi Chaim ben Isaac of Volozhyn.

The raw material is often desultory, originating sometimes in notes scribbled in the margins of the books he read. What gives his work unity is the originality of his approach. In his own terms he would have said that all he was doing was to encourage the 'correct' study of the Torah and Talmud – to get back to the original texts, to throw out guesswork and *pilpul* (casuistry), to establish the simple thread of *p'shat* (meaning) before turning to *d'rash* (commentary). He called also for a study of 'other knowledge', including the science of 'the Greeks', since by definition all true knowledge was consistent with – and would therefore amplify – the Jewish faith. A former pupil, Rabbi Baruch of Sklow, who translated Euclid into Hebrew at his request, quotes the Gaon as saying: 'For each single thing that one fails to understand in "the other kind of knowledge", one will lack a hundredfold an understanding of the Torah.'

There is a robust confidence in this attitude, and it is evident in all his work, notably that on the Talmud. The Talmud was, for the Gaon, a self-subsistent edifice of thought and practice. But if, as he clearly felt, it was the rock of Jewish life, one was called upon to use one's native reason to clear the ground of anything that impeded one's firm stance on this rock. The way to true understanding was through a careful analysis of textual variations in different sources to get back to the basic teachings. To follow this through involved a readiness to question all shorthand or fossilized formulations, a process which led him to criticism even of the Code of Law regarded with legendary reverence – the *Shulhan Arukh*.

He applied the same basic principles to the study of the Bible, immersing himself in questions of grammar and linguistics to dig out the original meaning of a text that might have become twisted by its use in rabbinic argument. The detritus of past centuries had to be cleared away in a relentless search for truth. It was an attitude to tradition which was respectful at heart but completely radical in its effect.

To one modern critic, Shalom Spiegel, the Gaon's instinctive modernity of thought in devising his own principles of literary criticism was the real stimulant to the Jewish breakthrough, in many academic fields, in the nineteenth century:

> If emancipation from blind submission to authority be a sign of modernity, then the Gaon, rather than the *Haskalah*, is the precursor of the modern Jew.[1]

The ideas implicit in the Gaon's approach to study expressed themselves with equal clarity in his struggle with Hasidism. But here, the social background has to be brought into the picture. In his Bible and Talmud studies, the Gaon could be a hermit, sitting in a curtained room and working day and night by candlelight; but with Hasidism there was a public issue. He could wrestle alone – as we shall see – with his own attraction to mysticism, yet had to deal with the movement publicly, owing to its direct and mostly baleful influence on the world around him.

Hasidism (*hasid* means 'pious') had emerged in southern Poland in the eighteenth century as a revivalist movement linked to stories of a mysterious figure, Israel ben Eleazar (1700–60), who became known to his disciples as the *Baal Shem* – 'Master (or

Wielder) of the (divine) Name'.* Legends proliferated about him and his followers grew in numbers, full of enthusiasm at being given new ideas, and a new kind spirit, for expressing themselves as Jews. The fervour of worship was held to be superior to study. All, however ignorant and poor, could achieve communion with God if they approached Him with surrender and joy, but there were certain Righteous Ones (*tzaddikim*) who were uniquely close to the Almighty and whose intercession could work wonders. The movement spread north, permeated with ecstatic worship and always highlighted by attachment to a local *tzaddik*. When it began to take root in Lithuania, the Gaon issued a number of edicts of excommunication, and the fight between Hasidim and Mitnaggdim ('opponents') was launched.

A Litvak cannot leave the story in this very simple form. Hasidism viewed simply as an idealistic expression of direct communion with God leaves out of account something less romantic – the long-entrenched role among Jews of magic, incantation and superstition generally. As far back as the period in which the Talmud was being formulated in Babylonia (4th–6th centuries A.D.), the Jews sought magic spells as protection from demons, plagues, curses, or tormentors. The rabbi was not merely a scholar but also a holy man who was likely to know the secret names of God and could talk with demons and the dead. His blessings could bring fertility, his curses death.

Much of this had been softened in later centuries, but it is no surprise to find the same faith in magic men surfacing in the remote and primitive areas of southern Poland in the seventeenth and eighteenth centuries. Bernard Weinryb's social history of the Jews of Poland provides lively detail. 'Baal Shem' was a general name applied to all such men and signified, in practice, 'a healer, quack doctor, miracle worker, or charmer'. They treated patients with folk remedies (herbs, ointments) or with amulets and incantations. Some of them could expel evil spirits, predict the future or perform miracles. The father of Hasidism seems to have spent the first part of his life in this role. At this

---

* More distinctively he was known as the *Baal Shem Tob* (Be-SH-T), which means "Goodly Master of the Name".

stage, he was less the other-worldly saint that legend projected later than a kind of workaday rabbi, occasional *shohet* (ritual slaughterer) and (in early American terms) a medicine-man with a gift for story-telling.

To get a glimpse, this way, of the social background, including the readiness of simple folk to accept the magic power of a *tzaddik*, suggests immediately why the movement would have been distasteful to a Vilna scholar, immersed in rational study of the tradition. This is not to say that Hasidism was necessarily wrong in its approach: it was different. And what we need to know, especially in relation to the Gaon, is how far Hasidism created (or stumbled upon) some new deep truths about man and God, and how far it has been a diversion, and a misleading one, from the abiding message of Jewish experience.

Superficially, the rift that emerged was a noisy and bitter quarrel about study, emotion and ritual: but the underlying issue was that Hasidism had an implicit theology which ran counter to established ideas.

To conventional Jewish thought, God was a personal Being, Master of the Universe, who had imposed a moral order on man by giving Jews the Torah. Through obedience to it, the Jew was aware of the concepts of right and wrong. The world of man was an arena of reality. Man was responsible for his own conduct. Nothing could mediate this in his duty to God.

In sharp contrast, the Hasid sought a transformation of daily 'reality' through mystery. To live in accordance with the divine law could never be enough by itself. One had to find a short-cut to God's will, and this was possible, for a Jew, through the mediation of a *tzaddik*, whose impulses were of a different order. The *tzaddik* had a private relation to God, each *tzaddik* in his own way. Ordinary men, attached to a *tzaddik*, were themselves transformed in living out the attachment. Every aspect of life – including the conventional concepts of right and wrong – could receive a new emphasis through him. One surrendered all decisions to him, confident that something miraculous would emerge. In this obedience, as Gershom Scholem, the great scholar of Jewish mysticism, puts it: 'personality took the place of doctrine.'[4]

According to Scholem, this role of the *tzaddik*, liberating and beneficial in its effect, was revolutionary to Jewish thought, even though it drew historically on mystical doctrine derived from the ancient lore of Kabbalah. The Kabbalah had acquired a new hold on the Jewish people in the sixteenth century through the work of an outstanding scholar-mystic Isaac Luria (1534–72). In his metaphysical scheme, the original perfection of the universe had been destroyed in primeval time, and the world we know is an expression of God Himself in exile, needing the help of man for its restoration:

> Sparks of the divine life and thought are scattered in exile over the entire world, and long through the actions of men to be 'lifted up' and restored to their original place in the divine harmony of all being.[5]

These ideas, Scholem shows, were implicit in the early Hasidic writings. Even for the most simple Hasid, 'the sparks' were everywhere, to be 'lifted up' through religious intensity. For the scholar, there were mysteries beyond this – the study of signs and portents in the letters of God's names, in numbers, in constellations. And the scholar could reach out beyond this into 'practical Kabbalah', the achievement of the supernatural, of which one might not speak to the uninitiated.

Kabbalah had a fascination for mediaeval rabbis; and the Gaon, reflecting this, was himself an ardent student of its doctrines, experimenting even in 'practical Kabbalah'.[6] How is one to reconcile this with his denunciation of the spread of Hasidism? Is it not, as the historian Heinrich Graetz thought, a fatal objection to any claim made for him as an intellectual – a rationalist? And what are we Litvaks to make of it when our hero is presented as the arch-Mitnagged?

Obviously, one has to give up defining the Gaon's attitude in black-and-white terms. Jewish life in eighteenth-century Vilna was too complex, in social as well as religious terms, for this. Yet the burgeoning of mysticism at that time does raise a broad issue which we need to evaluate for its ultimate meaning to Jewish life.

Some scholars, above all Gershom Scholem, extol the marvellous originality of the Hasidic view, which is held to have offered a creative alternative to the rabbinic tradition. The Gaon was a participant in Kabbalah yet took a different view, and one which to a Litvak, expresses more persuasively the force that sustained Jewish creativity in the ensuing centuries.

The central element in the Gaon's approach was his ability to see the Jewish tradition in the round, drawing freely from all its sources, but never going overboard on any new or fashionable developments running counter to the truth he felt in his bones. In our own time, Scholem has been so influenced by his brilliant researches into the history of Jewish mysticism as to see the Kabbalist influence on Hasidism as producing 'a wealth of truly original religious types'.[7] The Gaon was much more cautious. He knew the Kabbalah writings profoundly; and though his attitude showed respect, and even affection, it also included, as we shall see, an ultimate reservation.

One can see the issue at its clearest by considering the praise that Scholem gives to the irrationality of tzaddik-worship. The tzaddik, in his view, is the link for ordinary men between daily existence and an enthusiasm that unites man with the upper worlds, allowing him 'to rise higher than the angels and the seraphs and the thrones'. The fact that this enthusiasm is irrational is precisely its attraction. There are times when reason has to be dethroned.

Scholem quotes with approval the famous remark of a devout follower of one of the great Hasidic teachers, the Maggid of Meseritz: 'I do not go to the Maggid to learn Torah from him but to watch him tie his boot-laces'. This is not a remark, he says, which is to be taken literally, but it allows one to grasp the true force that a great religious personality is able to exercise merely by his existence. For the Gaon, there was holiness in the application of reason to the study of the Torah. Scholem asks us to understand the marvel when, with a tzaddik, there is 'a complete irrationalization of religious values (and) he himself becomes Torah'.[8]

We hear little from Scholem about the seamy side of the

tzaddik-cult. As a historian, he records that ultimately there was a reaction among some Hasidim against 'the unlimited emotionalism' that had developed. He seems to deplore this reaction: it was 'a departure from what was new and original in Hasidism'. However, the power that had been generated retained something valuable 'even after the spirit had departed, or, even worse, been commercialized'. The creative tension between a group of people and their *tzaddik* remains valid. 'What is lost in rationality is gained in efficacy.'

Everyone who reads Scholem is struck by the paradox that here is a profound intellectual applying his marvellous powers to the glorification of a system which, in his own analysis, exists by credulity. It is as if he is determined to break our conventional modes of thought while exploiting its most respected features – logic, precision, elegance of argument. The *tzaddiks* are to be symbols of our breakthrough. They are at home in the highly conceptualized world of Kabbalah, yet they speak not in reason but in riddles. In place of a disquisition, they tell a tale. We must all be prepared to surrender: 'a secret life can break out in you or in me'.

Scholem appears to be saying that we must give up the idea that rational thought is at the core of Jewish experience. The fact that mediaeval rabbis immersed themselves in Kabbalah is evidence, for him, that behind the intellectualism of Talmud study they were living out 'a genuine mystical life'. But one can take a different view of this. Professor Zwi Werblowsky, a pupil and great admirer of Scholem, has argued in a recent book it is a mistake to set the mystical (and psychical) experiences that were very common among rabbis 'over and against the sternly rationalist and moral type of rabbinic piety'. One should rather envisage

a religious attitude which, far from subscribing to the rationalist denial of mystical phenomena, actually takes them in its stride, as it were, but dismisses them as completely irrelevant to the spiritual life.[9]

Werblowsky justifies this acute gloss on the ideas of Scholem through a remarkable statement of the Vilna Gaon which clarifies uniquely what seems to lie at the heart of the Litvak heritage. We see from it that in the Gaon there was no puritanical denial of the power of imagination and poetry; yet there was an ultimate realism that kept man – the poet, the dreamer – at the centre of the experience.

The Gaon, as we know from his disciple Rabbi Chaim of Volozhyn, was not merely a prolific writer on Kabbalah, but also spoke of receiving psychic messages during sleep from *maggidim* (mediators) and 'visitations' from the prophet Elijah, the great mystic Isaac Luria, and others. God had provided sleep, he told Rabbi Chaim, so that man could create insights, while his soul floated in the air, that he could not obtain 'while the soul is joined to the body'; but he made it clear that 'knowledge' of this kind, obtained without conscious intellectual effort, was not wanted by him:

> I do not want my understanding of the Torah to come through any mediator . . . My eyes are to God alone: that which He wishes to reveal to me, and the share He wants to give me in his Torah through my hard labour of study – these alone I do desire.[10]

It is a pregnant remark. Man, aware of a sense of reverence and wonder, has to celebrate it in his own freedom. Reason, unique in man, is what God asks of him.

I am reminded, reading the Gaon's words, of a passage from one of John Donne's sermons. He had taken his text from *Psalm 62*:

> David asks the question with a holy wonder: *Quid est homo*? What is man that God is so mindful of him? But I have his leave to say, since God is so mindful of him, since God hath set His mind upon him: What is *not* man? Man is all . . .
> For man is not only a contributory Creature but a total Creature . . .
> He is not a piece of the world, but the world itself; and next to the glory of God, the reason why there is such a world.

If the Gaon was expressing a humanism of this kind, however unconscious of its full implications, it would be immensely significant for the centuries that were to follow, since Jewish experience, as it developed, bears strong marks of this attitude. As Jews emerged from the ghetto, the forces that shaped their history were too varied to be put into a conceptual straitjacket, but there is a line flowing from the Gaon that opens some understanding.

To describe the process briefly: ideas implicit in the Gaon were transformed – 'modernized' – in a way that left the ancient roots alive and potent. If we follow this clue, the contradictions and perplexities of Jewish emancipation begin to make sense.

The conventional approach is to see emancipation as the opening of a straight road to 'freedom', but the story cannot be understood this way. Jacob Katz, the frankest historian of Jewish/non-Jewish relations, has shown in *Out of the Ghetto*[11] that politically, socially and intellectually there was nothing uniform or predictable in Jewish emergence. The forces both within Jewish life and latent outside it were powered so much by strong elements of the past that change came only erratically, in ways that constantly defied *a priori* assumptions.

On the political front this is now widely understood, particularly in the wake of experience at the hands of Germany and Soviet Russia. But equally among the Jews themselves there was no simple breaking of the old mould. The most remarkable feature of nineteenth-century experience – in the sense of being so unexpected – was not the extent to which the Jews were increasingly 'normalized', but rather the way in which they reacted to 'freedom' by clinging to their old distinctiveness. As Katz puts it:[12]

> The disintegration that freed Jews from the bonds of traditional society ... was a dialectical process, which, by its very nature, generated the forces that halted and reversed the tide of dissolution ... Jews, having escaped from the traditional Jewish social unit, did not join non-Jewish circles but created new Jewish social entities ...

This is a judgment based on the experience of 'western' Jews. Within the Russian Pale, the great masses of Jewry limped along more slowly under the same influence and with infinitely greater separateness persisting.

Yet it is precisely from this distinctive reservoir of Jewish life that successive generations, as they moved 'outside', astonished the world with talent and vitality that seemed to have been nursed almost by design for a fertile role in western life, and a role that remained in some sense identifiably Jewish. It is as if creativity – whether in business, science or the arts – had particular power when it had roots in a social and intellectual background that remained authentic. In some mysterious manner, the Russian Jew carried the past with him – turning away, *breaking* away, yet always impelled to give it specific value. Reaching back to the days of the Gaon, one can identify two major ways – one moral, the other institutional – in which valid forces within the tradition seem to have reaffirmed the emerging Jew's self-respect and given him room for adaptation.

The first is in an area in which every Jew ultimately formulates his own working philosophy in relation to his past. For many it is exemplified in an attitude reaching straight to the Gaon – a recognition that the basic priority in conduct is man's responsibility for himself, his power and need to choose between right and wrong. We saw earlier what weight the Gaon gave to respect for reason. What we find when we look deeper, especially in his reaction to Hasidism, is how the use of reason enshrined for him a *moral* imperative. Re-examined with this in mind, his confrontation with Hasidism becomes more tolerant in one way, more decisive in another.

One needs to note tolerance to rebut the idea that the Gaon objected to the warm, earthy elements that Hasidism has reaffirmed for Jewish experience. If he had no taste for the folk-intoxication of the *tzaddik* world, it was not in the spirit of a hermit. His closest personal friend was Jacob Kranz, 'the Maggid of Dubno', a rough-hewn character famed for the popular appeal of his sermons.

It was not the common touch of the Hasidim that moved the Gaon to denounce them as 'foes of the Jewish people'. There was something decisively wrong, for him, in their moral stance.

Hasidism, as he saw it, was an abnegation of personal will. Even the ideas of the respected Hasidic scholar, Schneour Zalman of Lyady, were at fault on this. The near pantheism of his book *Tanya* not only obscured the separation between a personal Creator and His universe, but also blunted the moral choice for every individual between right and wrong. To surrender decision to the *tzaddik* was as mischievous to doctrine as the superstitious acceptance of his miracle-working power. The responsibilities of life could not be shrugged off by the virtual worship of a new breed of 'sacred' men who spoke in parables that were no better, very often, than gobbledegook. Clarity of language, rational analysis, a high seriousness that accepted mystery but never let it fog the mind – can anyone doubt that these elements in the Gaon's thinking have nourished later thought?

But how did these ideas emerge from a background strongly resistant to change? The clue lies in the Yeshivah system mentioned earlier – the establishment of a traditional base so 'safe' that thought could work itself free. That, with full allowance for paradox, was the social role, over the nineteenth century, of a remarkably influential rabbinical college, established at Volozhyn, some distance from Vilna, to give expression to the Gaon's teaching.

The Volozhyn Yeshivah was founded in 1803, six years after the Gaon's death, by his disciple Rabbi Chaim ben Isaac. Known as *Etz Chaim* in tribute to its founder, Volozhyn became the prototype for talmudic academies everywhere.

It is easy enough to see how a new institution of this kind, linked to the legendary influence of the Gaon, could become important for Talmud study. What is harder to understand is how it could break through its heavily traditional preoccupations to become a force in emancipation.

The curriculum of Volozhyn was novel in that it offered regular instruction through lectures and a deep involvement with the Bible, as a framework to the concentration on Talmud. But even so, it seems essentially narrow. Everything about it appears in sharp contrast to the liberating approach of the contemporary

Haskalah, whose leaders sought explicitly to expose Jewish life to 'modernity'.

But to see Jewish experience drawn in two opposite directions this way is to miss the effervescence and dialectic that lay at its centre. If one is looking for the sources of Jewish intellectual achievement in the twentieth century, *Haskalah* and Yeshivah have to be seen in balance and interaction.

In the century which followed the Gaon, the Lithuanian Yeshivahs had, at the most obvious level, ploughed on in isolation from the developing scene. More significantly though, they were providing throughout this time a constant stream of fervent intellectual power, a groping towards the world outside in the only terms that could possibly be valid for the great mass of Jews living in that time and place. To see the picture as a whole, one has to find ways of encapsulating the sense of ferment, the unending seepage, the power to adapt, the continuing transformation, as Jews broke out of the Ghetto. For this to work, the process of change had to be geared in some way to living institutions.

The Yeshivah was like a constantly operating refinery of the intellect, subjecting its raw material to endless processing, spewing out waste and desolation, but with a magic distillation at its heart. The students inmured within its walls were in a constant tug-of-war with past and present: the narrower their field of study, the more exciting for some of them were the prizes and delights that hovered beyond their immediate reach. For some it could lead to rejection of the heritage. For many more, men whose minds were disciplined to the past yet driven also by an intellectual fervour to move into worlds unrealized, it set up a rich counterpoint of dazzling interest.

If one sees this as an expression in some sense of a Litvak heritage, it is not because it remained narrowly localized. The movement of people and ideas was too complex for this. The Yeshivah leaders might frown on *Haskalah*, but the typical student – the Yeshivah *bochur* – was an addict of its books. Even the old Hasid/Mitnagged dichotomy was not always applicable. Many a bright young Jew of Hasidic stock would find his way to Volozhyn, hoping to get from it something like a secular education. Perhaps the most famous of them was the poet mentioned earlier, Chaim Nachman Bialik. He celebrated both its dreariness and its power in an epic poem *Ha-Matmid*, seeing his old Yeshivah as 'the anvil on which a people's soul is forged'. Another, the writer Micha Joseph Berdichevsky, found the intellectual atmosphere of his Volozhyn days surfacing later in a prolific outflow of books calling for a breaking of the Jewish mould, a transvaluation of values. Yet in the tone of his work – its vehemence and lyricism – there was a celebration of the *élan vital* which surely harked back to his Hasidic origin.

What Volozhyn had done was to provide for Berdichevsky, as for countless others, a sense of confidence on which to build. Isolated spirits, groping mostly in the dark, were drawn to something like a university, where ideas could be tested in fellowship. For the ensuing dialectic there had to be a firmly established set of values which one both accepted and fought. The legendary scholarship of the Gaon provided this.

By way of paradox, I will admit that the intellectual flavour of the Yeshivah was transmuted best by a man who never attended one – Chaim Weizmann, father-figure of Zionism and first President of Israel. Although I shall talk of him in the next chapter, I cannot leave the Gaon's world without considering briefly how Weizmann typified the Litvak tone of voice which became tangible, as time went on, almost as a by-product of the endless drone of Talmudic argument.

I think of Weizmann as the arch-Litvak of our time. If he was never a committed student of the Talmud, he had a deep knowledge of the Bible and Hebrew literature. But his special Litvak quality was something one would like to call a healthy form of scepticism – a readiness to question combined with a strong taste for irony.

It may seem odd to talk of irony and scepticism in relation to a man whose whole life communicated idealism and compassion. Nevertheless if one looks at the Litvak tradition, one sees how natural an evolution it was for generations of students torn

between love of their inheritance and bitterness at what it had produced.   The story is expressed in what we know of countless ex-
Yeshivah *bochurim* whose varied talents turned in many directions
– business, science, literature, politics – but always with this underlying conflict in their minds.   They would never lose the concentration and passion for argument that they had imbibed in the
Yeshivah, but would often see it all with a certain sadness, a feeling
that Jewish experience – for all the hold it had on them – would
always be a cloudy story, arousing questions in their mind that
God would find it hard to answer.

By definition, the Litvak has to have an open mind – to see
values even in a movement like Hasidism which is personally
unappetizing to him.   He likes to think that he is a questioner but
not a professional doubter, a reasoner but not a scoffer.   In this
sense he will admit that Hasidism is not to be shrugged off.   It has
brought an extra dimension of faith, art and devotion to the
Jewish scene.   It has fed into the Jewish body politic.   But is it
the lasting force that distinguishes the Jews, keeps them going,
renews them for the exploration of man's role on earth?

One can't expect a Litvak to be objective on this.   I thought I
had found some neutral support in a long essay on the Gaon by
the historian Professor Ben-Sasson of the Hebrew University, in
which he goes out of his way to enthuse about 'the *amor Dei*
intellectualis of the Gaon's circle, and the striking intellectualism of
the Gaon's personality'.[13]   But I then discovered to my chagrin
that Professor Ben-Sasson was not only a Litvak himself but had
actually studied at Volozhyn.   His evidence is clearly suspect, but
it does at least show how strong the bond is.

I said at the beginning that Hamlet can be regarded as an honorary Litvak, driven, for better or worse, by the sardonic intellectualism that Litvaks are heir to.   Shakespeare offers an interesting
gloss on this by telling us at the beginning of Act I that Hamlet's
father achieved military fame for his firm action against the
Litvak's traditional enemy: 'he smote the sledded Polacks on the
ice'.   Well, there it is.   In the end, we get it all from Father.

A JEW FROM PINSK

HOW far is one prepared to push Litvak pride? I will try for
the jackpot with a blunt statement that the State of Israel owes
its existence to a man whom I called, in the last chapter, the arch-
Litvak of our time – Chaim Weizmann, born just over a hundred
years ago in a *shtetl* near Pinsk.

To allot such credit to Weizmann is, of course, to invite a storm
of contradiction. What about the other founders of Israel –
Herzl, Ben-Gurion? And leaving leaders on one side, what about
Israel's agricultural pioneers, and her soldiers, and the dreams of
ordinary Jews for 2,000 years without which nothing would have
happened?

All perfectly true. So that if one wants to ascribe Israel's
existence to one man above all, one is looking beneath the surface
for a kind of leadership that absorbed everything else being done
and elevated it to a level of unimaginable distinction. This was
Weizmann.

If I call him a Litvak Jew, this is not just a geographical tag.
He saw his background communicating realism and drive, the
way, perhaps, that Scots do. 'Put some *Littwische Stimmung* into
it,' he wrote to a supporter who seemed unwilling to spend night
and day on Zionist work the way *he* did.

I feel that I know Weizmann intimately, though I only saw him
at a distance in real life, because during the last few years his letters
have begun to be published in a great flow of volumes, twenty so
far (1979), with perhaps another five to come. The joy is that
they are being presented without any kind of censorship. All his
human weaknesses are there for those who want to find them.
From another angle, they offer a kaleidoscopic picture of the
history of his times. But the overwhelming feeling that they
generate is of a different order entirely.

What the letters bring out is the source of the moral authority
that he exercised so naturally as the spokesman for his people.
His listeners sensed this on the great public occasions when he

spoke for Jewry before the bar of history. Centuries of Jewish experience seemed manifest in him; yet the vision that impelled him was personal, shaped by qualities of judgment and taste that flowed uniquely from his own nature. Behind each letter, whether it deals with matters of high strategy or the daily trivia of existence, one is aware of his preoccupation with the undying question: what does it mean to be a Jew?

At a superficial level, Weizmann might seem sometimes to be opting for an easy, sentimental answer. This great leader, brilliantly endowed at so many levels, never tires of saying that he draws his strength from remaining the simple Litvak he was at birth. 'I'm just a Jew from Pinsk' is how he puts it, and we warm at his loyalty, the strength of his roots. But this is not ultimately what his leadership meant. To be 'a good Jew' was never for him, as it has been for many, merely a matter of sentiment and nostalgia. Jewish existence, with all its attendant tragedies and miseries, enshrined for him innate qualities that had to be released, rescued and transformed through two of the simplest concepts of mankind – dignity and decency. If these were lost, Jewish life was meaningless – a tale told by an idiot. The birth of the State was not to be a base for power, or even just a safe haven. It was to be an assertion of moral values, or it was nothing.

Until the letters appeared, I had built up my picture of Weizmann from his autobiography, *Trial and Error*, which appeared in 1949. It is an appealing book in which Weizmann, having become the first President of Israel, is looking back warmly, tenderly, nostalgically – all passion spent – to the years of friendship, struggle and success. Its tone echoes the elegant portrait, often reproduced, by the English society painter Oswald Birley.

In the letters, especially those emerging from the early pioneering days, it is a different story. As he sits down every day, driving himself on with relentless fervor and will, nothing of the future is known, and we share his doubts, his fury, his agony. We see him not just as a great man but as an ordinary man, beset by trivia and frustration. It is all the more marvellous, then, that this daily record of effort and confusion is shot through with such a pervading sense of values, such unerring instinct on the path to be followed, even if he has to fight for it – as he often has to – alone. Behind the blood and fire that signalled Israel's emergence, we see in these early letters what qualities it took to turn the wandering tribes of immigrants, full of assorted motivations, into an incipient State.

Weizmann's life is divided, in terms of achievement, into two broad parts. The first covers the years from student days to the Balfour Declaration in 1917; the second is Weizmann as official leader, from the fight over the Mandate to the emergence of the State. In the first part, the marvel is how Weizmann, without any real executive status in the Zionist movement, exerts an astonishing personal authority from the sidelines, until the dramatic period when he is able, amid the upheavals of World War I, to steer the work with consummate skill towards the triumph of the Balfour Declaration. In the second part, he has become a legend, harnessing the financial support of world Jewry on a scale hitherto unimaginable, fighting on the diplomatic front with a blend of authority and instinct that was wholly his own, and throughout these bitter years building up the economy and institutions of the *Yishuv* (the settlement) in total confidence of the outcome. The climax in this case is 1948, a critical time for the emergent state, when Weizmann, brought from his sick-bed in London to the United States, turns the blaze of his influence on the United Nations and President Truman, and Israel is recognized.

In terms of public history, it is undoubtedly this second part which is the more important, covering, as it does, the build-up of a world-wide movement, the struggles in Palestine under the Mandate, and the unbearable problems of Jewish survival during and after World War II. But for me, responding so directly to the inner feelings of Weizmann as revealed in the early letters, it is the first part of his life which I find riveting. One is absorbed in the letters, with all their light and shade, as if one were reading a novel.

The years from youth to the Balfour Declaration are covered in seven volumes, containing nearly 3,000 letters.[1]   In the first three, we see what Richard Crossman described as 'the torso of greatness'. For while, as Crossman put it, they show the 'intellectual framework of Weizmann's Zionism fully articulated', we see him, in terms of personality, 'still an unbalanced – indeed an uprooted – intellectual, arrogantly sure of his ideas but only half-sure of himself'.[2]

In the three volumes which follow (IV to VI), Weizmann is, in one sense, still more uprooted, having left the warmth and contacts of European Zionism to build up his scientific career in England: but outweighing his recurrent sense of isolation is the opening-up of his personality to something entirely new for 'the Jew from Pinsk' – an environment that seemed to him to spell stability, freedom, and, above all, the long-term view. Little of this shows, for the time being, in the hectic letters he still pours out endlessly to Zionist comrades everywhere. But a sense of power is emerging – in the achievements of his scientific research, in political and social contacts, and in the feeling that the time is coming soon, particularly through his scientific work, when he will be able to plunge personally into the practical Zionism that he has been encouraging without let-up.

It is in Volume VII, beginning with the outbreak of war in August 1914, that the transformation is finally realized. Everything he has been, and worked for, and achieved in his own person suddenly becomes of crucial importance to his people. There is no magic waving of wands. Weizmann, as the volume opens, is still on the sidelines in the official sense. Throughout the book, which contains almost 550 letters, he is still infiltrating his ideas with a mixture of tact and bravado to fit in with the rapid proliferation of events. But in fact, he has taken over. The new direction is crystal-clear to him from the beginning. The road is going to be open to a Jewish Homeland at last, beginning with British suzerainty over Palestine. The Zionists must will it, though it runs counter to many attachments. The British Government must proclaim it as a debt which the world owes to the Jewish people. In all the buffering of international chaos and intrigue, Weizmann is rocklike at the centre, generating an authority that speaks for itself. On November 2nd, 1917, the Balfour Declaration is issued.

The first and last letters of these seven volumes, with thirty-two years between them, have a symbolic unity that lingers in the mind like the opening and closing notes of a symphony. The first is the letter written in 1885, when he was not yet eleven years old, to his *cheder* teacher, proclaiming – in halting Hebrew – his determination, as he sets off to enter the High School at Pinsk, never to 'throw off the garb of Judaism'. In a rambling postscript, he praises those who are inspired by Zionism, thanks 'the two patriots, Moshe Montefiore and Rothschild', and ends with a startling prophecy, often quoted since the letter was first published in Volume I:

> Why should we look to the Kings of Europe? . . . All have decided that the Jew must die. But England will have mercy on us. To Zion – Jews – to Zion let us go!

The last letter in Volume VII is written on the day of the Balfour Declaration, and is addressed – an extraordinary echo – to a Rothschild, the Lord Rothschild who is head of the family in England. The transformation has happened. Weizmann is now a unique figure in England, a scientist whose work has 'saved' the Allies, a statesman who has won the ear of Balfour, Churchill and Lloyd George. England, as he had foreseen, is ready to help. The disarray – the weakness and cowardice – is *within* Jewry, among the bourgeois, the half-hearted. It is with the support of the masses and a few Jewish 'patriots' at the top that he has successfully fought off the assimilationists. It is through Lord Rothschild that a Declaration, drafted basically by Sokolow, is sent hopefully to the Government. Fighting attempts to water it down, Weizmann is tireless in negotiation and in letters. When its issuance becomes uncertain, he gets it restored to the War Cabinet's agenda, and it is finally published, in the form of a letter to Rothschild. On the same day, Weizmann writes to him, in terms which evoke much more than the quiet words:

> When the history of this time is written, it will be justifiably said that the name of the greatest house in Jewry was associated with the granting of the Magna Carta of Jewish liberties.

There is a mutual *noblesse oblige* in this. Rothschild, who might have turned his back like others of his class, has acted as a free man. Weizmann, as the voice of Jewish history, is free to salute it.

Those who knew Weizmann personally never tire of trying to convey the nature of his authority. One hears usually of the intelligence he radiated, his insight, his swift and subtle mind, an air of absolute distinction, a look in his eyes that seemed to reflect the suffering of the ages. Ben-Gurion, trying to express this mysterious power, wrote to him once in a private letter:

> You are the champion of the Jewish people, not because you have been elected by a majority, but because you were born for it. The *Shechinah* of the Jewish people rests upon you.[3]

Golda Meir, trying to recover, at this distance, the feeling she had, has said: 'One can only call it awe. One was in the presence of a man outside one's ordinary experience.'[4]

It occurred to me, when I was in Israel a little while ago, that there was one element missing in these familiar judgments. Like many others, I tend to see Weizmann conditioned by the Jewish verities in which he had grown up. But he was basically a scientist. Where did this fit in? I tried to find out, in Israel, what part science had played in his life.

Talking to scientists and reading what they gave me, I soon began to realize that a man activated by a whole vision of life never separates himself into separate compartments. Weizmann had started as an organic chemist, a field which at that time had moved into a position of aristocracy in the scientific hierarchy in seeming to have tapped at last the underlying secrets of nature's operation in sustaining life. The outstanding symbol of this was Pasteur's epoch-making work on fermentation as a living process. A development of this was the use of micro-organisms as agents in industrial chemistry, through which specific products could be 'released'.

Weizmann's work in this field led to the application of his research to the manufacture of acetone during World War I, which was the first time in history that a bacterium had been used for large-scale production of industrial chemicals. But for Weizmann it was only one aspect of a wider scientific preoccupation with the future of man's ability to transform the resources of nature so that food and new products could be synthesized on a vast scale, to set man free at last from poverty and starvation. Those involved with Weizmann saw his work as a scientist expressive, in two fundamental ways, of his power and wholeness of character as a Jewish leader.

The first was its moral implication. Ernst Bergmann, who worked intimately with Weizmann for years, said of him that in directing so much of his scientific research towards the betterment of economic conditions for the colonial peoples, 'he wanted to convey to the world the Jewish capability of contributing to the progress of humanity'.[5]   Aharon Katzir, the distinguished scientist who was assassinated by Japanese terrorists at Lod in May 1972, saw in Weizmann the rarest type of scientist – a man who, in living out his scientific instincts, 'set standards for human behaviour'. The attitude of men of this quality to scientific exploration reaches down to the fundamental position of man in the universe:

> The subject matter with which such men deal . . . requires a fine intuitive orientation in an undefined and unknown world. . . . What they create is not a philosophic structure based on a logical sequence of ideas: it is their life-work itself that is summed up in the form of an operational philosophy.[6]

Ephraim Katzir, a scientist like his brother and subsequently President of Israel, talked to me of Weizmann's talent in terms which helped me to understand how his wide-ranging grasp as a Zionist leader was a perfect reflection of his scientific approach. Weizmann, he said, was not a great original in the world of science, but had a remarkable genius in seeing connections between different fields of discovery and intuiting ways of applying these in practical forms.   It was marvellous, attending one of the regular staff meetings at the Weizmann Institute in Rehovot, to see how every scientist present was drawn into total admiration and participation through the synthesizing influence of his personality. Intellect expressed itself in a unique amalgam of idealism and reality.

One senses the identical reaction among the widely assorted friends who became his disciples in Zionism. They saw a mind at work that was flexible and sensitive. Men of Weizmann's calibre, Aharon Katzir wrote, 'forego the pleasures of children's dreams and are ready to grapple with reality directly'.[4] But though the aim was always practical, it was subsumed under a passion of boundless aspiration for his people.

One must emphasize 'for his people'. Egotism in the crude sense was totally foreign to him, strange as this may sound in the light of the fact that he was dogmatic, intolerant of critics, contemptuous of the second-rate, and bore himself as a natural leader. Yet there is no paradox in this as one reads the letters. The driving force was not ambition for himself, but the determination to rescue his people from psychological degradation. What he sought for them was not some kind of sabre-rattling independence, but a visible sense of quality, expressed, as I said earlier, in dignity and decency. It was precisely because he saw the opposite qualities so prevalent in the Jewish world that he poured out anger and satire, like some prophet of old. The Jews had become victims of history, not simply in persecution and slaughter, but by finding the decencies within them subjugated to the need for subterfuge and opportunism. Emancipation was not 'equal rights' but the freeing of Jews from this baleful legacy. One didn't exploit Jewish leadership to have personal power: one gave oneself with everything felt in the blood to bring about a revolution in Jewish life.

Indifferent as Weizmann was to formal pietism, every word of the Bible, every prayer of his youth, was vibrant in his mind. In every crisis there was a touchstone of conduct to be reached for, an attitude embedded in the ancient tradition. To Balfour – to everyone – Weizmann, despite his sophistication, seemed a total Jew. They sensed that his loyalty to the past was, paradoxically, the true base for achieving the revolution in Jewish life to which he was committed.

. . . . . .

Nowhere is this paradox more tangible than in the contrast between Weizmann and the man who was (and still is in many ways)
the prophet of Zionism – Theodor Herzl. In 1896, when Herzl's
Der Judenstaat appeared, taking the Jewish world by storm,
Weizmann was a young man of twenty-two. Like everyone
else he was totally captivated by the majesty, the dramatic aura of
the man who, in establishing the Zionist Congress, gave form and
unity to the age-old dream of a Jewish Homeland. A sense of
veneration remained even when Weizmann began to feel, as he
soon did, that Herzl's approach enshrined a fatal flaw. Herzl,
who had appeared on the Jewish scene with the brilliance of a
comet, seemed unable to understand the grassroot work that had
to fill out the political bargains he hoped to achieve with his melo-
dramatic sorties. To think, as he did, that one could 'buy' a
homeland with the money of rich Jews and develop it through a
Chartered Company, left out of account the inner transformation
that had to be won.

It is this that Weizmann keeps insisting on remorselessly in his
early letters. He pleads for cultural programmes to transmute the
Jewish loyalties of youth; for schools and colleges (using Hebrew
increasingly) to transform the technical base in Palestine; for
practical ventures, even of the simplest kind, fired by Zionist
idealism instead of charity. By the time the Balfour Declaration
was issued, the groundwork for this had been laid; and one can
see, looking back, how sure Weizmann's instinct was, even when
he was being compelled, from the sidelines, to be critical of the
leader.

As early as 1903, he had the temerity to challenge Herzl on these
points in a huge letter of some 8,000 words, concentrating with
prophetic insight on two crucial issues: the need, for the future, to
preserve the movement from the domination of rabbinism, and
the need to fight in Russia against the pathetic and indeed tragic
belief of young Jewry that they would win freedom and equality
through immersion in revolutionary socialism.[8] Behind the
arguments on practical detail, brilliantly elaborated, was the
underlying conviction that Herzl's mentality, despite its
prophetic expression, was not authentically Jewish, and that

this would have increasing significance for the future if Zionism was to become a practical, as distinct from a purely messianic movement.

We know about Weizmann's ideas in this early period because of the letters he wrote almost daily to his fiancée Vera, and continued to write, after they were married, whenever work or travel kept them apart. Herzl, for Weizmann, fitted into the distinction he always drew between 'East' and 'West', which meant between 'real' Jews (those with a gut relationship to Eastern Europe) and the timid ones, open to alien influence. It was, of course, quite wrong to put Zionists into water-tight compartments in this way, but it was a convenient shorthand in the letters which he poured out to Vera and his friends. The vehemence of his style at this time was not, however, simply that of a young hot-head, as Herzl (virtually ignoring his memorandum) seemed to think. It was, in fact, the most direct clue to the innate powers which he was to display with such calm mastery when he could take the reins into his own hands. It is exemplified in two early moments of drama.

The first, from the autumn of 1903, is on 'Uganda' – Britain's apparent offer of a large settlement area for Jews in Africa. At the Zionist Congress in the summer, Herzl is for accepting, while 'the Russians' oppose it. But in Weizmann's view, his colleagues are being ineffective in exposing the real fallacies. Nor are they hammering home the true alternative. He is not yet thirty, but he plunges in with a virtuoso display of every analytic power he has. Somehow he manages to get to England for a whirlwind visit. With one hand, he begins organizing a great Jewish intellectual stock-taking in the form of a university Seminar which will assemble top Jewish scholars and scientists to establish the essential nature of Jewish existence – the cultural tradition, the practical prospects. With the other hand, he pursues a one-man diplomatic campaign to wrest from British officials the damning facts which will explode any remaining faith in 'Uganda'. He is without money, support, or knowledge of English, but this wild foreigner seems to have powers that open doors – *and files* – to devastating effect. In great excitement he writes to Vera:

> I am burning with desire to see you now and talk with you . . .
> I went to see Johnston* . . . If I were to publish the entire content
> of the conversation, a mortal blow would be dealt to the "Africans".
> . . . You see, my child, how diplomacy is conducted. Our
> leaders merely spoiled things and made fools of themselves. I am
> convinced that Herzl would speak of "enormous successes" were he
> to know all I know now. (Vol. III, p. 53-4)

Back in Geneva, he pours out a stream of passionate memoranda to his comrades, bringing the whole subject to life in immense factual detail and with brilliant personal sketches of the people he has met. From time to time in these letters, which continue for months, he reveals the sardonic tone that many were to experience from him in later years ('Herzl is a clever operator . . . He has weapons at his disposal that others would not even dare to consider'). But within the tactical struggle he reverts constantly to the deep principles which alone give meaning to what he and his group are trying to do:

> Seven years of Zionist activity [he writes in one letter, III, p. 80] have
> finally taught us that we have sought in vain to construct a unity out
> of heterogenous elements . . . One group conceives of Zionism as a
> mechanism, and is ignorant of its connection with the soul of the
> Jewish people. Consequently it seeks to manufacture Zionism
> either through diplomatic journeys or through fund-raising appeals
> . . . The other group understands Zionism to be the life-giving force
> both actual and potential: the free development of the nation finding
> its highest expression in the idea of statehood.

With what one can only call passionate logic, he fights against the comfortable idea of a 'pact' under which the East European masses supply the 'content' while Western leaders manage the external forms. This policy has failed because it inevitably lacks organic force:

* Sir Harry Johnston had been Special Commissioner of the British Government in Uganda.

For the West Europeans, Zionism has remained a cliché, completely devoid of Jewish content, unstable, wavering and hollow, finding its highest expression in so-called diplomacy, and in 'Jewish Statism' that smells of philanthropy.

And here, in 1903, Weizmann projects the practical emphasis that was to be of momentous importance for the upbuilding of the nascent State. It was wrong to wait for the perfect political framework: 'Jewish content' meant absorption in practical work immediately:

> The policy of waiting implies a death sentence for the movement. We know that work in Palestine is feasible; we know that by means of slow and systematic activity in the spheres of culture and colonization it is possible to create a force in the land. We therefore demand that all our energies be directed towards examining this question and giving it reality ... Our colonization must be collective and strategic.

From this he moves on to detailed plans on organization, publications, lectures, enrolment of volunteers. It was too much, at the time, for the comrades. He is furious while he waits endlessly for a response. But one sees in this passionate drive the clue to his later triumphs.

For a different kind of drama, tragic in essence but with an element of farce, there is the crisis in October 1905, when pogroms break out in Russia in the wake of the revolutionary movements of that year. By this time, Weizmann has been living in England for more than a year, with his scientific work in Manchester going very well. He has also been active in English Zionism. He has already met Balfour and will shortly be meeting him again for what will prove a momentous talk. But all this growing success vanishes from his mind as he hears of the pogroms. 'The terrible news!' he writes to Vera in Geneva (IV, p. 192). 'God! I am so distraught. I firmly believe that it is a crime to be here conducting chemical experiments while slaughter takes place over there ...' Two days later he is writing again:

'My dear: the pen is shaking in my hand, my brain refuses to function: everything is tinged with blood . . . I am alone among strangers. Oh Veruchka, it hurts so much. Again and again, thousands slain, thousands wounded, weeping, wailing and such helplessness . . .'

The next day he is even more distraught:

I have always regarded myself as a commander, but what kind of commander if I am not with the army? This is my fifth day of suffering the torments of hell . . . What a pathetic situation . . . to be here, reading the newspapers and teaching Englishmen chemistry!

But if he is simply letting himself go with Vera to ease his feelings (as he admits), he loses no time in pulling himself together for practical action, again in typical style. In a long wild letter to an older Zionist, Ussishkin, in far-off Ekaterinoslav, he denounces the Jewish leaders in England who are doing their best, he says, to prevent the immigration of these persecuted Jews to England, and are even reported – wrongly, in fact – to be lending money to the wicked government of Russia:

For the past month [he tells Ussishkin, IV, p. 200] I have been working without respite, travelling, campaigning, rousing the public conscience of Jews and Christians. I plan to use my influence to undermine the authority of the Rothschilds and the gentry who have behaved in a base and cowardly fashion in this terrible hour . . .

He has a great plan that needs Ussishkin's help. There is to be a massive anti-pogrom Protest Rally in Manchester in two weeks time, to be addressed by British political leaders (Churchill, in fact). He (Weizmann) will move a resolution attacking 'the cowardly behaviour of certain Jews who consider themselves to be the official representatives of the Jewish people'. These Rothschilds, he says, are putting it around that the pogroms are the work of mobs and that the Russian Government itself is friendly to the Jews. Ussishkin should write a letter for the meeting denying this. Such a letter would have a dramatic impact:

I implore you again and again [he writes]. We are at an historic moment and cannot afford to miss it. We Zionists can gain control over all English public opinion. After the meeting a deputation, myself included, may go to see the Prime Minister and the King.

It is fascinating to compare the Weizmann who could write a diatribe of this kind with the seasoned leader who, ten or eleven years later, has become the trusted intimate of some of these same Rothschilds, does in fact meet the Prime Minister (and the King), and operates with calm vision and strength. Yet even in his heated exaggeration, we see his sure instinct at work. He was totally right about the origins of the pogroms; and he foresaw accurately that a crucial problem for Zionism would arise in England over the opposition of the assimilationists – 'Montefiore and all that bunch', as he called them.

At that stage he still felt totally frustrated – analysing, demanding, negotiating with tireless energy, but to a great extent in a vacuum. But it is not difficult to see the signs even then of the Weizmann who was to become a legend, operating, to quote Isaiah Berlin, with a:

> serene and absolute conviction that made it possible for him to create the strange illusion among the statesmen of the world that he was himself a world statesman, representing a government in exile, behind which stood a large, coherent, powerful, articulate community.[9]

It is often said – Lloyd George himself said it – that it was Weizmann's brilliant work during World War I in keeping British guns firing which led the Government, out of gratitude, to issue their declaration of support for a Jewish Homeland. Certainly it is true that when the U-boat victories cut off almost completely the supply from the U.S.A. of acetone – the solvent in making cordite – it was Weizmann's fermentation process which saved the day. Recruited overnight into a top position as scientific adviser, he organized the flow of acetone on a huge scale from converted breweries and specially built factories, first in England and then overseas, with the greatest administrative and scientific ingenuity. But this began only in the spring of 1916. His most remarkable contribution to the birth of a Jewish State had come in 1914, on the day war broke out, and it lay not in what he said to British statesmen but what he did to the Zionist movement.

If ever vision was decisive, this was the occasion. With the outbreak of war, Weizmann saw with absolute clarity how all that the Zionists had dreamed of and worked for could now be channelled into reality. A revolutionary change in direction had to be imposed. Everything at that moment put Zionism in the opposite camp to the Allies. Palestine was controlled by Turkey. The Zionist office was located in Germany. Jewry in the U.S.A. was pro-German at the top of the social scale, and at the bottom violently opposed to Russia, the ally of Britain and France. To turn all this round involved not merely insight, but tireless and brilliant diplomatic skill. This was Weizmann's achievement.

One sees this to dazzling effect in Volume VII of the letters. It is startling to watch him moving in the British Establishment with total freedom and dignity. But, if at the top level in government and public opinion he was negotiating as a leader, he was fighting at other levels to make this leadership possible. The letters show what a knife-edge he lived on while the outcome was building up.

First, he had somehow to maintain contact with the official Zionist leadership, steer it away from German involvement, make something positive out of the Russian connection, keep in order the valuable but mercurial talents of people like Sokolow and Jabotinsky, and line up the Americans in a role that was to be decisive. Holding this complex of international forces in his hands, he had at the same time to protect his base in England, where personal interests and rivalries posed particular dangers, in view of the impact they might have, at close hand, on the British Government.

We see him at work on the European front, fighting off potential mistakes by the scattered Zionist leadership from the moment war breaks out. On the American front he brings all his force to bear, as we see in a letter to Shmarya Levin in New York as early as October 1914 (VII, p. 21):

> I am convinced that the outcome of this catastrophe will be a British and French victory. I cannot and do not wish to envisage any other outcome. Turkey has roused the Allied Powers against her and will have to pay for this. I hope that in that case Palestine will come

under English influence, and England will understand the Zionists better than anyone else.

In a moving passage, with thoughts that he was often to repeat in the years ahead, he sets out his approach:

> As soon as the situation clarifies, we could with a clear conscience point out to both France and England the abnormal and cruel position of the Jews, who have soldiers in all armies, who fight everywhere, and are recognized nowhere.
>
> We can draw their attention to the positive achievements and potentialities of the Jews and to our desire and ability to create from all the suffering, dispersed Jews, a force which could serve progress and civilization. We could show the interest of all those nations now fighting for small nations in securing for the Jewish nation also the right to exist.
>
> We shall be understood in England, and in France, and in America. Only a few rich and assimilated Jews, both here and in other countries, will not want to understand us. The force of our moral claim must be self-evident, and the political conditions for the realization of our ideal will be favourable.

Shmarya was a close friend to whom he could voice inward doubts as well as hopes:

> With feverish anxiety [he says] I am watching events, which have for me a deep hidden meaning: it is the struggle of the pagan Siegfried against the spirit of the Bible, and the Bible will win. Will this great period find a sufficiently worthy generation? Will Jewry understand all the greatness of this historic tragedy? I hope it may.

One is half-tempted to say 'the rest is history': but if one can, in fact, trace the emergence of an independent Israel to the moment of Britain's decision in 1917, there were too many world dramas *en route* to pretend that the outcome was now determined. Nor can we look at Weizmann himself in too simplified a way. In the letter to Shmarya we see him as a master of logic and strategy, but if we are to gain intimacy with him through the letters, we must meet him not only as a driving, creative force, but as a quiet man, with a peculiar power to communicate feeling.

It is indeed in this form that we can find the answer to the

question raised earlier: why was it that Britain moved into the
role of sponsoring the Jewish Homeland? Certainly it was not in
payment to Weizmann for his scientific help, valuable as this was.
Nor does any student of history believe today, that putting Jews
into Palestine was motivated solely by the advantage Britain saw
in winning Jewish support during the war itself and for later.
However strongly this was argued in Foreign Office minutes,
there was a simpler factor that turned the scales – an issue of
humanity.   Walter Laqueur, in his *History of Zionism*, reminds us
of something we are apt to forget in the aftermath of Ernest
Bevin.   In her palmier days, Britain could be swayed by simple
generosity, and in this spirit 'take decisions which were of no
obvious political, economic or military benefit'.[10]   Principles
counted: Balfour and Lloyd George believed that the Jews had
suffered at the hands of Christendom and deserved reparation.

Richard Crossman, taking the same view in *A Nation Reborn*,
saw this as Weizmann's particular contribution:

> His achievement was to charm British statesmen out of their usual
> concentration on national self-interest, and persuade them to take a
> great risk for a good cause ... At the height of their power, they
> looked into the tragic eyes of this Jew, and felt their conscience
> stirred.[11]

Weizmann's critics have always fastened on his British attachment
to argue that it inhibited the aggressive fighting spirit which
proved vital for the emergence of the State of Israel.   To say this
is to misunderstand what Weizmann's feeling for Britain really
meant.   At no point did the love he had developed for his
adopted country curb the passion with which he fought the
Jewish cause.   It was to help this fight on the *spiritual* plane that
he turned to England for what he thought he saw in its tradition;
and he was prepared to go a long way to let this influence ripen
among Jews.

Patience and compromise were certainly strong elements in
Weizmann's character, but never in the form of subservience.
The attachment to Britain was never a limitation to his Zionist

dream, but precisely the opposite: a call to the pursuit of qualities which Jews needed, in his view, to give validity and dignity to an existence impaired and unbalanced by centuries of abnormality.

At no point did Weizmann look on the British uncritically. How could he? But fallible, timid and indeed treacherous as they could be, there was something in their tradition which spoke with immense appeal. Coming from the maelstrom of Eastern and Central Europe, he was deeply impressed, as the letters show, by the sense of freedom and fair play which he had never before seen so prevalent as a way of life.

Above all, the British took the long view, and how penetrating this was as a principle. To give way in a crisis to desperation and fanaticism was to surrender the very aims one was fighting for. One looked instead, in the British spirit, for what was practical and possible. One was flexible. One used one's imagination. This was no abnegation, but on the contrary a harnessing of effort to results that were otherwise beyond one's reach. A people that could work this way had shaken off its abnormality and could face the future.

Yet if this was a cast of mind that gave Weizmann a unique affinity with England, he was far too authentic a Jew to change inwardly in loyalties and sentiment; and we see in the letters – sometimes warmly, sometimes painfully – how typical he was, despite his apparent freedom, in experiencing the age-old conflict of personality that all Jews seem heir to.

In one form, it made itself tangible in his attitude to the Jews themselves, miles away from the familiar 'self-hate', but expressed sometimes in ways that sounded perilously like it. His love for the Jewish people – his proud identification with them – was absolute; but it went with a clear recognition that there were many Jews – individuals or groups – that he loathed, not, one might say, on a *personal* basis, but because they expressed authentically and horribly some degrading tendencies that impinged on his ideal. They were no worse than non-Jews, but that was not the point. Being Jewish was something beautiful, ineffable, in its true expression. To betray it was a crime.

This conception of what being Jewish should mean lay at the heart, as we have seen, of his scientific research into the nature of life. It governed all the work he did – single-handed in the early years – to try and establish a university where this mysterious ancient force within the Jewish tradition could be recovered and distilled into a modern, living form. The university seminar that he had begun working on as early as 1904 was to be its first expression. Writing to his dear friend Catherine Dorfman, he is rapturous over his plan (III, p. 57). 'Imagine,' he tells her, 'the best Jewish elements holding a series of courses, say in Zurich for six weeks, on topical Jewish themes.' The subjects he was planning to cover with his chosen team were, in fact, a hodge-podge of Hebrew literature, Bible criticism, Jewish colonization, chemistry, Spinoza, Jewish statistics. However, the sense of aspiration was tangible, and was realized to the full when the 1913 Congress finally endorsed his plan for a university, and gave him authority to pursue it.

In contrast to his love for those who can understand his cultural purpose, we see his disgust with those surrendering to materialism. On a visit to Warsaw in 1911, he writes to Vera (V, p. 247) about the joys of meeting family and friends there and how horrible it is 'as soon as one steps over the threshold'. The poverty is devastating, but it is the *spiritual* degradation which appals him:

> Jewish life here is a *Totentanz, danse macabre*. Ostentatious over-dressing, over-flowing cafés, gaiety and amusement, while the screw turns tighter and tighter, the circle of misfortune gets narrower.

Endlessly, in his letters, it is the vulgarity of the bourgeois which disgusts him, but he is equally intolerant of those whose vulgarity is, one might say, intellectual. In his student days, arguing through the night in Geneva, he had fought against the Jewish Marxists and the early Bundists who felt it necessary to reject Zionism in order to espouse 'the brotherhood of man'. He was repelled morally by their eagerness to betray their people, but he saw it also as intellectually bankrupt, self-deceptive, inauthentic.

By the same token he was implacably opposed to quasi-intellect-
ual argument from the extreme right, which linked itself to the
virtues of naked force.   When resistance turned to terrorism, it
seemed evil and 'un-Jewish', however patriotic its motivation.
The truth is that he had little stomach for any manifestation of the
mailed fist.   And it must be admitted that sometimes this left him
exposed in an ambivalent position during the dramas accompany-
ing the emergence of the State.

Isaiah Berlin has written that 'the State of Israel was constructed,
whether it knows it or not, in Weizmann's image'.[12]   In its
underlying origin, certainly, but not always in the way it developed.   Events generated a momentum that gave statehood,
especially after the Six Day War, certain qualities of jingoism,
materialism and complacency far removed from the vision he had
nourished.   To be a Jew could never mean justification through
the trappings of power.   It exasperated Weizmann that his own
people did not seem to feel this.

In this mood, he was liable to fall back nostalgically into
Yiddish, a prime vehicle for what one might call loyal exaspera-
tion.   At one level, Israel had introduced a spirit of normality into
Jewish existence, at another, the Jews were still, and would remain, a peculiar people, capable of ruining everything by a crass
narrowness that bore the mark of the *Galuth*.   On his death-bed,
in words recorded by his loyal friend Meyer Weisgal, it was
within the sardonic intimacy of Yiddish that he murmured
thoughts of this kind:

> Yidden sainen a klein Folk, ober a groiss Folk.   Sei sainen a miess
> Folk, ober oich a Schein Folk.   Sei sainen a Folk vos boit, un a Folk
> vos zerstert.   Sei sainen a genialer Folk, un zu selber Zeit a narrisch
> Folk.   In seier Akshoness-digkeit sei kennen durch brechen a Wand
> ober der Loch in Wand wet stendig blaiben kukendig oif sei . . .*

---

* The Jews are a small people but a great people.   They are an ugly people
but also a beautiful people.   They are a people that builds and a people that
destroys.   They are a people of genius and at the same time a silly people.
By their obstinacy they can drive through a wall, but the hole in the wall
remains gaping at them.[13]

One hears the Litvak speaking. The rueful wit is so typical. One wonders, sometimes, if this kind of wit will survive in Israeli life. At one time one was not sure. Now, with an unexpected revival of Yiddish also, it seems powerful enough, part of the process of coming to terms with, instead of rejecting, the past.

Certainly it is one of the joys of these letters that we see Weizmann sparkling with humanity in the midst of all his troubles. Sometimes he can be very sharp, as when he says to the famous English writer Israel Zangwill in an early exchange: 'You may be the historian of the ghetto, but you are not its psychologist.' Sometimes he is like a character out of Sholom Aleichem, bewailing his constant lack of funds. 'I used to think of myself as a Baron Hirsch without money,' he writes to a friend. 'Now I am a Weizmann without money.'

The way he writes to his friends is, in the end, the most heartwarming side of his character. The two Zionists he most admired in the political realm in these early years were Ahad Ha'am and Ussishkin, a symbolic pair, in effect, since the one seemed to Weizmann to express infallibly the undying *spiritual* meaning of being Jewish, while the other stood like a rock for the *practical* upbuilding of the Homeland. Yet though he wrote continuously to these two, and relied very much on their reaction to everything he said, there was more respect than jollity in his relationship to them. For jollity, there were the old comrades from student days. When he is depressed, he writes to Catherine Dorfman, wishing they could all be on holiday together. 'How I would like to recall the old days: how good they were: how young we were: how everything has become stale since then.'

Shmarya Levin, subtle and endlessly entertaining, was a particular favourite: and it is a remark of his, in *Forward from Exile*, that helps us to understand, indirectly, what qualities there were in Weizmann that all seemed to feel. Shmarya is writing not of Weizmann but of another Zionist leader, Nahum Sokolow – an encyclopaedic scholar, immensely talented. He says:

Sokolow was a swift swimmer in a calm sea, but he was no diver, and he never brought up the pearls that are under the surface of the waters. He envisaged all life, but did not penetrate it. He was witty and intelligent, but not passionate.

And Weizmann? He was passionate; he penetrated life; and he brought up pearls.

III: GOLDEN LANDS

Jerusalem U.S.A.
England in Style

JERUSALEM U.S.A.

I HAVE been exploring Jewish experience so far, in this book, from my base as an Englishman, a Litvak, and a lover of Israel. Quite powerful roots to draw on, one would think. Enough to keep one busy.

But one has only to mention the word 'America', to realize how flat and empty Jewish life would be today if one didn't draw also on that strange and teeming world across the Atlantic. I have, admittedly, a special interest. America is a symbol of power and fulfilment even if one has never been there, or simply paid a brief visit. In my own case, I lived and worked there for years. I belong to the place. I was reborn there.

'O my America! my new-found-land.' This is exactly what one feels, even if, unfortunately, John Donne had something quite different in mind when he wrote the words. The poem is called *On Going to Bed*. It was his mistress whom his roving hands discovered, with a sense of freedom and delight that opened up a new world of happiness. But the metaphor lives on, with all its overtones, for anyone caught up in the boundless excitement that America has generated for its people, and most particularly for its Jews. It is easy enough to salute Israel as an expression of Jewish vitality, but can anyone doubt that the achievement of America's Jewish immigrants in creating a vivid and wholly original culture has, equally, a striking place in Jewish history?

It was not difficult, during the Bicentenary rejoicings of 1976, to envisage the Jews taking their place proudly on celebratory platforms with their ready-made prayer *Sheheheyanu*, thanking God 'who has kept us alive, sustained us and brought us to this day'. A Jew outside has to join in. What we salute is not just the marvel of American fulfilment in general, but the forging of what is almost a new Jewish civilization.

The Jewish experience in America has been unique in two major ways. The first is that we can see, looking back, that America provided the physical base – almost as if Providence were at work – for the transfer of a mass settlement of Jews from their earlier 'Heartland' in Central and Eastern Europe. If this had not happened, building up from large-scale migration from Europe in the latter part of the nineteenth century, the murderous aim of Hitler to annihilate the Jewish people could have succeeded in large degree.

But the move to America was more than a transfer of population. The real wonder lies in the interaction of American and Jewish life. By a kind of miracle, America had something to offer its Jewish immigrants that was tailor-made to the fertilization of their own longings and genius. Not that this was a one-way process; the Jews came, in time, to have a deep influence on the host country. But if one seeks the causes of Jewish fulfilment and distinction in so many American fields, it looks – to put it provokingly – as if Jewish history had been waiting throughout the centuries for America to turn up.

This alone seems to explain the unique creativity and 'success' of Jews in America. It is not that the Jews were innately cleverer, more hardworking, more idealistic – and wittier – than other immigrant groups, as some like to think. The special factor in their role lay in a peculiar hunger for that kind of transforming process that America alone could offer. There was a visible amalgam of drives in which the age-old question of what it meant to be a Diaspora Jew was explored and deepened in the context of a society that encouraged an escape from the conventional limitations to thought and action. The issues in being a Jew in a basically Christian world took on a different perspective – a different vigour. The old passions were there, but pressed now with greater freedom. America, emerging as the greatest power on earth, was full of perplexity on how to interpret its manifest destiny: the Jews, involved in this as Americans, felt the outcome intensified by their own traumas.

Even in these general terms, one can see why something unusual was likely to emerge from the Jewish settlement, once it had become large and rooted. There had never been, in the world's history, a community of Jews so deeply and powerfully settled in a rich society. There were parallels in ancient Babylonia, Alexandria and Spain, but with a crucial difference. Here, for the first time, they were not peripheral as a community but an integral part of what they had helped to create. In exploring their own problems as individuals and as a people, they had some-thing relevant to say to their fellow-Americans.

There is a paradox in this that is not yet resolved, and perhaps never will be. The Jews, for all their eager absorption of America, were always looked on – and still are – as 'different', often disliked, and always in some sense unassimilable. But this was a *social* reaction. In the *cultural* field, it became accepted that the very distinctiveness of the Jews – preoccupied though they were with their own special problems – was releasing something which had character and value, and with communicative power. America was always ready to listen to the different voices which spoke up from within her. At different times there was some-thing like a message for all Americans coming from New England writers, from the South, from the Mid-West. The Jewish voice, when it finally emerged, had something of this quality, but with a different kind of carrying power. It brought with it not only a local or regional experience (though it certainly did this in relation to New York) but a tone that, for a very good reason, was to intensify the spirit already rooted there. America became recept-ive to what might have seemed at one level alien because, as the Jews matured in this new society, they found themselves drawing, from their own past, on moral and intellectual qualities which had, in fact, long fed the American life-stream.

It is in this sense that one can talk of a special Jewish element in the character of the present American *ethos*. On the surface it may seem odd. America has drawn its generative power – qualities of courage, imagination, hard work, religious faith, intellectual brilliance, dry wit and warm-hearted vivacity – from virtually every nation on earth. Every difference of origin is a source of living tradition. The German-Americans, the Irish, the Swedes, the Italians, the Poles, the Armenians and countless others are all vividly aware of undying links with their countries of origin, and translate this into the strongest of communal feelings. And what of the Black peoples of America, whose sense of community has become, in recent years, a vibrant aggressive force of immense consequence, transforming many aspects of American life. To claim more for the Jews may seem perverse, and one has therefore to define rather carefully what is meant. Briefly, it is that the Jews have become significant not from the *outside* – by perpetuating nostalgia or foisting something divisive or disturbing on American thought – but rather by enriching something already there. There are plenty of paradoxes in this. Let me try to spell them out.

The special Jewish place in the American cultural bloodstream has two elements in it, both, in a sense, accidental. One is that the Jews have found themselves particularly responsive to what is the deepest influence in all American life – the British tradition. The other is that the immigration from Russia brought with it echoes of a culture that was life-enhancing in a quite different way but was already feeding into American experience.

On the Russian factor, it was precisely at the period when the mass of new immigrants were beginning to find their feet – the beginning of the twentieth century – that the giants of Russian literature and the power of Russian artistic creativity had begun to stir Western feeling. The Jews, even if only half-aware, were immersed in it. It was often transmuted for them in Yiddish, but still immensely potent. Once they had found a way of speaking from within their new culture, they would carry the older heritage into it, just as, centuries earlier, they had been the bearers into mediaeval Europe of the lost Greek culture which they had absorbed, in Arabic, during their settlement in Moorish Spain. In all these senses one can fairly say that there were accidents – or cultural paradoxes – behind the Jewish influence in America.

The Russian element that the Jews injected is so obvious as hardly to need exposition. The affinity to the British tradition is less spoken of, but in a way more significant.

On the general role of the British tradition in American life, does one have to justify the assertion that it outshines all the hyphenated cultures in which America is so rich? Politically it has become fashionable – and perhaps realistic – to deny the survival of a 'special relationship' between Britain and the U.S.A.; but it is absurd to close one's eyes to the bonds of language, literature, law and sentiment. Every American, even if full of vestigial hatred like those of Irish descent, inherits and deepens the received British tradition. In the same process, the British are constantly affected and enriched by what comes from America. The difference between this and the much weaker inter-relationship of America and Germany (or Italy) is not difficult to explain. With Britain and America, we are not dealing with uprooted nostalgia – as expressed, say, in the delightful Italian street-festivals of New York City – but with the mingling of living and common cultures. In a recent book, Stephen Spender called this shared tradition: 'an immense common life of the past, sustained within the permanence of the works of imagination'. There is nothing static or complete in attitudes or feelings on either side. Both countries are reacting individually to their current experience, but the involvement is there. The British element in American life is part of an unfolding process, constantly exemplified in thought and motivation.

But what of the Jewish affinity to this tradition? Socially, there is a large and lasting gap between those born into the WASP background and the Jews: yet intellectually and morally there is a bond which has asserted itself over the years, symbolized by the emergence of a critic like Lionel Trilling whose work reached deep into these common qualities. Perhaps the Bible is at the root. The old American writers were drawing naturally on English literature, and English writers had absorbed the Bible into their blood. If *Moby Dick* has something of the epic power of *Paradise Lost*, we know what sources Milton himself drew on. American immigrants of the second generation, eagerly absorbing the literature of their new land, all felt the immense sobriety, elegance and moral power of the Anglo-Saxon tradition. For the Jews among them, as their own writing began to emerge in novels and criticism, this strain received particular expression, as if their strong desire for identification was drawing on a built-in quality from their own tradition.

The central element in the WASP *ethos* – Protestantism – had a particular appeal, though once again through a strange paradox. In any striving towards religious understanding, orthodox Judaism should feel particularly akin to Catholicism. The concept of sin, and the authority of priest and rabbi are obvious parallels, and the style of worship is often identical. To take only one example, the Mass arouses the same holy intensity as two central rituals of Judaism – the *Kedushah* (sanctification) in the daily service, and the *Kaddish* recited for the dead. Yet historically Jews have a profound fear, even hatred, of Orthodox Christianity in all its forms, as if its expression of primitive faith, and especially worship of the Virgin Mary, is an unbearable offense to reason. Without doubt, there is an echo in this of the hatred of idolatry expressed in the Bible. By contrast, the Jews are usually quite at ease with Protestant Christianity. The transition was particularly satisfying for those who could now forget the confrontation of the orthodox faith of Czarist Russia. They saw Protestant America as a blessed relief from the inquisitions of the past and reached out hungrily towards its culture.

They did so, at least, once they had come to terms with it through their schooling. In the more immediate foreground they were dominated – and continued to be – by the kaleidoscopic folk memories they had brought with them from Russia. One can identify in these feelings the agonies of exclusion and fear, overlaid by the rapture with a new freedom. But ultimately the distinctive mark of Jewish expression was a consciousness of history. In material terms they might be absorbed in scraping a living or building a fortune, but this could never be what life was about. It is surely because the Jew could never see the story of his people as something finite, or played out, that the search for its meaning became so engrossing in its expression.

Yet it was America which made it all possible. For some American Jews, their double view – as Americans and Jews – could be inhibiting, even paralysing; for others it was an enrichment.

They saw America as a culture which encouraged them to let go with everything they felt, every aspect of their reason, every side of their nature. They could be authentic to themselves in every field of endeavour, drawing on the particular amalgam of experience that had come their way to assess what being an American Jew of this age meant to them. Inevitably, their achievement would have a flavour all its own. Some observers, unable to shake off ancient hatreds, would find it distasteful for precisely this reason. Others would recognize it as a product not just of the Jewish tradition but of the American dream – that freedom of the spirit which welcomes individual expression, enlarges it, and gives it universality.

I have been talking of American Jews as if there were a consistent story beginning with the first settlement of 23 Jews who arrived in New York – or rather New Amsterdam, as it then was – in 1664. In one sense, perhaps, this might be true. The ups and downs of Jewish settlement from those remote Dutch days did reflect underlying factors which were always to be typical of the American background and the Jewish dream, but by itself this is like looking at French history during the last 300 years without regard to the French Revolution. American Jewry had its revolution, as we all know, in the 1880s. Without this, it would have gone on under an *ancien régime* – a leadership of settled Jews harking back in spirit to the bourgeois timidity of the German Jewry from which they had come.

The immigration which brought these German Jews to America had begun to gather pace from about 1820. This was the age in which German-Jewish peddlers (among many other types of new settlers) moved westward to lay the basis in trade, mining and ultimately banking for some of the great American fortunes. In this period of swift expansion, American prosperity rose to new heights. The Jews became increasingly prominent, with a heavy emphasis on their German origin. In moving to America they had brought German culture with them – its self-assurance, even arrogance. No Germans liked Jews, but the Jews liked every-

thing German, especially music. For the synagogue, they had
brought a formula from the Fatherland in the shape of Reform
Judaism – a plan for acculturation through keeping a low profile,
denuding worship and observance of anything which was alien,
old-fashioned, unscientific. This was to be the way to social
acceptance. It was one way in which America was better than
Germany, for there was no need to baptise. One could be a
German-Jewish-American and proud of it.

It could have remained a hyphenated existence like that of other
immigrant groups, had it not been overtaken by the desperate
horde of Jews who began to pour in from Russia following the
outbreak of pogroms in 1881. Between 1880 and 1925, when
new immigration laws damned the flow, about two and a half
million Jews entered the country. The heaviest concentration
was, of course, in New York City. By 1920, it had a Jewish
population of more than one and a half million. Today, the
Jews of the New York Metropolitan Area number two and a half
million, which is thirty per cent of the population. Without any
doubt, it is from this strong concentration in what is the cultural
capital of America that the special Jewish influence radiates, for in
America as a whole the Jews, just below six million in number, are
less than three per cent of the total population.

New York, then, holds the key: but we shall never understand
how the influence worked itself through unless we look at the
character of the settlement that suddenly launched itself into this
city. It was not most significantly a question of numbers, although the inflow was certainly dramatic. In 1880, there were
only 80,000 Jews in New York; in the next twenty years the
number rose by half a million. But numbers were not the sole
factor, as one can see from a comparison with other dense settle-
ments of immigrants in America – the Irish in Boston, for
example. In the middle of the nineteenth century there was a
huge emigration from Ireland following the potato famine. In
the decade from 1847, more than one and a half million emigrated, with America – and especially Boston – a main focus.
The Irish continued to arrive in the years which followed, and
Boston was revolutionized. From a home of Anglo-Saxon

Brahmins, it became heavily Irish in politics and religion. There is no sentiment for the Old Country stronger than among the vast population of Irish-Americans, no kinship loyalty more enduring. But there is little Irish *cultural* influence, as far as one can tell, in the thinking of America as a whole. Even after its Irish transformation, Boston's abiding influence remains that of the Anglo-Saxon Brahmins.

I sometimes think that if one is looking for illustrations of the way in which the *Jewish* irruption became so decisive, the closest to a parallel manifests itself in the phenomenon mentioned earlier – the explosion of Black sentiment. It is a paradox even to suggest this, since the historical, intellectual and social differences are so obviously enormous. Indeed, it could be argued that the Black explosion is not a parallel to Jewish sentiment but its exact opposite, not seeking to deepen the existing tradition but to reverse it. Yet the Black movement is relevant.

Black liberation was once a Jewish pre-occupation; today, the Jews are a special focus of Black hatred. If there was thesis, and then antithesis, there will never, one feels, be synthesis. Yet in some deep sense there is a parallel, which some Jewish writers have tried – unsuccessfully – to exploit. Jews and Blacks, wrestling with what they feel to be the injustice of their fate, have caught the imagination of America – and the world – with some kind of universalist overtones. And there is a parallel, too, in the paradox embedded in their new vigour. One can sum it up in the famous catchword: 'only in America'. Both peoples have been self-obsessed, and some have been led, though in very different ways, into bitter hostility to the society of which they are a part. Yet it is America which has nursed them and nourished them. As we say in the *Sheheheyanu* prayer, it is America which has given them life, sustained them, and brought them to this day. Certainly for the Jews, the more one examines the inward element in their story, the more one sees how it could only have been realized as it has by a creative and human power unique to America itself.

The arrival of the East European immigrants in the 1880s was, at first, a story of total confusion. In Czarist Russia – the main source of the outflow – the Jewish masses were already experiencing deep social change. At one level, it is true, they were locked in rigid exclusion from the world around them. Apart from a small scattering of rich Jews, traders, agents, and a growing number in the professions, they lived in close settlement in cities and *shtetls*, all Yiddish-speaking, traditionalist, poor and fearful. The impulse to escape became overpowering for two main reasons. First, with a great growth in their numbers, they were close to starvation. Second, the pogroms were mounting: they lived in terror. Looked at in this way they seem remote, buried in the Middle Ages, ignorant and helpless.

But this is nothing like the full picture, as we saw in discussing the legacy of the Vilna Gaon. Though desperation was the hallmark of the Jews, there were forces at work, especially among the young, breaking the old mould. In Yiddish, or in the original languages, they were avid readers of nineteenth-century literature, and were creating their own. Ideas fought for expression – the dignity of man, the brotherhood of all man, the need to be free. Some saw the solution in a return to the ancestral land. For many more, this seemed reactionary and they threw themselves into a Jewish labour movement, with poweful cultural overtones. Others moved wholly into *Russian* revolutionary movements. For all of them, there was one common preoccupation – fierce, relentless, intellectual argument. Perhaps centuries of Talmud argument had trained them, though surely the Russian background, in which a political harangue might last six hours or all day, was relevant. The Jews had responded to Russian culture, in so far as they could reach it, with the same enthusiasm they showed later in responding to America. They were bursting with ideas – imaginative, intellectually stirred, poised for change.

None of this, we may be sure, was known to the prosperous, cautious German-Jews of New York when hordes of Russians began pouring out of the steerage holds into Ellis Island. The local Jews saw these kinsmen quite simply as poor, ignorant and alien: somehow or other they had to turn them into Americans. With some distaste, but in a humanitarian spirit, they set up organizations to help with food, education and general welfare, though the gap – felt on both sides – was immense. The immigrants huddled together in primitive dense conditions downtown; the rich Jews moved uptown. For several decades there could be no affinity. The immigrants viewed the German-Jews with awe, but also with a certain amused contempt. They called them *Yahudim*, which marked them off from 'real' Jews, who were *Yidden*.

The ultimate outcome, as we know, was astonishing. As with immigrants from so many other countries, America took hold. The main thing was that there was work – long hours, terrible conditions, but offering a way out. The immigration process, with all its marvellous achievements, was never a simple story – history without tears – but a crude kind of epic, full of paradox. Though uprooted, the Jews had the warmth of family and *landsmen* (home-towners) for support. In the strange world outside, cruelty was mixed with kindness, poverty with opportunity, corruption with justice, coarseness with idealism. This mixed pattern is still the essence of American life; with the Jews, who suffered and responded in mind, the paradoxes have received full expression.

From the beginning the Jewish immigrants were not passive recipients of American favour but active participants in their own style. Irving Howe, in his brilliant *World of Our Fathers*,[1] sees the difference from other immigrants lying in the way the Jews brought a fully structured society with them. He puts it this way:

> The Irish, Italian and Slavic immigrants were the dispossessed elements among their peoples. All they were able to bring with them were caste sub-cultures. The Jewish immigrants were different. They were not a class but a dispossessed *people*, all of Jewry in microcosm. They deposited on American soil their full culture, gripped in the throes of a transition from ghetto to freedom.

At the centre of being a Jew is the Bible; but what these immigrants brought with them was not subservience to a theology but *Yiddishkeit*, a cultural framework which starts with the Bible but has a wider set of social values. For *Yidden*, the pain of life is annealed in kinship, and ethics draws on this, turning on the obligations of what might be called Jewish decency. There is a familiar phrase which expresses this: *'es passt nicht'*: there are things which it is not 'seemly' for a Jew to do. It may seem vague, but it has meaning: it is a guideline.

It was with this underlying attitude – a broad set of feelings stretching into politics, literature, art and ethics – that the immigrants, living through a colossal social and economic adjustment, were able to hold on to the things they valued. In the first phase of the new settlement the instrument was Yiddish, and at its peak in the 1920s the intensity of Yiddish life was overwhelming. There were five Yiddish daily newspapers, innumerable book-shops and a great range of political organizations, side-by-side with a proliferation of *shuls, cheders* and *yeshivahs*. Most particularly, there was the Yiddish theatre, with productions ranging from sentimental hotch-potch to Shakespeare, Chekhov, Strindberg and the rest, graced by stars like Maurice Schwartz, Molly Picon, and the Adler dynasty.

Yiddish may seem to have made it parochial; but as this new settlement moved into full command of English (assisted by American-born children) the flavour of its culture began to have a wider effect, especially in the political field. The Yiddish news-papers had inculcated what one can only call a Russian obsession with political ideas, and this continued to be an obsession of the Jews. In every Red Scare – and they were frequent – Jews were picked out for infamy. The Communists certainly had a hold, though the stronger element in political writing by Jews became a hatred of Communism from what one might call the sophistic-ated Left. Both elements were due to feed into American life with great intensity during the Depression and Roosevelt's New Deal. In successive and sometimes bewildering turns of flank, it was a battleground in which no quarter was given: and the results are tangible in all serious American-Jewish writing.

The New Deal was in many respects the watershed. By this time many of the second generation were college-trained and ready to be absorbed (like other immigrant descendants) in the social experiments which were transforming America. It was an accident, but a lucky one, for the Jews that they were ready just when America was poised for a great argument – a shake-up that challenged the past with new concepts. Some doors opened to the Jews, others were forced open in a drive from them that drew heavily on their inherited culture, with its Russian overtones. The theatre was a particular case. In the Thirties, there was a sudden outburst of talent reflecting many strands in the Yiddish tradition. The Theatre Guild grew stronger. There was the Group Theatre and then the New Deal's Federal Theatre, all dominantly Jewish, and expressing a missionary zeal, in straight plays or satires, that was both artistic and political. Many of those involved in these ventures moved on into stardom. It was a breakthrough for authentic Jewish talent, due to be enriched from another source by actors and writers from Jewish holiday camps – 'the borsht circuit' – where people like Danny Kaye, John Garfield, Moss Hart and Doré Schary first found their feet. Hollywood was already overwhelmingly Jewish on the production side. It now rose to its 'golden age' with a variety of Jewish talent in the *artistic* field, with disastrous results when Jewish idealism, in that strange hothouse of wealth and guilt, became decidedly parlour-pink and brought much trouble on its head.

Plays and movie-scripts overlap with novels, but in this particular field the pace of development was different. There were inevitably novelists (as there were playwrights) who happened to be Jewish but made their mark without this being significant. Edna Ferber, colossally successful, believed, above all, in providing a good read, and many Jewish writers followed this neutral path. But the phenomenon we are dealing with is the exploration by Jews of their own situation. Here, the results, to begin with, were very disappointing. With a few notable exceptions, the trend was towards Marxist realism. Books like Michael Gold's *Jews Without Money* were just full of hate – anti-capitalist, and in effect self-hating anti-Jewish.

It was not until World War II that novelists emerged who could give full rein to the powerful Jewish element in their nature with imagination and love, fully aware of all the horrors and contradictions, but finding a voice that was their own, true to history and to the human issues which life on earth generates. If their work had this serious concern, this didn't mean that it was pompous.   On the contrary, it drew on the already established vein of New York humour to good effect.   There was wit, irony and vivacity in abundance, but there was also awareness, feeling and intelligence. Each writer explored himself and the immediate world around him, but it carried a wonderfully communicative power.   The experience of a Jew, in some respects restlessly alien, could stir everyone's intellect, enrich everyone's imagination.

There is no way to explain why a burst of creativity erupts at particular times, but there are always some clues in the social situation.

In the last thirty years – i.e. since the end of the War – the social basis of American-Jewish life has been virtually revolutionized. In the Thirties, despite the New Deal, the Jews were still in mid-stream as Americans, longing to get ashore.   Today, the sense of rootedness is stronger.   Young Jews are now overwhelmingly the children of American-born parents, and in an age in which many of the old limits of discrimination have been shattered. The greatest symbol lies in college life.   Quotas have been abandoned, even, it seems, in the Ivy League.   Jewish students are said to form eighteen per cent of Yale and twenty-five per cent of Harvard.   Even more remarkably, fifteen to twenty per cent of Faculty posts in America are held by Jews.   The same libera-tion has spread into many fields, notably in business and govern-ment.   Dislike and discrimination have by no means vanished, but in the issues of daily life a Jew feels on firmer ground.

By the same token, he is now free to talk about his feelings as a Jewish-American reflectively – without pressure or inhibition. His Jewish consciousness has come alive with vibrant power in the aftermath of the Holocaust.   As an American, fully at home at last, he has shared in the swings of feeling that have dominated postwar thought – the pride in American power, transfused with doubt at what it may have led to.   He has absorbed it all, and wants to talk about it.

An outpouring of novels has been one result, in moods varying from satire to high intellectual purpose. The ground is firmer underfoot, but a sense of bafflement is evident in new forms. What some want to express is distrust of the very 'safety' now open to them. Comfort, they are saying, thins the blood. Society – often in the shape of a Jewish mother – has tried to emasculate them. They are afraid, not for themselves as Jews, but for the future of a world in which individual values are swamped by huge impersonal forces – the computer, multi-national corporations, or just the mindlessness of the media. As one critic has put it: to win in such a society is to lose – to lose is to win. To be the hero you have to be something of a *schlemiel* – a dope – but with divine longings. Big ideas – Marxism or Progress – are out. What one is after is to get back, as it were, to the Torah, to simple virtues, to the discipline of thought. History has to have a meaning, even if one keeps tripping over one's feet in finding it out.

It is an approach tangible in all the best novelists, different as they are in the form of what emerges. For its clearest expression, both intellectually and emotionally, one turns always to Saul Bellow. Opening his latest novel, *Humboldt's Gift*, almost at random, one finds a sardonic aside – it is the asides which matter most – on the pretensions of all manipulators. The author's main character Citrine is spending an evening in conversation with Humboldt, and pauses to sum it up:

> There came a time [he says] when, apparently, life lost the ability to arrange itself. It had to *be* arranged. Intellectuals took this on as their job. From, say, Machiavelli's time to our own this arranging has been the one great gorgeous tantalizing misleading disastrous project. A man like Humboldt, inspired, shrewd, nutty, was brimming over with the discovery that the human enterprise, so grand and infinitely varied, had now to be managed by exceptional persons. He was an exceptional person, therefore he was an eligible candidate for power. Well, why not? Whispers of sane judgment plainly told him why not and made this comical. As long as we were laughing we were okay.

For the other side of Bellow – or is it the same side? – there is a brief remark on the same page about his girl-friend Demmie:

There was a lot of agony in Demmie.   Some women wept as softly as a watering can in the garden.   Demmie cried passionately, as only a woman who believes in sin can cry.   When she cried you not only pitied her, you respected her strength of soul.

Bellow, and all the others, are not writing for a Jewish audience but for everybody; yet their writing is Jewish.   They have seen through society, but are still engrossed in a search for meaning. This quality emerges clearly in contrast to a new fashion in American writing which one might say is non-Jewish – writers like Kurt Vonnegut, Thomas Pynchon, or Donald Barthelme. Superficially these writers might seem equally to be rejecting the horrors of the establishment, but it comes out in them, both in content and literary style, as despair at all coherence, a plague on all houses, turning history (as someone has put it) into a comic-strip, with no intention of being anchored in reality and meaning. It is a far cry from the kind of alienation that critics have seen in American-Jewish writing, expressive of the predicament of man in modern industrial society.   In these newer writers, alienation in the *medical* sense – the rejection of responsibility – is where everything seems to be leading.

In the last book before his death, *Sincerity and Authenticity*, Lionel Trilling tackled this question squarely.   To his despair, he saw irresponsibility – even madness – being elevated into a virtue in some areas of American thought.   It is an outcome, he showed, of the view that a man with something to say cannot be 'authentic' to himself as a responsible member of society, but only by letting go in total self-indulgence.   For Trilling, the meaning of life has to emerge in ordinary experience, 'in going to weddings and funerals', or, as Jesus did, 'in reasoning with rabbis'.   From a different position, there is the same humanism in a writer like Alfred Kazin, with his marvellous feeling for what is rhapsodic, as well as tragic, in life.   Naturally, some Jewish critics, like Leslie Fiedler, have taken off for the wilder horizons; but mostly they deepen *traditional* virtues to powerful effect – Jewish, in a sense, even though their work is addressed to American consciousness as a whole.

This general influence of Jewish humanities is itself bolstered by a separate phenomenon in American-Jewish writing – an astonishing outburst in recent years of scholarly, as well as popular, writing on specifically Jewish subjects. Books have poured out endlessly on Jewish history, sociology, folklore, rabbinic learning and theology, a vivid reflection of the unique role that American Jewry now plays in the world. There is also a fruitful interchange with academic work in Israel. Together, a wholly new form of exposition has been established, directed first to the huge audience of six million Jews in America, but indirectly to all of us.

One has no idea how far this new civilization of American Jewry will also develop patterns of Jewish religious observance that will be significant for the rest of the Disapora. There have been enormous changes since the days when German-American Jews opted for timidity. The Russian immigrants were orthodox at first, but have moved into different positions, in religion as well as politics. Since the War, orthodoxy has been rampant in new style, especially with the settlement of Hasidim in large numbers. One of the strangest sights of New York is to walk along 47th Street between 5th and 6th Avenues – the diamond centre – and see the dense throng of men in *pe'os* (ringlets), fur hats, and long black coats (the Hasidic dress), oblivious to everything except Judaism and diamonds. One recovers, for a moment, the tone of the first great Russian invasion, and contemplates what happened to it in American hands.

I cannot tear myself away from talking of American Jews without some tribute to the unique social humour which their experience has generated, especially in New York. Here, then, is a story from Judd L. Teller's delightful *Strangers and Natives*.[2] Since it brings together Mayor LaGuardia, the labour movement, racketeers, orthodox Jews and an Irish judge, it is surely relevant.

The time was 1936. The *shochtim* (*kosher* slaughterers) of New York had formed a union, with a closed shop: but some *shochtim* claimed that they were being refused membership, and therefore work, because the union was racketeer-dominated. The racketeers, drawing their rake-off, had put in a speed-up which met demand with fewer slaughterers. The unemployed *shochtim* argued that the speed-up violated rabbinic law, so that the poultry being sold in New York was, in fact, not *kosher*.

LaGuardia summoned both sides to a hearing, but before it began, he called in some Jewish journalists covering City Hall to ask them how a speed-up could make the poultry non-*kosher*. He was told that, to ensure no pain, the knife used by the *shochtim* had to be very sharp and without a nick, which is called a *p'gam*. The law says that the *shochet* has to break off constantly to test his knife, running the blade against his fingernail to make sure it hasn't got a *p'gam*. LaGuardia then called in the disputants, and asked those already in the union to produce their knives. He went along the line, passing his fingernail along the blade in each case, and then announced, in his famous squeaky voice: 'There are more *p'gams* in these knives than there are needles in a porcupine.' The *shochtim* still holding jobs were dazed by this expertise. The Mayor was right: a speed-up *was* against the law. They threw out the racketeers, and admitted the unemployed *schochtim* to the union.

As this was New York, the story didn't stop there. Two separate groups of rabbis now came forward, each claiming monopoly control of slaughtering, and therefore of the fees. The case went to the New York Supreme Court before an Irish judge, with rabbinic argument – in Yiddish – dragging the case on for months. Of such are the joys of New York.

What would the first twenty-three Jewish settlers in New Amsterdam have made of it? For that matter, what would they have made of Mark Rothko's huge empty canvases, or of *Portnoy's Complaint*? Are we quite sure we know what to make of it all ourselves, and we have had two hundred years to think about it.

ENGLAND IN STYLE

O NE can respond whole-heartedly, as I do, to the American-Jewish scene without losing one's attachment to England. Indeed, it may be that an English Jew is only free to enjoy America so much because he has England to come back to.

Jewish life, it must be admitted, is pretty tame here compared with its rumbustious excitement in the U.S.A., but peace and quiet are, after all, the qualities that American tourists admire so much in England generally. They also come here in droves to savour the surviving relics of a once-glorious heritage: and as it happens, this is one area in which English Jewry has something to offer too. The great aristocratic days, by which one means the really eccentric days, may be over, but there is still a good deal of fun in it, and for once the story can stand four-square with that of America – perhaps even five or six square, as S. J. Perelman might put it.

I may appear to have been somewhat off-hand, in the last chapter, about the American-Jewish aristocrats – the great German families who took off on their rise to fortune in the middle of the nineteenth century. But to assess them properly depends on where one stands. Looking back from today over the last hundred years, it is the *Russian* immigrants who rivet one's attention, not only for their achievement but for the way they represented the mass of Jewry – the non-famous, the inchoate multitude of ordinary Jews. This, one feels, is where the roots lie, and one identifies with them. One likes to think of them as alert, warm-hearted and idealistic. One knows, at the same time, as Weizmann saw so ruefully, that they can be stupid and materialistic, with an eye as open as anybody else's to the main chance. But there they are, the warp and woof of Jewish existence. In the American scene they turned it all into a miracle.

With this miracle in mind, the *ancien régime* which the impoverished Russian Jews finally displaced seems small beer, certainly in creativity. Yet if one dismisses the great German-Jewish families this way, it leaves out an essential part of the dialectic. Even more, it leaves out an equally valid aspect of Jewish history – the way it has always thrown up a few enormously wealthy *nedivim* (princes) side-by-side with the crude and poverty-stricken masses. Above all, it leaves out the fun which one can always extract from tales of the really rich. One is almost ready to say that here again America is the greatest: but maybe, as I have already suggested, one should wait to see what England has to offer in this field.

The raw material for comparison is available happily in two delightful books. In 1967, *Our Crowd* by Stephen Birmingham took the American reading-public by storm.[1] Its sub-title, 'The Great Jewish Families of New York', might have suggested a collection of pious family chronicles, but nothing could be more misleading. *Our Crowd* was both serious and funny – a highly ironic picture of the one-time life-style of a closely-knit group of the fabulously rich.

The family names are bywords in American life, not only for wealth but also for the immense support they have given to cultural and socially progressive causes – Loeb, Sachs, Guggenheim Lewisohn, Seligman, Rosenwald, Morgenthau, Lehman and the rest. Within a few decades of their appearance they were at the pinnacle. Their New York mansions included, 'Otto Kahn's sprawling palace, Jacob Schiff's castle, the Felix Warburg's fairy-tale house of Gothic spires'. When they moved to their vast country estates, it was in private railway cars 'carrying chefs, stewards, butlers, valets and maids'.

One would never understand New York without taking in stuff of this kind, but it is always more than period history. Many of the ironies move over into our own times. First, one is aware, reading of this gargantuan wealth, that there were social barriers that could still not be overcome. From another angle, there is a bitter-sweet amusement in comparing the attitude to wealth of the *really* rich with that of the *nouveaux riches* of today. For 'our crowd', there came a point after which the supreme virtue was not

display but modesty. 'One spared no expense to be incon-
spicuous.'

If their self-confidence was rock-like, it was not without a flaw
or two on the Jewish question. There is irony here, too, in the
way this was resolved. Their philanthropy towards suffering
fellow-Jews all over the world was always immense; but for a
long time they fought shy of active identification with world
Jewish causes if this seemed to impinge on their status as Americans. The Holocaust and Israel changed all that. Today, their
conscience as Jews is as vibrant and absorbing as it was when the
founders left their humble Jewish homes in Germany.

But in the meantime they have lived through splendour in a
style all their own. They had a true sense of *noblesse oblige*: and
if they were snobs, it came as naturally to them as to the out-
rageous Mitfords of England. If a name was mentioned, they
had a simple criterion: 'Is it someone we would visit?' But if this
established 'our crowd', it also carried a deeper meaning: do these
other people live by rules – by a code of conduct we can take for
granted? Not that their own group always behaved themselves,
but there is an idea here that one doesn't wholly dismiss.

Could anything from the other side of the Atlantic match this?
A few years after *Our Crowd* appeared, a British author, Chaim
Bermant, decided to have a try with a book he called *The Cousin-
hood*.[2]

The scale, of course, had to be smaller. Nothing is ever as big
as America. *The Cousinhood* – highly entertaining – is a study of
seven very wealthy and interconnected Jewish families that rose to
dizzy heights of fame and influence in nineteenth-century Britain.
Reading it, one thought at first that the thesis was going to be:
anything 'our crowd' can do, we – the Cousinhood of England –
can do better. In fact, however, one soon became aware – as one
might have expected – that the history and style of the English
families were vastly and significantly different from that of the
German-Jewish aristocracy of America.

Superficially, the subject matter of both books seems identical.

In Britain – as in the United States – a few Jewish immigrants arrive, move swiftly from trading into finance, and in no time at all – partly because of dynastic intermarriages – are fabulous powers in the City, launching vast issues, opening up new countries, amassing great fortunes, acquiring huge estates. Behind it, there is a specifically *Jewish* drama. Mighty as these rich families become, they are still *arrivistes*, fighting for full acceptance by the Gentile world. At the same time as they struggle for a new image, they are restrained by a strong sense of loyalty (in varying degrees) towards the Jewish background from which they have emerged. What might have remained a dilemma is resolved finally in the same terms as in the U.S.A. In the ordinary course of events, there would have been an inevitable one-way seepage of Jewish identity. Yet when everything might have disappeared, the sense of being Jewish came back into its own, and with a new *élan*, through the emergence of Israel. Peoplehood over there – supported with true enthusiasm – became a safe and satisfying surrogate for an otherwise unconvincing kind of Jewish identity over here.

In many ways, then, *Our Crowd* and *The Cousinhood* cover the same ground, and the characters, of course, sometimes overlap. But the difference in locale is fundamental.

In the American story, the opportunities were both greater and less than in the British scene. American growth in the middle of the nineteenth century was gargantuan: and the life-style of those carried forward on the wave had a richness as flamboyantly American as their vast financial deals.

Yet the America which knew no bounds on what could be achieved in economic terms set harsh limits on what could result socially. The families of *Our Crowd* may have opened up America with finance and dazzled it with benefactions; yet in many ways, the top prizes they sought lay beyond their reach. They were larger than life but could fail at the Social Register, or even a box at the Opera. More seriously, it was an existence out of the mainstream of active politics until relatively recent times.

In almost all these respects, the atmosphere of *The Cousinhood* is very different. Great fortunes – sometimes dazzlingly great – surface in its pages, yet the overall picture is much more intimate – almost parochial at times – in keeping with the scale and style of England itself.

The timing is different, too. Unlike *Our Crowd*, the story reaches a peak in the first part of the nineteenth century, and had begun earlier, in the second half of the eighteenth century, with the arrival of a few key immigrants who put down firm roots in British trade and finance from this time on, and – to their great profit – were thus in a position to play a part in meeting the huge needs that arose for finance and supplies over the whole of Europe during the Napoleonic Wars.

The essential quality of the *Cousinhood* families – especially in their first century – lies in the meaning one gives to the phrase 'putting down roots'. They were not opening up a new country, as in America, but trying to find a place – albeit a place with a special flavour – within an existing pattern. This way was open because the built-in conservatism of British life was self-confident enough to admit oddities from outside. This meant that almost from the beginning, immigrants who made the grade financially, could be given a role as a natural, acceptable, and convincing element in the British scene – always provided, of course, that the newcomers never tried to claim that they were *really* or *fully* English in the way Lord Derby was, or the village blacksmith.

This paradox – that the Cousinhood was totally British (or, rather, English) yet ineradicably alien – survived countless different forms of expression. It was lived with, resented, obscured, and enjoyed in varying degrees. It had the great English virtue of never trying to push things to a logical conclusion. One could feel a hundred per cent English (or more), participate in political life, settle in some quiet country seat, intermarry with the aristocracy, and win the Derby. The price-tag to make it acceptable was to acknowledge – however silently – one's ultimate difference. England was full, as it still is, of rich and talented foreigners, taking on the local patina forcefully, brilliantly, amusingly. Eton, the clubs, the racecourses, even the Palace – they were all open, but on terms.

Was it the old English sense of lineage, or just convenience, that caused these Jewish families to become so fantastically interwoven? The *Crowd* families intermarried to a certain extent, but the Cousinhood took it further, and with one particular oddity at the centre that is worthy of note.

The magic names that everyone knows are Rothschild and Montefiore; but, in fact, the marriage alliances that forged the Cousinhood were built to begin with on a humbly-named Mr Cohen – Levy Barent Cohen – who had arrived in London in 1770 and become so rich in the City by the end of the eighteenth century that a new immigrant called Nathan Mayer Rothschild was very happy to marry his daughter in 1806. Six years later, another Cohen daughter, Judith, married young Moses Montefiore. Ultimately, then, this is a Cohen Cousinhood.

However, flamboyance was in the wings. The Montefiores, though only second-generation immigrants, were already linked in marriage to the long-settled Mocattas, as well as to the Goldsmids, bullion dealers with the Mocattas (as they still are) on a vast scale.

It is the Goldsmids, perhaps, who in some ways generate best the early period flavour of the Cousinhood. Interspersed among tales of their huge – and sometimes catastrophic – financial deals, we read of their taking several of the Royal Dukes with them to synagogue, and entertaining King George III and his Queen at their country house at Morden. Nelson, who visited them frequently with Lady Hamilton, had to sit silently there one night after dinner for what seemed to him hours, while Moses Montefiore, the most devout of all these characters, recited the Grace after Meals in Hebrew, and at its full length.

The Rothschilds went on marrying Montefiores and the special clan of Cohens. At the same time they were marrying into an endless stream of cousins of their own in Paris, Vienna and elsewhere. But this was to be only part of the Cousinhood.

Up in the north of England – in Liverpool – a local cousinhood of families called Samuel, Yates (Getz), and Franklin had graduated from commerce to finance and was preparing to move south.

The preeminent member of the first London generation – due to be ennobled later as Lord Swaythling – established the merchant-banking firm of Samuel Montagu and married a grand-daughter of Levi Barent Cohen. One of his sons married a Goldsmid, his daughter a Montefiore connection. His nephew Herbert Samuel, who became an outstanding political leader (ennobled as Viscount Samuel) was thus an integral member of the now proliferating Cousinhood.

A quite separate Samuel family, which had immigrated in 1750, grew to fame in the person of Sir Marcus Samuel, the founder of Shell Oil (he was ennobled as the first Viscount Bearsted), and attached itself to the Cousinhood through marriages in the next generation. The Sassoons, descending on England from the far reaches of the Empire, established a link with the Cousinhood by marrying into the Rothschilds. It sounds as if one can go on and on, with every English Jew a Lord.

Allevei! – as the Yiddish word has it so poetically. 'If only 'twere so.' One had only to drive in one's brougham from Mayfair to the East End to find, without any surprise, a very different story. There they were, the flotsam and jetsam, the teeming multitudes, refugees from the pogroms, alien and poverty stricken.

One has to remember something else, too. Although honours began to accumulate around the Cousinhood from the days of Sir Moses Montefiore (knight, 1836), English Jews, powerful as they might be in the City, were still excluded from some expressions of citizenship, including the right to sit in Parliament. Emancipation in this sense arrived only in 1858, and even then was grudging, as if expressive of the fact that Jews were to have not a normal but a special place in English life. Perhaps it was in unconscious recognition of this that the first Jew allowed to enter Parliament – symbolically, a Rothschild – sat in the House of Commons for the next fifteen years without once opening his mouth. It was important to get over the hurdle, but not to push things too hard after that. Jews might be virtuous, useful, even distinguished, but there was still something unusual about them.

. . . . .

No one expressed this oddity better than Queen Victoria herself. She had been a personal friend of Moses Montefiore since 1835, two years before her accession, when her mother had rented a modest summer house next door to him at Ramsgate and been given the key to his spacious gardens. Yet despite this long friendship, she seemed to feel that City money, when made by a Jew, was somehow tainted. This, anyhow, is what she wrote to her Prime Minister Gladstone in 1869, when he kept insisting that the leading Rothschild be given a peerage:

> The Queen really cannot make up her mind to it. It is not only the feeling of which she cannot divest herself against making a person of the Jewish religion a Peer; but she cannot think that one who owes his great wealth to contracts with Foreign Governments for Loans, or to successful speculation on the Stock Exchange can fairly claim a British Peerage.

Yet if the conviction persisted – even after the peerage barrier finally fell in 1885 – that Jews would always remain in some sense alien, this oddity, when fully acknowledged, seemed precisely the condition for the great social freedom that prevailed. Unlike the position in Germany at this time, where conversion to Christianity was an essential ticket to many rights, the British had no taste for it, and the Cousinhood rarely went in for it, except in so far as it fell 'naturally' on some of their children or grandchildren through a marriage outside the faith.

If one tries to identify what particular flavour was added to Cousinhood activities by the British background, two points come to mind, one serious and the other frivolous.

The first was an acting out of their leadership role in consonance with the feeling, embedded deeply in British life, that the Jews, as the People of the Book and heirs of the Holy Land, had a special religious significance for mankind. This respect for the Jews went deep in Christian life. As a result, Jewish leaders had ready access to public support in moments of crisis.

One sees this in the vehement response of public opinion at the time of the Damascus Blood Libel in 1840, which centred on the allegation, surviving from mediaeval times, that Jews killed Christians, especially children, to use their blood for Passover rituals. It surfaced now in Damascus, following the mysterious disappearance of a Capuchin monk. No body was ever found, but a number of Jews were arrested and charged with the crime. In prison, they were tortured and 'confessed'. Sixty-three Jewish children were seized to extort information on where the blood had been hidden.

The shock to civilized opinion was immense, especially in Britain. In Parliament, and at a mass meeting at the Mansion House, there was a demand that British power and prestige – very significant in those days – be used to secure the release of the arrested Jews. When Sir Moses Montefiore set out on a journey to the Near East to make these demands personally to the Sultan of Turkey, he was received by Queen Victoria before he left, and again after his triumphant return.

Behind this – and the similar outcry at the time of the Russian pogroms in the 1880s – lay a streak of pro-Jewish sentiment that was to find momentous expression in the Balfour Declaration. The idea of the Jews re-establishing a national centre in their ancient homeland had been treated romantically in English writing in a variety of different forms in the nineteenth century, so that when Chaim Weizmann expounded this vision to British political leaders with prophetic ardour, there was a ready soil for its nourishment.

Within all the negotiations, there was an assumption of a special relationship. Britain, still the world's major power, could afford to display a romantic benevolence towards a people who had suffered so much. On their side the Jews, and especially Weizmann, felt that there was something in British history, and the British character, which fitted harmoniously with Jewish aspiration. There was to be mutual advantage also, it was thought, in *political* terms: but a personal warmth transcended this.

Within the Cousinhood, there was, inevitably, considerable apprehension as to what a Jewish Homeland might do to their dearly prized British status. It took a confident man, Lord

Rothschild, head of the family, to show his disdain for such timidity by throwing his full weight into the Zionist struggle. It was to him – in a calm assumption of all the indefinable realities of the Cousinhood – that Balfour wrote on November 2, 1917, telling him, in eight historic lines, that the British government had decided to facilitate the establishment in Palestine of a national home for the Jewish people. 'I should be grateful,' he added, and it sounds almost like an afterthought, 'if you would bring this declaration to the knowledge of the Zionist Federation.'

If this serious side to the British involvement with Jewish experience had historic political results, the frivolous involvement with the Cousinhood at play is not to be underestimated as a significant part of the picture. From the very beginning – as we saw with George III and Nelson – the British establishment was very ready to enjoy the hospitality that these new-style financiers were in a position to offer: and if it lacked the flamboyance that emerged later in America, it had a cachet all its own. There is an ironic passage in *The Cousinhood* describing a ball given by Baroness Lionel de Rothschild[3] at their suburban estate at Gunnersbury in 1838 as part of the festivities for Queen Victoria's coronation. A banquet was laid on to start the affair in the evening for the five hundred guests:

> The baroness sat between two dukes of the blood royal – Prince George of Cambridge and the Duke of Sussex. Also present were the Duke and Duchess of Somerset, the Duchess of Richmond, the Duke of Devonshire, the Marquis of Londonderry. There were two ex-Prime Ministers in the gathering – Wellington and Melbourne – and a pair of future Prime Ministers, Russell and Disraeli. Every glittering name in England seemed to be present, and not a few from Europe – Prince and Princess Schwarzenberg of Austria, Princess Esterhazy from Hungary, Marshall Soult from France, a sparkle of German princelings . . .

The balls, the house-parties, the matchmaking, and the political intriguing that distinguished the Victorians increasingly absorbed the Cousinhood. A thoroughly raffish tone was added when the

Prince of Wales established his own lordly set, with racing, gambling, and every kind of lavish adventurousness.

The Prince had a penchant for odd characters, and also needed financial support. Rothschilds and Sassoons were included in the Court favourites, together with fabulously rich railroad and mining tycoons like Baron de Hirsch and Sir Ernest Cassel. In a sense, one moves outside the Cousinhood here, since these particular millionaires were not *echt* British, despite the Prince's favour. However, it extends the canvas entertainingly enough, as when one reads of a hunting party that Baron de Hirsch staged for His Royal Highness in 1891 at his estate in Hungary where the guests, who included Lady Randolph Churchill, Winston's mother, slaughtered more than eleven thousand head of game in a five-day *battue*.

It comes as a jolt to remember that there was a serious side to this flamboyance. Baron de Hirsch may have enjoyed spending a few millions in having fun with the Prince, but he gave away many more millions for the support of the Jewish poor, including great benefactions in Palestine and his enormous project for establishing Russian Jews as an agricultural community in the Argentine. No genuine Cousinhood members operated on this scale. Most of them went in for quiet propriety *à la* Forsyte. If, in early days, the romance of huge fortunes set its own style (as in Disraeli's picture of the Jew 'Sidonia' – a Rothschild-like character always on hand in *Coningsby* with his preternatural wisdom and munificence), the *persona* of the Cousinhood emerged in the present century with a distinction that has virtually nothing to do with wealth and exists solely in terms of intelligence and public service.

A Rothschild was, perhaps, a good symbol of the change – the Lord Rothschild of the Balfour Declaration, who made his mark not as a financier but as a naturalist. In this new tradition, the present holder of the title is a scientist by training who has also held the prestigious post of Head of the Prime Minister's 'Think Tank' at 10, Downing Street. Of the Montefiore dynasty, Claude, who died in 1938, was an outstanding theologian. Hugh, descendant of a collateral branch, became a Christian (he calls himself a 'Christian Jew', or perhaps it is a 'Jewish Christian'), and has been elevated to a Bishopric in the Church of England. The family ruefully regard this as the cross they have to bear.

Dilution of the tradition is inevitable, yet the high purpose of those Victorian decades has left an inextinguishable mark. It is rather satisfying that of all the glamorous Cousinhood names, the humbly Jewish name of the founder – Levy Cohen – has gone on, generation after generation, with its own *éclat*. The Cohen clan – a roll-call of extraordinary variety – climaxed in the present generation in the person of Lord Cohen of Walmer, probably the most distinguished public servant of Britain until his death in 1976.

In moving this way, the Cousinhood have – perhaps to their surprise – fulfilled the real meaning of a Yiddish concept referred to as *yichuss*.

Yichuss – originally an Aramaic word meaning 'pedigree' – denotes the overwhelming respect which one accords instinctively to someone of high descent. But there is an angle to it that is all-important. In the Jewish tradition, the pedigree that counted was not of wealth but of learning. A rich man had his place in the scheme of things – above all because he was in a position to help the poor. But this was ephemeral. The *yichuss* that mattered was being linked to a long line of scholars. Here was something eternal. One might be rich or poor, a saint or a scoundrel, but if one had *yichuss*, one was above the common herd. One carried within one something of the distinction that had preserved and elevated Jewish life through all the ages.

I know someone who is an Abulafia. The family have kept intact the links of their descent from a clan that moved from the Holy Land to Spain in the twelfth century and produced an unending galaxy of rabbis, philosophers, poets, financiers and statesmen whose story illuminates centuries of Jewish existence. Closer to our time, there is the instinctive respect accorded to the prodigiously talented Schneersohn family, which claims descent from the great Hasidic scholar, Shneour Zalman of Lyady (1745–1813).

But if there is one *yichuss* that tops everything it is being linked, as so many Litvaks claim to be, to the family of the Vilna Gaon: and here, for illustration, I come back to the Jewish aristocracy of England – new style.

One of the most engaging men of England in the last half century was Israel Sieff, a leader of the great Marks and Spencer business, and ennobled as Lord Sieff. If he was personally wealthy – as he may have been – this was not where his distinction lay. What everybody felt about him was his intellectual warmth, his tireless concern for human welfare, his radiant response to every aspect of culture, and the wholeness of his Jewish character.

He tells us, in his *Memoirs*,[4] that his great-grandfather, who was a rabbi, talked to him as a child about the family's origin in Vilna. The most important thing about Vilna, the old rabbi said, was that in the eighteenth century the greatest Jewish scholar in the world taught there – the Gaon. The Sieff family was, in fact, descended from the Gaon's brother Joseph. 'We should be very proud,' he said, 'to be part of the family of the Vilna Gaon.'

Lord Sieff clearly liked this – a pedigree to be proud of. It was, of course, only part of the wider *yichuss*, that he was a Litvak.

IV: ADDING IT UP

Seventy Years On
Jesus
How Faithful?

SEVENTY YEARS ON

THERE comes a point, after looking at different facets of Jewish history, when one wants to add things up. It's clear that one can get the feel of Jewish experience from a wide assortment of starting-points if one is prepared to follow each one through: but is there any way of taking stock of everything?

Just seventy years ago, a wholly original attempt to do just this was made in the form of a massive *Jewish Encyclopaedia*, produced in the U.S.A. and completed in twelve huge volumes in 1906. It was endlessly informative.

But this was Jewish history up to the end of the nineteenth century, and in the present century the material that goes into a global view has surely been revolutionized. Foremost in one's mind there is the Holocaust and the birth of Israel. This alone seems to call for a new evaluation of what being a Jew means. Side-by-side with this, there has been an astonishing breakthrough in the field of scholarship, affecting every facet of Jewish experience in the past. A fresh conspectus was clearly called for, and it was given form in 1972 in a totally new work – *Encyclopaedia Judaica*, published in Israel with the help of a world-wide team of scholars, and set out in 16 volumes, 11,000 pages, and a brilliant array of illustrations.[1]

Does this colossal amount of information help one to add things up? No one will read through a work of this kind expecting some clear-cut answer. Yet something new and unified does emerge as one turns the pages, led on from one subject to another. I've been doing this for eight years now, and can at least report on how it has affected my own feelings.

The range of the work is certainly daunting. It sets out, as its predecessor did, to survey the whole of Jewish life from the most far-off times to the present day, assessing the religious faith of the Jews, their experience in every part of the world, the ideas they have generated both for themselves and those around them, their sense of kinship as a people and their immense variety individually.

To be coolly factual on all this would be hard enough, but the approach has also to embrace elements that transcend facts – above all, a sense of wonder and paradox. Here is a people obsessed with material problems yet full of dreams; avid for change, brilliant at innovation, yet clinging to the past; longing to become unnoticed yet refusing to disappear; the eternal victim – the eternal survivor. The encyclopaedia itself becomes a paradox. Its subject may be a small people, but the canvas is of Western man. The Jews are peripheral but at the heart of things; absorbed in each background yet rising out of it to express the most generalized spiritual problems of humanity. It started in the Bible, it is equally evident today, and it is the hallmark of Jewish experience in many of the ages in between.

An encyclopaedia does not formulate ideas this way, but they emerge through the treatment of individual subjects. There is a challenge to each contributor to break fresh ground, to re-examine the past, to systematize the experience of their generation as a step towards establishing a new outlook. The historic example of this approach is the great French encyclopaedia of the eighteenth century. In the field of Jewish experience, something of the same intensity emerges in this new encyclopaedia from Israel.

If one looks for guidance on how to make sense of all that has been happening, the sources that a new encyclopaedia can draw on are now immense. For the distant past, archaeological discovery has opened up a new understanding of Jewish origins. For later periods, scholars have immeasurably deepened traditional Hebrew studies, and created a new approach to the study of Jewish social history. For the Holocaust and its background, the documentation is enormous, almost unassimilable: and the same is true for Israel. For all the historic issues of Jewish life, philosophers, linguists, historians, political scientists, economists and sociologists have been labouring in their highly specialized fields. It is a perfect moment in time, and Israel is the perfect place, for the distillation of so much new experience and knowledge in the form of an encyclopaedia.

Nothing new in Jewish life obliterates what has gone before. This is true of Israel itself: and it is equally true that one gets a deeper understanding of the approach conveyed by the new encyclopaedia if one compares it at key points with its seventy-year-old predecessor, the old *JE*.

One of the most interesting aspects of the change is in the field of Bible scholarship. Any discussion of Jewish experience has to ground itself on an attitude to the Bible, and the *JE* of 1906 was very conscious that it had to formulate a new position on the issue. In the foreground were the startling new theories of non-Jewish scholars. The 'Higher Critics', breaking up the Pentateuch into separate documents, were asserting that the Patriarchs were fictional projections of later times. The Psalms were largely 'Maccabean'. Everything was 'late'. The uniquely sacred character of the Bible was being called into question by parallels in other ancient literatures. Religious ceremonies were being 'explained' through anthropology and folklore. How was all this to be handled?

The *JE* found a satisfactory solution. With every Old Testament book or character, the straight Bible story was told first, followed by a separate section giving a full account of all the legends on the subject, and then by a section summarizing, rather cautiously, 'the critical view'. The reader knew exactly where he was. The 'straight' part – on Abraham, let us say – was a summary of the familiar Bible account. The legend section was very original in systematizing so many vaguely remembered stories. But to read the 'critical' section was, for a traditionally-educated Jew, almost like eating a ham sandwich:

> The biography of Abraham in Genesis is probably to be regarded as legendary ... The stories of Lot, Hagar, and Keturah are ethnological myths ... Circumcision was not adopted by the Israelites in the way here represented; the story of the attempted sacrifice of Isaac is a product of the regal period ...

Even to read it was daring. To believe it, even tentatively, was blasphemy. But it opened the mind.

All is very different in the new encyclopaedia. Seventy years have passed. Critical theories, familiar now to the most devout, are looked at in a much cooler, less horrified way. Where a Jewish scholar still feels impelled by unshaken faith or vestigial sentiment to hold on to some form of fundamentalism, he is likely in most cases (though not all) to aim at refuting the critics in their own terms, rather than by outright refusal to consider any possible alternatives to the traditional approach. For most serious scholars, however, some position in the middle is assumed, allowing them to accept any conclusion that textual criticism may point to, provided critical techniques are applied without preconceived theories and with full regard to the wealth of information that has become available from other fields. A major factor here is the breakthrough in archaeology, as a result of which much that was once obscure in the Bible text can now be seen to be explicable by parallels with other cultures of the Near East.

Repeatedly, in the new work, one finds these modern Jewish Bible critics working their way through to a very strong affirmation of views which sit comfortably with traditionalism, though not with fundamentalism. Their attitude is workmanlike rather than theological. On Abraham, for example, the 'legendary' aspect mentioned by the old *JE* has more or less gone. Abraham as a person may not yet have been identified, but:

> the evidence of a sociological and onomastic nature that has been accumulated since the discoveries at Nuzi, Mari, and elsewhere tends to show that the Abrahamic traditions are more likely to be authentic reflexes of a true historic situation than retrojections from a later period.

The article on the Pentateuch as a whole takes this approach much further. Opening with a fully-documented acceptance of the idea that the Pentateuch has to be seen as an amalgam of four 'sources' (J, E, P, and D), the author establishes first that the editing (and much of the content) of the first four books reflects the David-Solomon Age, and Deuteronomy the time of Hezekiah-

Josiah. He then goes on, however, to take the material further
back into history. 'The traditions that serve as the basis of the
pentateuchal literature began to be crystallized ... as early as the
period of the Judges.' Wellhausen's view that the Priestly
elements (P) are very 'late' (Second Temple) are baseless: 'the
sacral institutions ... are known to us from early biblical literature'. Indeed, the whole idea of separate 'sources' can mislead:
'in spite of differences and contradictions ... a common underlying legal and historical tradition can be observed'. Even more
surprisingly, he ends up with Moses giving Israel the Law at
Mount Sinai: 'the basic premise underlying this tradition, i.e. that
Moses was the first legislator and, as such, responsible for the basic
legislature of Israel, is undoubtedly true'.

To get back to tradition this way is, of course, not enough for
the fundamentalist. The article carries a postscript by an orthodox rabbi emphasizing that the traditionalist still believes that the
entire Pentateuch is 'a unitary document, divinely revealed, and
entirely written by Moses' (except for the last eight verses recording his death). Yet even with this demurral, one feels that the
basic Bible articles in the new encyclopaedia convey the open-
minded tone of modern study, reflecting a significant change in
Jewish consciousness since the days of the old *JE*.

The Bible, though central to Jewish feeling, is only one subject on
which one expects a new Jewish encyclopaedia to transform one's
earlier concepts. One is not let down. Turning the pages, one
is constantly struck by the originality which it introduces into so
many fields, all with wide ramifications.

If one starts with A for 'Archaeology', the guidance given on the
subject as a whole does not simply reflect its relevance for Bible
studies. The Jews, especially in Israel, are fascinated by archaeology in its broadest aspects. Its massive treatment here seems to
lift the reader out of the many sad subjects that are inevitable –
alas – in a Jewish encyclopaedia, to a level of sheer pleasure and
adventure. Perhaps in the same breath one should add A for
'Art', since the reproduction throughout the encyclopaedia of

many marvellously illuminated manuscripts of the Middle Ages reflects a wealth of discovery, and irradiates in colour what were once thought of as the Dark Ages of Jewish life.

Another subject quite transformed in grasp today, as a result of massive detailed study, is the history of individual Jewish communities throughout the world. This is a product of the intensive effort in the present century to establish a well-founded social history of the Jews and a valid theory of their economic role.

The great authority on this subject is Professor Salo Baron of Columbia University, whose multi-volumed *Social and Religious History of the Jews* has transformed previous thinking. Here, in a long article, part of 'Economic History of the Jews', Baron covers the story from ancient times to the fifteenth century, refuting, with a wealth of illustration, the hoary notion that Jews of those ages led very restricted lives.

For much of the period there is no formal material to draw on, so that the picture has to be constructed indirectly, often to amusing effect, out of odd remarks in the Talmud or the rabbinic *responsa*. We learn about tanning as a Jewish occupation in rabbinic times because the rabbis decided that a tanner's wife could use the awful smell as grounds for divorce. The great success in date-growing in Babylonia is revealed when the Palestinian Rabbi Ulla, arriving there, exclaims: 'A whole basket of dates for a *zuz*, and yet the Babylonians are lax in studying the Torah.' The role of scholars as businessmen comes out when we hear of three famous rabbis of this time amassing great wealth from the brewing of beer.

On a broader plane, Baron shows us the conditions which made the Jews into merchants, with little emerging about 'innate' qualities. Sea-ports and caravan routes are more relevant. In the early Diaspora, when conversion to Judaism was common and therefore produced Jewish communities everywhere, these places turned into trading centres through contact with Phoenicians and Carthaginians who brought with them the commercial skills for which they were famous.

A more dramatic moment came with the rise of Islam. Before this, Jews (including converts) living in Arab countries were largely peasants. We begin to understand, in Baron's exposition, how 'the new political and socio-economic revolution for the first time converted a predominantly agricultural Jewish population into a people of merchants, moneylenders, and artisans'. It was through Islam also, we learn, that Jews were first put into their fateful role as tax-farmers. The Koran was interpreted to mean that non-believers could be tolerated if they accepted a special duty to provide 'tribute'. In different circumstances the Jews in Christian Europe became 'the King's Treasure' to similar effect.

Yet if the Jews were in this way conditioned by others, they retained a vivid sense of independence, with much more freedom (e.g. in owning land) than is often thought, and able to feel that the rules of commercial life had to fit in with their own law (as interpreted by scholars) and their own social rules. To a very great extent – it seems a surprising conclusion – they were free and inner-directed as a people even if, as individuals, they might feel driven by the pressures of the external world.

Some of the same ideas emerge in the study which follows, by a different scholar, of Jewish economic history from the sixteenth century to our own day. Going beyond the familiar exposition of Jewish migrations and international contacts as a key to their role during the emergence of industrialism and capitalism, the author takes us into the socio-economic structure of Jewish communities everywhere, giving full play to class motivations and tensions, though without the dogmatic Marxism of Raphael Mahler's *History of Modern Jewry*.

These are merely two articles of many which bring together the pioneer work of scholars on the variety and independence of community life as a new approach to understanding Jewish history. An article on 'Autonomy', for example, is full of surprises. To take a single illustration, one thinks normally of the Jews in Spain as participating fully in public life until the fateful decision in 1492 that they were to be expelled. We learn here, however, that they were always a very separate community: 'self-rule achieved heights rivalled only in the Muslim lands and by the Councils of the Lands of Poland-Lithuania'. A separate article on

'Judicial Autonomy' shows what wide powers Jewish authorities throughout mediaeval Europe had – even, in some circumstances, covering capital punishment (mainly for 'informers'). One begins to understand the tremendous internal political and social struggles that would be generated in this special kind of existence, but one feels, also, how it explains the cohesion of the Jews and their powers of survival.   There was social strength in this background, which gives substance to Ahad Ha'am's remark that it was a period in which the Jews had 'freedom within slavery', in contrast with Jewish life after emancipation – 'slavery within freedom'.

Is this just a neat epigram, or does it bring out a real change, during the last seventy years, in our concept of the past?   It is certainly an idea that one wants to pursue.   Were mediaeval Jews 'free' in a sense one had not envisaged?   I have found a way of considering this through a masterly article in the encyclopaedia by a writer I have already mentioned in this book, Professor Hillel Ben-Sasson of the Hebrew University of Jerusalem.   The clue he offers is to put the emphasis on individual Jews and the enthusiasm they brought to their daily existence.

In the story told by most historians, the Diaspora is dominated by Jewish homelessness and suffering.   This is the 'lachrymose' approach, which Ben-Sasson finds unacceptable in that it leaves out the dynamic which kept the Jews going.   What matters for him – as for Salo Baron – is the personal quality of life in the vast variety of backgrounds in which the Jews lived.   If Jewish literature emerging from the Middle Ages concentrated on lament, leaving a tale of sorrow, the scholars of today evoke a very different picture from a study of community archives and private letters long ignored.   Jews certainly suffered in the Middle Ages, but this was the lot of most of the multitude, with the Jews no worse off *on the whole* than anyone else.   Salo Baron has, indeed, put it even more strongly in his *History*.   'It is quite likely,' he says, 'that the average mediaeval Jew, compared with his average Christian contemporary ... was the less unhappy and destitute

creature ... not only in his own consciousness but even if meas-
ured by such objective criteria as standards of living, cultural
amenities, and protection against individual starvation and dis-
ease.'[2]

It is this attitude which becomes manifest when one reads Ben-
Sasson's encyclopaedia article. The tragedies are there, but
Jewish history is presented as a story of individuals, confronted as
all human beings are with the insoluble problems of attaching a
meaning to man's existence, but coming to terms with life (when
life was possible) through family and local affections, the drive to
keep going, intellectual and social diversions, and above all the
pleasures and frustrations of 'the search' – the struggles with conflicting loyalties, the responses to new movements and ways of
thought, the feeling of being involved in something beyond
oneself.

There is a sense of dignity and freedom about this which one
has to set against the unspeakable horror which surfaced later, at a
stage in history in which the Jews were supposed to have been
freed from the slavery of the Middle Ages. But here, too, Ben-
Sasson evokes a sense of courage which helps one through the
grim story. 'The executioners,' he writes, 'were dehumanized
beyond recovery. The victims were intended to reach this state:
but Jewish vitality and spirit, and the demonstration of Jewish
brotherhood, quickly brought back most of the survivors to
personal integration and proud human stature.'

Personal integration. It is a phrase that one tries to cling to as one
hears on almost every page of the encyclopaedia some echo –
implicit or resounding – of the Holocaust. Threaded through the
story are photographs, almost all taken, obviously, by the Nazis
themselves. Any single one of them would be enough. The
text, one might say, is redundant. But there is an unending problem for the Jews themselves, not only in how to live with the
memory, but how to think of the way in which those who were
caught up with the tragedy bore themselves. We have lived
through a period of thirty years in which the documents have
built up. Nothing has diminished the general horror, but we are
gradually accepting that among the millions who were trapped,

the moral problem for those who had to 'cooperate' are probably
forever beyond our judgment. In the main article in the encyclopaedia on the Holocaust, Jacob Robinson tries to 'explain', to
show the rationale, to instil some charity in us where we want,
somehow, to turn away in grief. He cannot entirely succeed
because it is a problem which is ultimately beyond any categories
of assessment in normal civilized terms. In our minds, we have a
postscript – the rescue of survivors, a new life in many lands, and
above all the creation of Israel. If any final evaluation were
possible, it would have to take all this in.

The truth is, of course, that no final evaluation *is* possible. The
virtue of an encyclopaedia is that it allows one to escape from
confronting the big unresolvable issues all the time. One turns
with relief to those many byways of interest that never appear in
the broad judgments that most publicists go in for.

Perhaps it is more correct to say that we all form for ourselves
some broad verities that we live by, but are always ready to be
surprised – and delighted – by the detail behind them that we have
never been aware of. This is undoubtedly true of Israel itself.
Here, as one turns the pages, the magnitude of its achievement is
expressed in a richness of detail that gives it a fresh colouring.
We have a good picture in our minds of leaders like Weizmann or
Ben-Gurion: but the texture of Israel comes to life with a different
kind of appeal through meeting here an endless array of people –
many virtually unknown – who have played their part. Nor
is the Israel story mainly a question of Israelis. The articles and
pictures take one back, without a break, to an understanding
of Zionism and the multi-faceted movements out of which the
national revival took shape.

The same is true of the broad issues of Diaspora history, some
of which I have been discussing in this book. If one wants to
relax from generalization to let Jewish life speak to us selectively
for the understanding that this can bring, one seems to learn more
by turning the pages of this encyclopaedia at random than by all
the learned definitions, for never was alphabetical serendipity

richer. One goes on one page from the movie star Kirk Douglas (born Issur Danilovich) to the great Hasidic leader Dov Baer, the Maggid of Mezhirech (d. 1772). One learns next of Dra, a region in South Morocco which is said to have been an independent Jewish state in ancient days, and where Jews farmed land with the help of the descendants of black slaves until modern times. A little lower down, the American labour leader David Dubinsky is followed by the great historian Simon Dubnow, murdered by the Nazis in 1941 – in this case a coming together of two men motivated by a common humanism despite the huge difference in their lives.

Sometimes there is a parade of history in a single family name, with the passions of the time coming to life in astonishing form. Mordecai Meisel, who lived in Prague in the sixteenth century, financed the wars of the Emperor Rudolph II, and was the first Jewish capitalist of Europe. He spent a fortune redeeming Jewish captives from pirates, but in the end, in a quarrel over his wealth, his entire family was excommunicated. From the eighteenth century we met Moses Meisel a rabbi who managed miraculously to keep friendly with both sides in the classic struggle between the Vilna Gaon and the Hasidic leader Sheour Zalman of Lyady, but came to a sticky end after being accused during the Napoleonic invasion of secret contracts with the Russians. In the nineteenth century there is Dov Meisels of Cracow – rabbi, banker (through a rich father-in-law), and ardent Polish patriot, urging his congregants to fight against Austria in successive revolutions, and supplying arms to the rebels. The Jews as Polish patriots! One has to keep remembering how deep these national attachments have been. As if to symbolize the irony, we are led through the same name into the final moment of this story. Maurici Maisel was the last President of the Warsaw Jewish community. When the Nazis invaded in 1939, he fled. For those who remained, one of the saddest and most heroic pages of Jewish history was about to be written – the doomed uprising of the Warsaw ghetto.

One question that I have not been able to answer, despite my constant dipping into the encyclopaedia, is the root question of all: who is a Jew? Anyone producing a Jewish encyclopaedia has to confront this, to decide who is to be included. Jewish history is full of Jews who at some stage opted out – privately or publicly, timidly or brazenly. The editors took a simple decision: include everybody.

The question is very relevant when one tries to compile lists – as the encyclopaedia does – of Jewish achievement in every field of human endeavour. By putting everybody in, whether or not they continued to think of themselves as Jews, one can presumably be led to some conclusions about the relation of 'innate' Jewish talent to fields in which, on the face of it, the achievement of Jews seems spectacular.

What about medicine, for example? The very long article on medicine traces Jewish achievement back to Talmud times and all through the Middle Ages. Is it brains (not very convincing), social ambition, or some lofty Jewish desire to help the suffering? Certainly medicine has been the field of a high proportion of Jewish Nobel laureates. But then, oddly enough, so has high-energy particle physics. Is one supposed to ascribe this to a powerful Jewish urge to search for the Ultimate? It may be gratifying to be lofty in this way, but looking at one long list after another (Jews in architecture, art, chemistry, music, sport, the theatre, and so on), one recalls that there have been quite a lot of Jews around in modern times, especially in the dynamic atmosphere of urban centres, and they had to do *something*.

Perhaps we should be grateful – or complain? – that while the editors thought it right, as it no doubt is, to include a list of Jews in criminology, they do not give us a list of Jews in crime. It is true that we are provided with individual entries for distinguished gangsters like Bugsy Siegel and Lepke Buchalter, but in general such discussion as there is of the incidence of crime among Jews is conducted anonymously. To be fair, the encyclopaedia is not entirely mealy-mouthed on this subject. It acknowledges, for example, the lamentable Jewish role, some years ago, in the white-slave traffic in Argentina (with links to Eastern Europe), showing also the strenuous and successful efforts of Jewish welfare organizations to remove this blot. And it also reports, in predictable fashion, that the variety of crimes in Israel has become as wide there as anywhere. In other words, the Jews are now normal.

Jews in chess provide a good list, though it may surprise some to learn that the Jewish contribution to chess on an appreciable scale dates only from the middle of the nineteenth century. However, there is one great field which, according to the encyclopaedia, can be definitely and almost absolutely identified with the Jewish genius – the movies. Here are all the alleged Jewish characteristics working at full blast – enterprise, imagination, financial acumen, artistry, vulgarity. The list of Jews in the motion-picture industry rolls on for pages, offering pleasant surprises (to one reader at least) in being able now to welcome to the fold Leslie Howard, Erich von Stroheim, Peter Lorre, Tony Curtis, and Anouk Aimée. We may smile at Hollywood, but it is at least more satisfying as an episode in Jewish history than, say, the Jewish contribution to public relations, where the encyclopaedia invites us to take in the memorable fact that it was a Jew, Edward Gottlieb, who coined the slogan: 'Which twin has the Toni?'

Am I any closer, having lived for years now with this immense work, to deciding what Jewish experience adds up to? I certainly have a clearer idea about the amazing changes in Jewish life in the present century, but seventy or eighty years cover, after all, only a small part of the story.

For the meaning of the story as a whole, I rest content with the richness that reaches one almost in haphazard fashion as one turns the pages. E. M. Forster must have had the Jews in mind with his 'only connect'. Unless one's bones are as marrowless, one's blood as cold, as Banquo's ghost, it is virtually impossible to check a fact in a work of this kind without being led on through a name, a quotation, a sense of surprise or a feeling of identification into endless further and inter-connected exploration. This is, in fact, how the rabbis studied the Torah, letting one subject or one anecdote lead to another, not with any expectation that a final pattern would emerge but for the fulfilment offered by the search. The sign of death is to be left, ghostlike, 'with no speculation in those eyes'. One has to go on asking questions. As for the answer, one will never know precisely where one fits in. It is enough to belong.

JESUS

I THINK it will be obvious why I cannot try to add up Jewish experience without bringing in Jesus.

The Jews have always been immensely suspicious of Christianity, both as a religion and for the effects on them of Christian societies: but their feelings about Jesus have been more ambivalent. If much that was tragic for them was done – to some extent – in his name, he himself was not always held responsible. Even to those kept away from the New Testament by a massive wall of fear and ignorance, there was a sense that Jesus was a Jewish teacher who had somehow taken the wrong path.

In more recent centuries, as Jews began to grow up more freely in Christian societies, the Jesus story came into their consciousness in more positive forms. The absorption in a common culture brought endless echoes of the picture presented in the Gospels – the appeal of his sayings, the nobility of his character, the poignancy of his death. It was never easy to respond wholeheartedly: the Jews were labelled, after all, as the villains of the piece, and had to fight hard to deny their own – irrational – sense of guilt. They needed a split mind to be able to accept on its own terms the overpoweringly Christian elements in the European tradition of art and music while at the same time accentuating the *Jewish* aspects of their relationship to the Founder.

For some, it was enough to accept the centrality of Christianity to European culture – as with Bernard Berenson expounding the Renaissance paintings of the Virgin, or Leonard Bernstein throwing himself with devout fervour into a performance of the St. Matthew Passion. More characteristically, many Jews have responded to Jesus in a manner that reflects their own Jewish feelings. To Chagall, Jesus could be painted as a rabbi of Vitebsk, surrounded by the familiar floating figures of that legendary town. Alfred Kazin, in *A Walker in the City*, recorded an even stronger ecstasy of personal vision when, as a young boy, a copy of the Gospels was thrust into his hands:

For now we see through a glass, darkly. I tasted the rightness of each
word on my tongue . . . *Blessed is he, whosoever shall not be offended
in me.* Offended in him? I had known him instantly. Surely I
had been waiting for him all my life – our own Yeshua, misunder-
stood by his own, like me, but the very embodiment of everything
I had waited so long to hear from a Jew – a great contempt for the
minute daily business of the world; a deep and joyful turning back
into our own spirit . . .

The ambivalence can never be fully resolved. Even for
Christians, the approach to Jesus is compounded by childhood
memory, folk-history, poetry, and many other indefinable
influences. No one can detach himself from his own involvement with history to deal factually with a subject which carries
with it such clouds of mystery. Christian scholars have long
shown, for example, that the Gospel material which furnishes the
broad picture of Jesus was composed after his time, and is so full
of gaps and contradictions that it cannot in itself provide any
reliable historical picture of him at all. But most of these same
scholars, attracted to the subject by their prior faith in Christianity,
feel able to determine by instinct and training what comes authentically from Jesus himself as distinct from what was grafted on
much later by writers drawing equally from the myths and
mysteries of the Greek and Near Eastern World.

Jesus is, then, both the most misrepresented and the best known
of men. The religion which grew out of his life and death
centres on doctrines – death to expiate the sins of mankind,
resurrection, the Second Coming – which depend, for Christian
scholars, not on facts but faith. Yet applying this faith, as it were,
in retrospect, the Gospel sayings, fragmentary as they are, acquire
a complete validity of their own, yielding a figure who can be
known intimately, and whose vision and sense of destiny, as
spelled out in the Gospels, have been felt by untold millions to
be completely consonant with the Christological doctrines
emerging later.

Jews can easily sympathize with a circular view of this kind
since it echoes the attitude to their own history of those who are
unable to accept a fundamentalist approach to their origins yet see

a mystery in their faith which, as it were, makes it all come true. On Jesus, the clearest expression of this attitude emerges in a book called *The Founder of Christianity* published by an eminent Christian scholar, C. H. Dodd in 1971, four years before his death.[1] Professor Dodd fully accepted the unreliability of the Gospels as documentary history in the ordinary sense. Yet he felt that they allowed him to tell the life-story of the Founder quite convincingly, for two main reasons. First, the Evangelists, remote though they were from the events, were drawing on what might be described as social memory: 'the church *remembers* that on a certain night its Founder said and did certain definite things, briefly reported'. Second, details 'remembered' this way, but hard to understand, often 'came true' in a later context. A good example would be the miracle of the loaves and fishes. Dodd was fully prepared to admit that 'none of the attempts to make the story intelligible or credible ... carry conviction', but he asked one to note that it was presented 'as a mystery'. It was a mystery that was to become clear later when John related this bread to the bread which Jesus gave to his disciples at the Last Supper, with the words: 'This is my body.' By moving backwards and forwards, Dodd implied, one united both Jesus and Christ.

Jews understand the Christian dilemma, but themselves face a much more direct problem – how to evaluate the alleged factual elements in the Gospel story in which the Jewish establishment of the day, and the Jews forever, are guilty of everything. In this view, the rabbis of the time – the Pharisees – must have hated Jesus because he exposed them as nothing but narrow hypocrites. The Temple leaders went out of their way to condemn Jesus in their Sanhedrin and hand him over to the Romans for execution. At this point, not just the establishment but all the Jews turned against Jesus, baying for his death. Without any doubt, this presentation has been the root cause of Jew-hatred throughout the Christian era. A Jew of today, inheriting the burden, feels that the original story must have gone wrong somewhere. History can't be reversed, but at least it should be understood. What can the scholars tell us now about the facts?

The key seems to lie, first, in understanding the Pharisees. I

mentioned earlier (pp. 67–8) how fiercely Jewish scholars have
attempted to rebut the vilification of the Pharisees as presented in
the Gospels. This approach has been increasingly accepted by
many Christian scholars, following particularly R. Travers
Herford and George Foot Moore. It is fair to say that the general
view today is that far from being hypocrites and ethically bankrupt in their blind adherence to the 'the Law', the Pharisees were a
closely-knit brotherhood of high moral standards, preoccupied
with the study of a long-established oral tradition of how the
Torah was to be interpreted in daily social life, and intensely
observant of this tradition as a means of expressing the holiness
that it enshrined. It is true that this view has to be based on
rabbinic teachings written down some centuries later; but the
richness and inner consistency of the tradition handed down seems
to support the view that it went back authentically to the teachings among Jews at the time of Jesus.

If, then, the Pharisees have to be seen as a moral brotherhood,
there was no rift but an affinity between them and Jesus. It is
easy to elaborate this view. As noted earlier, much of what Jesus
is recorded as saying – especially in the Synoptic Gospels – can be
paralleled by authentic Jewish teaching as evidenced both in the
literature of the proceeding century and in the later rabbinic
writings. The style of his teaching echoes the Jewish 'Midrash'.
Even the Gospels show his respect for 'the Law', which he 'came
to fulfill', despite his familiar image as a trenchant critic of scribes
and Pharisees. Is he then to be brought back into the mainstream
of Jewish history as a typical ethical teacher, with the supernatural
elements of the Gospels – miracles, expiation and resurrection –
played down as unauthentic, or was there something in his teachings and actions which took him out of the normative Jewish
religious tradition, and thus foreshadowed the unbridgeable gap
in outlook which developed later between Christianity and
Judaism?

An early protagonist of the latter view was Joseph Klausner,
who argued in his *Jesus of Nazareth* (written originally in Hebrew
in 1922)[2] that while every single word of the sayings of Jesus can
be paralleled in Jewish writings, there was ultimately something

'un-Jewish' – and fallacious – in concentrating so heavily on ethics itself, in contrast, say, to his contemporary, Hillel, a rabbi who was preoccupied with interpreting the practicalities of the Law in ways calculated to help the good society to improve itself. It made better ethical sense, as it were, to be kind to strangers, as ordered by the Torah, than to proclaim an unreal abstract doctrine of loving your enemy.

What made Jesus unacceptable (in Klausner's view) was the conviction which came into his mind after his baptism that the Kingdom of Heaven was at hand, due to replace the existing system through a miraculous change to a divinely-ruled brother-hood of men in which all moral and social problems would *ipso facto* disappear. A faith which is 'not of this world' runs counter to Judaism which 'is definitely *of this world*', calling for moral regeneration in the familiar circumstances of daily life. If – though it has never been proved – the Pharisees objected to Jesus' teaching, there was good cause, according to Klausner. He was taking Judaism along the wrong road, as the later development of Christianity was to show.

It is worth recalling this highly simplified attitude to illustrate the enormous change that has come over Jewish thinking about Jesus in the years since then. If there is one prevalent view now, it is that Jesus was an authentic Jew in every sense of the word, completely true to the background into which he was born. This is not to say that the scholars now agree on how this helps to paint the life-story, for the background itself is shown to contain factors not allowed for earlier, and which the scholars interpret with differing emphasis.

Some put great weight on the political struggle to overthrow Roman overlordship. Others are concerned with the increasing recognition that Jewish life was permeated by many of the mystical and apocalyptic ideas which Klausner was trying to play down as 'un-Jewish'. The sources available for Jesus as an historical figure are still the late and fragmentary accounts in the Gospels of his acts and sayings. They can still only be moulded

together speculatively and with imagination. But as the background itself is now richer, Jesus emerges more solidly as a figure
of his time, even if, in some accounts, his link to contemporary
events is interpreted differently.

Perhaps the most startling of the new projections is the emphasis
now given to Jesus in some books as a conscious and active
political rebel, confirming the view that it was the Romans of the
time, and not the Jews, who had to counter his influence and
therefore executed him in the interest of law and order. This
approach attracted much attention through a book by a Christian
scholar, Professor S. G. F. Brandon of the University of Manchester – *The Fall of Jerusalem and the Christian Church* (1951).[3]
That the condemnation of Jesus was by the Romans, who saw him
as an active rebel leader, was brought out with equal cogency,
though with somewhat different emphasis, in a work published in
1961 by a Jewish scholar, Paul Winter – *On The Trial of Jesus*[4] – in
which the quarrels with the Pharisees alleged in the Gospels were
examined in great detail and shown to be unhistorical.

There is no difficulty in understanding how the Gospel writers
came to present Jesus as a victim of hatred by his fellow-Jews. In
the forefront of their mind was the projection of a mystery –
the death and resurrection of a man who was God. Faith was to
turn on this, and on its corollary – the Second Coming. The idea
that God came to earth to save mankind transcended everything.
It was a concept of shattering magnitude to which everything in
the story had to be tailored.

In describing the lead-up to the Cross, the Gospel writers had
memories and legends to draw on, often used factually and with
great effect. It was in the historical *focus* that they failed. There
was an overriding need to absolve the Romans from responsibility
for the death of Jesus, since their favour had to be won. A strong
Jewish hostility was therefore imputed. The Gospel writers had
no direct understanding of Pharisee teaching, and could therefore
retail sayings of Jesus without realizing how Pharisaic they were.
The scholars today can explain all this, but the damage has been
done. In the popular mind, Jesus and his fellow-Jews are still
thought of as having been deadly enemies.

The Jewish writers who feel that this is the heart of the problem are by no means at one in considering how to demonstrate its falsity. One recent book *Revolution in Judaea: Jesus and the Jewish Resistance* (1973)[5] set out to show not only that Jesus was in tune with Jewish feeling, but that he became, as an active political leader, 'the sole hope of a great number, perhaps the majority, of the Jewish people'. The author, Hyam Maccoby, believes that when Jesus spoke of 'the kingdom of God' being at hand, this was 'not a spiritual kingdom situated in the remote heavens or at a remote point in time, but an earthly kingdom situated in Palestine in the immediate future'. Seized by this vision, Jesus actually had himself crowned as the 'prophet-king' and then began 'a royal progress towards his capital Jerusalem'. The object was 'the ejection of the Roman forces', not by an army – which he didn't possess – but through a miracle. Naturally enough, he was arrested by the Romans as a rebel and executed.

There is a very different approach in a work by an Oxford scholar, Geza Vermes, called *Jesus the Jew* (1973).[6] Dr. Vemes starts from the same basic position that Jesus has to be understood through his Jewish background, but achieves this through a meticulous re-examination of the phraseology – however vague – of the Gospels. His method is to study key words and phrases in order to see how they can be properly interpreted in the light of what is now known about Judaism in Jesus' time.

The ultimate aim of Dr. Vermes' study of Jesus is to see where his exceptional religious influence came from. The one thing we can be sure of is that Jesus was a man of strong personal independence. Another side to his character that emerges with great clarity is his gift for healing the sick and deranged. On both, there is a clue in his link with Galilee. It was an area that maintained a strong tradition of independence, suspicious of both the Jewish and the Roman authorities in Jerusalem. Basically,

> once the Gospel report concerning his person and work is analyzed, the secondary traits removed, and the essential features inserted into the context of contemporary political and religious history, Jesus of Nazareth takes on the eminently credible personality of a Galilean Hasid (pious teacher) . . .

As exorcist and healer, he was similar to others. As a preacher, it is true that he preferred audiences of the poor and uneducated, and 'spoke with authority' rather than by deriving everything from rabbinical ordinance. But if he was more relaxed about the Law than the Pharisees, 'there is no evidence of an active and organized participation on the part of the Pharisees in the planning and achievement of his downfall'.

To what extent did Jesus regard himself as having a superhuman role? Certainly he thought of himself as a 'prophet', but this was a term that had no precise definition. It could cover both a teacher with insight, and a precursor of the Messiah. The title 'Lord', by which he was addressed, had no divine significance. The persistent use of the phrase 'Son of Man', thought by some to lead back to the oldest Christological traditions, is shown by Vermes to have had no relation in Jesus' time 'to an eschatological or Messianic office-holder'. As for being the Messiah, Vermes remarks:

> Strange though it may seem, Jesus' own teaching on the subject of the Messiah, even if the obviously inauthentic passages are included, amounts to very little.

After a long analysis of all the various meanings attached to the concept of the Messiah at that time, we are reminded that 'Jesus never asserted directly or spontaneously that he was the Messiah'.

Was he tried by the Sanhedrin for blasphemy? The evidence is against it. Was he then a political rebel? The idea of Jesus as a Zealot 'fails to convince'. But Galilee is where rebels came from. 'Zealot or not, Jesus was certainly charged, prosecuted and sentenced as one', and probably because he was a Galilean.

After all the arguments, one begins to feel drawn back to a contemplation of Jesus as a mystery, not in the sense of having been divine, but for the unending power on man that his story has generated. The moral sayings in the Gospels have, in this sense, always been valid. One wants, somehow, to purge them of the hateful anti-Pharisee envelope in which they were presented, and be left with a myth that has become the common property of mankind.

An odd little book, *Jesus*, published in 1969 by David Flusser, Professor of Comparative Religion at the Hebrew University of Jerusalem,[7] came close to achieving this, largely, perhaps, because it offered a series of epigrammatic and rather scattered reflections instead of a solid analysis in the manner of most scholarly books. This seems to be – for I have never met him – a reflection of Flusser's personal appeal, as described by Edmund Wilson in his book on the Dead Sea Scrolls. To Wilson he was the world's most engaging conversationalist, with a mind that could lead him 'to make connections and draw conclusions that nobody else has or would have thought of'.

It is a well-known fact that brilliant conversationalists seldom produce large systematic works. But they are enlivening. In this case, Flusser's approach, wandering here and there to cover highly selective aspects of the story – Love, Law, the Son of Man, etc. – enables us to explore with him many issues that will always lie in the mind on Jesus.

How was it, for example, that the form which Christianity took was so inimical to the Jewish conception of 'the Law'. It was all due, in Flusser's view, to the accident that the new faith spread *westward*, into Europe:

> Had Christianity spread first to the eastern Asiatic religions, it would have had to develop a ritual and ceremonial law based on the Jewish law in order to become a genuine religion.

It was all due to Paul, then, who felt that it was the will of God to spread Christianity to the Graeco-Roman world where 'liberalism' (i.e. absence of rituals on food, etc.) was the norm. Jesus himself had no basic quarrel with the attitude of the Pharisees towards the Law, though he stressed, as they did, the importance of a moral interpretation of the ritual. His saying on purity ('not what goes into the mouth defiles a man, but what cometh out') is not a revolutionary remark but 'a piece of popular moral wisdom'. As for the famous criticism by Jesus of the fanatical observance by Pharisees of the Sabbath, Flusser recalls a parallel remark in one of the rabbinic books: 'The Sabbath has been handed over to you, not you to the Sabbath.'[8]

Much of this is familiar; and where Flusser really helps is in considering how it was that Jesus, while drawing only on contemporary teaching, managed somehow to give it a new kind of emphasis. On the relevance of the Dead Sea Scrolls, for example, he links sentences from the writings of the Qumran sect to the apocalyptic *Testaments of the Twelve Patriarchs*, in order to show that in the two centuries before Jesus Jewish religious thought had already moved beyond the strict 'right and wrong' of the Bible towards a subtler view which allowed for the 'good and evil struggle within the heart of every man'. The Golden Rule (of Hillel as well as Jesus) was in that period coming to mean that you had to love your neighbour as yourself 'because he is like yourself'. More deeply still, love of God – 'the first great commandment of Jesus' – was 'in harmony with the spirit of contemporary Pharisaism'. The concentration of Jesus on love was therefore not new, though it was immensely significant as part of his 'total preaching':

> From ancient Jewish writings we could easily construct a whole gospel without using a single word that originated with Jesus. This could only be done, however, because we do in fact possess the Gospels.

This is a pregnant remark. It leads Flusser on to what he considers the 'really revolutionary' view of Jesus, the 'unconditional love' which can embrace sinners and even one's enemies. In this, according to Flusser, he was rejecting some doctrines of the Essenes – notably their separation from the world and their mixed attitude of hate and love – but accepting ideas from *The Testaments of the Twelve Patriarchs* which, while not Essene, 'belong to the fringe of the Essene cult'. It was ultimately an 'Essene discovery' that evil can be overcome with good:

> It is only human nature to love the one to whom one does good. . . . Those groups who lived on the fringe of Essenism outgrew the

Essene theology of hate, and hence affirmed these very consequences of doing good to one's enemy.

It was from this same 'fringe' that Jesus took over two key ideas – that evil must not be resisted by physical means, and that the 'good news' has to be addressed particularly to the poor and out-cast. If one asks for some evidence on what was 'within the fringe' and 'beyond the fringe' at that time, Flusser's answer might be that one has to start with an imaginative concept of what underlay Jesus' unique influence, and pick phrases here and there from the sectarian writings that fit this picture. One gets nowhere by adopting a mechanistic attitude: the impact of Jesus does not lie on the surface but is bound up with paradox. Indeed, he says something like this in discussing how Jesus could produce 'the transvaluation of all values':

> We might say that Jesus' concept of the righteousness of God is incommensurable to reason: man cannot measure it, but can grasp and understand it. It leads also from the Sermon on the Mount to Golgotha, where the just man is to die the death of a criminal. It is at once profoundly moral and yet beyond good and evil.

I wonder, sometimes, how to take remarks like this. Almost every book on Jesus falls into purple prose at some point, giving way to the seductive joys of oblique suggestion or outright paradox. For half the time, with Flusser, we are asked to weigh things up through the concrete discoveries of modern scholarship, but in the same breath we are told to surrender to a mystery in order to understand what Jesus was saying.

At one point, for example, he asks whether 'the man Jesus' may have thought, at his trial, that like other prophets he would be granted some kind of immortality. Clearly the phrase 'the man Jesus' in the middle of a scholarly discussion, is a way of suggesting that there hovers in the air the idea that Jesus was also *more* than a man. The same double approach lies in his claim that there is a special reason why Jesus is particularly important to current times:

Today we are receptive to Jesus' reappraisal of all our usual values, and many of us have become aware of the questioning of the moral norm, which is his starting point too.   Like Jesus, we feel drawn to the social pariahs, to the sinners.   When he says that we must not resist evil because, even by our denial, we only encourage the intrinsically indifferent play of forces within society and the world at large, we men of today can at least understand.

Does Flusser mean – as he seems to – that the wheel has some-how come full circle with our discovery (through scholarship) of the historic Jesus coinciding – through the workings of Provi-dence? – with the same kind of doom-laden age, to give validity at last to his sayings?   It is a lively idea, but needs faith to make it ring true.   The time-worn (unscholarly) picture of Jesus has surely been just as powerful in other ages.   Where did 'uncondi-tional love' receive purer expression than in the selfless devotion of many missionary Christians to the poor and sick in a very un-apocalyptic age – the nineteenth century?

One is left to make up one's own mind, accepting scholarship, accepting the mystery, and fitting it all in, somehow, with the richness of experience – both creative and desolate – that has come in the wake of Jesus to Jew and Christian alike. Flusser, at least, makes no bones about asserting views for which the only authority is his own instinctive feeling, counting on the art of the spoken word.   How can one resist the conversationalist who says so blandly to Edmund Wilson: '*Les chrétiens sont derangés: les juifs sont derangés aussi: moi, je ne suis pas derangé.*'

HOW FAITHFUL?

I CAN imagine a reader feeling that I have talked a lot about Jewish experience without dealing, as yet, with what is surely the central issue – the relation of a Jew to his ancestral religion. I plead guilty and will now make amends. But if I have hesitated so far to offer some explicit ideas about this, I am following an old tradition. Throughout history, we Jews have addressed ourselves to God morning, noon and night but have never been too keen to define the faith in theological terms.

This attitude survives and is not as odd as it may seem. It is certainly not a sign of a lack of strong feeling about what our faith is telling us. It would be more accurate to say – leaning on paradox – that the ideas that reach us through our faith are too important to define. There is an analogy in one's response to a poem. To summarize its meaning objectively is to miss its real power. The meaning only takes shape as the poem is read. The ideas that are created in that act are linked to words, associations and feelings that move the reader in ways that transcend a simple analysis of what the poet is saying. The meaning is never static or finite. Even when the words themselves have become routine, one is poised, hearing them, for fresh understanding.

Something like this lies behind the reluctance of Jewish thinkers over the centuries to agree on the dogmas that their religion expressed. The routine of prayer and practise may be objective, conveying thoughts and principles of conduct that seem, at first, reducible to definition. If, despite this, they fought shy of credos, it was because being a Jew carried with it a cloud of history and feeling that went beyond the would-be precision of theology. No one wanted to draw a hard line, in accepting God's power, between 'fact' and myth. When definitions were attempted, it simply led to controversy.

The work of the outstanding Jewish philosopher Maimonides is a good illustration of this. Maimonides, born in Spain in 1135, symbolized Jewish experience very aptly in that he drew deeply as a young man on the stimulating Moslem culture of Spain yet had to spend most of his life in Egypt as a refugee from Spanish-Moslem fanaticism.   It was not the first or last time that a Jew, responding deeply to a host culture, was rejected and fled, carrying the culture with him.   One thinks of Germany.

Within Jewish life, Maimonides set out on a programme of supreme all-embracing definition.   He had absorbed everything of the Bible, the Talmud and subsequent literature: and his training as a philosopher incited him to impose a coherence on a background teeming with law, legend, instruction and argument. His aim was to identify basic principles in clear terms for the guidance of the man-in-the-street, without in any way impeding sophisticated study by the scholarly élite at a higher level.   At the heart of his project was the desire to justify everything in the tradition in words that would not offend reason.   Where there was conflict, he offered a 'sensible' compromise, separating the essential from the extraneous.   Where tradition was stated in anthropomorphic terms – as on Revelation or Prophecy – he asked for it to be understood philosophically, or as metaphor. The strength of his mind and personality was so dominant that he became a legend to his time and to subsequent ages.   Yet there was no universal acceptance of what he was doing.   To rival scholars, his gigantic and masterly consolidation of rabbinic law was often looked upon as dogmatic.   By what authority did he allot priority to this law or practise, and less to some other?   Even more so, there was doubt about the way he framed the principles of Jewish belief.

He had identified 'Thirteen Principles',[1] covering everything in the tradition – belief in God's unity and incorporeality, Revelation through Moses, God's knowledge of the acts of men, reward and punishment, the coming of a Messiah, belief in resurrection. Expressed in very simple terms, these ideas were seen by every Jew as basic to a tradition he was at home in; yet even here there was conflict if one tried to spell out what each principle really meant. In what terms could one accept that every word of the Pentateuch was literally written down by Moses at God's dictation?   Did *t'hiyyat hametim* (the reviving of the dead) mean the immortality of the soul – which is a poetic idea – or the physical resurrection of the body, which is how many Jews conceived it? Maimonides preferred not to be pressed with refinements of this kind when offering guidance to the man-in-the-street.

It was as if the 'principles' were there as signposts to an historic faith rather than truths to be accepted by every Jew in exactly the same sense: and this, indeed, is how Judaism continues to convey its meaning. In every synagogue – orthodox or reform – the congregants sing a hymn, known by its first word *Yigdal*, which is a charming expression in verse of Maimonides' Thirteen Principles. Only the most pedantic would raise their eyebrows at this or that phrase in it. One is celebrating, as one sings, a living tradition which bears a thousand interpretations. The most pronounced secularists can join in happily. To sing of Moses and the Torah and the Messiah is to sing about Jewish history. Listening to the song evokes memories of childhood. Travelling in far-off places, one hears the same words everywhere as an echo of Jewish unity.

This is not to say that being a Jew is simply a matter of sentiment. It is, rather, an experience one is born into. Religion hovers in the air, immensely serious for some, less serious for others, but never defining a Jew through adherence to a clear set of beliefs. Judaism opens the mind of a Jew to areas of existence that lie beyond the daily practicalities, but dogma is not its characteristic. Faith expresses itself in the shared experience of an unbroken tradition. If there *is* a credo, it centres on history, to establish that what a Jew is really listening to is the voice of the ages.

There is, in fact, a credo of this kind that was recited originally when a Jew brought the first-fruits of his land to the Temple in Bible times, and is now read annually at the Seder ceremony of Passover. The key words are in the form of an affirmation, summarizing what was then thought of as lying at the heart of the Jewish historic experience. In six brief verses (*Deut.* 26: 5–10), the pilgrim recalls that his ancestors were rescued from Egyptian slavery by 'the God of our Fathers' who gave them a rich land ('flowing with milk and honey') from which these first-fruits are given to Him in gratitude.   In later centuries, the Temple setting was transformed into a folk recital of the words – in synagogue readings or at the Seder – in endlessly varied circumstances: but God's act in history – the Exodus and its sequence – remained central and unchanged as the pivot of Jewish experience.

If one is looking for a more theological-sounding credo, dealing with the actual nature of God and his relation to the Jews, the rest of the same chapter of *Deuteronomy* gets closest to it.   The pilgrim, making his offering to the Temple, affirms that he has helped the stranger, the fatherless and the widow *in accordance with God's commandments*.   The priest, welcoming this declaration (and the gift of the first-fruits!), expresses the benediction that the pilgrim's obedience ensures.   Because he has avouched the Lord to be his God, walking in His ways, keeping His commandments and hearkening to His voice,

> the Lord hath avouched thee this day to be his very own people . . . and to make thee high above all nations that He hath made . . . that thou mayest be an holy people unto the Lord thy God.

Here we move from the specific events of the Exodus to a relationship with God that is put forward as governing all time. The phrases used here have been a recognizable framework of Jewish experience ever since, with an additional fillip in English from the old words of the Authorized Version which, in this verse, saw God identifying the Jews as His 'peculiar' people, instead of, as we now translate, His 'very own'.   Certainly the idea of 'the chosen people' is a phrase that the Jews have lived with. Even the Jews who resist its literal meaning can see it as symbolic. They are well aware that their experience has been distinctive – in pride and horror, in hate and love.   Yet this is not how the verse really speaks to the Jews as a credo.   They lean more on the phrase in the last sentence – 'an holy people'.   They do not see it as sanctimonious, but as carrying an air of self-determination – a role freely chosen, a sense of independence and resilience which is recognizable and enables one to live with the irony of 'high above all nations'.

When one says that most Jews do not make a habit of spelling out their religious credo, it is important to note that this applies equally to the orthodox among the Jews and those less traditional in practise.   For the orthodox, the credo is, so to speak, taken for granted.   It acquires life not in words but by the way a Jew *acts*, in strict obedience to the commandments affecting ritual and social life which were given by God to Moses, who wrote them down in his Five Books.   Some of the commandments do, indeed, tell the Jew what to *believe* – e.g. in the absolute unity of God and the need to love Him, expressed in the famed words of the *Shema* (*Deut.* 6:4–9).   The rabbis always felt free to develop this by speculating on the attributes of God and his relation to man, but their main object was to ensure that a Jew knew precisely how to follow the practical routines which are the expression of obedience and love.   This is clearly the aim of the Talmud which opens – significantly – not with the analysis of a credo but with the most detailed discussion, running on for many pages, of what is the exact time at which the Jew should read the *Shema* as part of the daily evening service.

The less orthodox, who do not lean so heavily on the *rituals* encumbent on the Jew, are obliged, almost by definition, to spell out beliefs more explicitly.   But it is not all that easy to turn a flexible version of a fundamentalist faith into a clear-cut credo. The doctrine of 'the chosen people' is a case in point.   The orthodox read in the Bible that God chose the Jews 'above all nations' and accept this literally as a fact.   The less orthodox, ask- ing 'why' and 'how', are left in perplexity.   A contemporary American rabbi of distinction, Arthur Hertzberg, who is 'conser- vative' rather than 'orthodox', says in his book *Judaism*[2] that the conception of the chosen people is ,'the truest key to understand- ing Judaism on its own terms', but he goes on immediately to admit that no one dare assert that he knows what it means!   The closest he gets to an explanation is that God chose a people, 'for the task of strict obedience to His will, as an instrument for His Hand'.   The orthodox Jew might comment: if you believe some- thing as unprovable as that, why can't you accept the mystery in its literal Bible form?

It looks as if one needs less doctrinal terms to understand what being a Jew means today. The Jews are a people of passionate faith, but religion in the conventional sense does not exhaust the meaning of this word.

If one seeks a new meaning for Jewish faith, it has, somehow, to embrace both religion and humanism. To be Jewish is always more than nationalism, even among the most secular Israelis. One has to be equally careful not to see the fondness for some ancient rituals as merely sentiment. There is something in the air today among all Jews which might be described as a quasi-religious faith in the Jewish people. It has a numinous glow which is reflected on secularists as much as on explicit believers in God.

I am, of course, generalizing on the basis of personal judgment, but when I consider what seems to me a broad pattern of the thought and behaviour of 'free-thinking' Jews, I cannot help feeling that the Jewish attachment bears many of the old marks. It is true of all people, however indifferent to formal religion, that they are moved at some point by the sense of wonder and veneration that religion expresses. What is striking about Jews is that they continue to import into this universal feeling something of the old Jewish intensity. However sceptical they may be of the literal tenets of orthodoxy, they meet regularly, or on set occasions, for ceremonies that put them firmly in a Jewish context, drawing on familiar, comforting prayers to the Creator of the Universe. Their existence as a people celebrates the belief that the words of the Bible – however archaic – recapture for them the intimacy that the Jews of old felt with this Being. Within this framework, they seem to accept that there is more than pragmatic authority for the ethical standards of life – the responsibility for one's conduct, the absolute of right and wrong, with its corollary of sin and atonement. In the agonies of life and death, they look for comfort to a mystery that is beyond comprehension in realistic terms and yet is apprehended as a Presence to whom a Jew turns in the spirit of his ancestors.

One might describe this as a vestigial survival from the period, not so long ago, in which Jews lived overwhelmingly in strongly Jewish communities, cut off intellectually and socially from modern life. If this were all, however, it would be a weakening heritage, whereas the Jewish attachment, in all its forms, has taken on new life in this century, almost, one might say, with the force of a revolution. The reasons are not hard to identify.

In the first stages of emancipation from what was still mediaeval in the great Heartlands of Jewish life – notably in Eastern Europe – everything seemed to be working for a weakening of the bonds. The one countervailing force was the new concentration of Jews in the U.S.A., in which the social cohesiveness of Eastern Europe was in some measure given fresh life. But though this was a powerful movement in itself, it was in a socio-political framework which envisaged emancipation as 'merging'. America was to be, above all, a melting-pot.

In recent years, this ideal has undergone a transformation in America as a whole. The reinvigoration of ethnic roots is the current tendency. But long before this movement became part of the American scene, the Jews had begun to undergo a revolution of this kind in their own thinking, flowing from the immeasurable catastrophe of the Holocaust, and the subsequent emergence of the State of Israel.

The impact of these momentous events on the consciousness of Jews living in emancipated conditions has been incalculably great. America dramatizes it most powerfully because of the size and power of its Jewish community; but the effect was universal. The Jew could no longer see himself as part of a steady progress of mankind towards a freer and higher form of living. Something unutterably evil had burst on the world, destroying every assumption of human progress. In the midst of this evil, courage had created an unprecedented adventure of hope in the ancient Holy Land. No Jew – certainly no Jew with a spark of imagination – could follow these dramas merely with sympathy, and without direct involvement. For many Jews, the intensity of their reaction was amazing to themselves. They had been aware of their fellow-Jews as in some sense kin; suddenly, they were identified with them to the deepest core of their being. In one bound, every

Jew, however 'liberated', was brought back into the heart of Jewish experience.

The most obvious result was the harnessing of energy and wealth on the freest possible scale towards rescue and support in physical terms. But as part of the same process of shock, Jews had to re-examine the character of the attachment which had received such bewilderingly strong exemplification. Its traditional form had been religion, and for some Jews this was how their new absorption in the Jewish fate had to be expressed. They had to identify with the source, however different in temper from the contemporary scene. Reason was no longer adequate. Had it ever been adequate to explain the emergence of the Jews, the quality of their life, their resilience and survival? The force that had kept the Jews alive had been faith, as expressed for all time in the Bible, in prayers, in ritual, in ordinance, in legend, in parable. One could not explain how this had worked, but it was a reality that was its own justification. One therefore identified with it, accepting that in the past the Jews had survived through religious faith and practice, and that this must carry a valid message for the future.

With this feeling at work, there has been a fresh impetus in the postwar period towards a strengthening of orthodoxy. Pietism and ritual are its basic manifestations, but with corollaries that move the believer into wider fields. In some cases, the new trend has given an impetus to old-fashioned 'learning' in a widespread expansion of Talmud study; in others, mysticism has come to the fore with a revival of Hasidism. At a different level, it has given a new kind of aggressiveness to orthodoxy already in existence, as in the uncompromising attitude of the orthodox in Israel, for whom every *political* action is now to be tested and justified by the words of the Bible taken literally.

The aggressiveness of orthodoxy in Israel has highlighted the contrast there with secularism; and this is a useful reminder that the new weight given to quasi-religious feeling in an aroused Jewish consciousness, has by no means swept aside the rationalism that had become increasingly dominant among Jews of the last century and the first decades of the present one. The heritage of

Enlightenment has been a dogged belief in the power of man using his innate resources of intelligence to set the world to right. There seems little doubt that many Jews of today find themselves nestling in this form of secularism. Yet it is equally evident that they never regard this as the whole story. There has to be room, somewhere, for the kind of faith that expresses the spiritual quality of Jewish kinship.

At one level, this intense identification by so many Jews today with their people is elementary decency: to be born into this kinship and stand aside, after all that has happened, would be an obscenity. At another level, however, it undoubtedly has some of the mystic quality which is the underlying element of religious faith. For one thing, Jewish loyalty is not 'rational': it has its own necessity. For another, it takes the believer into a realm of apprehension which offers insight of a particularly intimate kind. To identify with the Jewish people of today opens up the past, not through analysis but through a willingness to participate in the dreamy but satisfying parables and legends through which Jews of all the centuries gave shape to their feelings about Jewish existence. In much of this, the idea of God was not a theological but a poetically human concept. Above all, there was never any sharp division in Jewish thought and folklore between the holiness of God and the holiness of His people. God had appeared in the Bible as the benefactor of His people. He was manifest in the form and fate of His people. To those Jews of modern times who are seized with the feeling that their people has its own, completely compelling *raison d'être*, the story of the past is seen in this shadowy way without theology but with the patina, nevertheless, of ancient faith.

The theologian anxious to pinpoint Jewish religious beliefs will doubtless find all this very shaky. To suggest that Judaism is not really reducible to a set of absolute doctrines might seem to be robbing this ancient religion of its real character. It cannot be denied that there is something in this: but it is not a watertight argument, as emerges when one examines the attitude that many ardent, believing Jews have adopted to the faith they inherited.

The issue comes neatly to a head in a major book by a modern Jewish theologian, Rabbi Louis Jacobs, called *Principles of the Jewish Faith*. The author's aim is to rebut the idea that Judaism is simply an attachment, weak or strong, to familiar rituals – 'a way of life' – without an underlying structure of explicit religious doctrines. He agrees that 'there have been very few systematic and highly organized authoritative statements of what Jews must believe'. The Bible and Talmud – 'the classical sources of Judaism' – are non-speculative in character, being concerned, above all, with correct *action*. It would be wrong, nevertheless, to conclude that Judaism was 'unconcerned with belief'. The practises of traditional Judaism have religious principles behind them which can and must be identified. 'Judaism is not a form of behaviourism.'[3]

In the course of his argument, Rabbi Jacobs quotes the view of a distinguished scholar, Solomon Schechter (d. 1915), that Judaism must have implicit dogmas; but when one gets a little closer to Schechter, one finds that he is very reluctant to go along with any definition of them that has been produced. It seems to be his view that in the Jewish faith, the respect for history envelopes or overtakes theology. Even the ordinances of the Bible are to be accepted in these terms, and he gives a rather startling example:

> Jews do not keep the Sabbath so much because it is in the Bible but because of the emphasis the Biblical injunctions concerning the Sabbath receive in the history of Jewish life, thought and experience.[4]

Many an orthodox eyebrow must have been raised in shock at this blunt assessment: but it leads into a kind of theology which is not hostile *au fond* to the implicit ideas of orthodoxy. Schechter, though suspicious of rigidity and dogmatism, had an overwhelming respect for the mystery of Jewish survival. The moral and cultural values which it expressed flowed for him not from ancient authority but from the constantly developing ideas of what he called *k'lal Yisrael* – the Jewish people, past and present, as an entity. This concept – he translated it engagingly as 'catholic

Israel' – matches exactly the feeling so resonant in our time that identification with Israel is a new form of Jewish faith. It can express itself in an attitude to life which is God-oriented or secular; but it seems to draw from history, kinship and the passion for Israel, an amalgam of feelings close enough to what many would describe as religious.

It might seem tempting to leave it that way, with the implication that more tightly defined theological argument need not be considered. But if this would express what many Jews feel, one knows that it doesn't fully cover the picture. There are enough Jews – and they are very vocal – who are driven by the feeling that the over-riding theological issues of God and man – with the ancillary issue of God and the Jews – are too powerful to be pushed inside a quasi-religious faith in Israel.

One oddity about this is that the expression of these ideas takes very different forms in Israel and the Diaspora. I call this odd because it had always been assumed – or hoped – that the existence of Jews in their ancient Holy Land would generate a new and deep understanding of Judaism that would, by definition, be authentic and appealing for Jews everywhere. 'From Zion the Torah will go forth, and the word of the Lord from Jerusalem.'

In the event, there is no automatically valid common ground. Significant ideas and attitudes that have developed in Israel are strongly conditioned by the unique homogeneity there of Jewish life, while in the Diaspora something more characteristic of Jewish history – the Jew living among non-Jews – continues to be a dominant factor, yielding sometimes a freer and more dynamic outlook. Let us examine this difference of approach a little more closely.

Every visitor to Israel is aware of the power there of orthodoxy, and in forms that are related to the new factor of Jewish independence.

At the extreme, there are the fanatically orthodox who look upon the State as a wicked presumption, since God alone, and in His own good time, must be trusted to bring about 'the redemption'. There is a section of Jerusalem very much on the tourist map – Mea Shearim – in which many of these Jews live in an apparently timeless vacuum, perpetuating in dress and Yiddish speech an era in seventeenth-century Poland where Jewish life was totally inward-looking, uncorrupted by any willingness to accept the world as it is. The style of these sectarians can be quite ugly in expression. The onlooker is apt to find them alternately picturesque and disturbing, fascinating and ghastly; but they are, in the end, a tiny minority.

Far more significant in influence are those, no less orthodox in practise, who believe passionately in the State, and see it as a means of giving authority to the ancient tradition. Public law affecting social life in all its details is to be governed by the ordinances of Bible and Talmud. Every inch of the territory promised by God to the Patriarchs is immutably Jewish. Political argument with neighbours must start with this as an axiom.

Less stridently, but equally reflecting the ethos of Israel rather than the Diaspora, there is a strong sentiment among many Israeli Jews which attaches them firmly to an orthodox religious outlook even though in other respects they are as modern as any secularist. They just like to be 'fully' Jewish. Israel, for them, is a country in which one can be naturally Jewish in thought and practise without having to adjust to cultures, which, especially in the Christian world, carry alien overtones in the religious sense. It is not easy to say how widespread this attitude is, but it is certainly an important feature of Israeli life. It is in no sense a rejection of 'modernity'. One finds it, sometimes unexpectedly, among scientists, artists, philosophers – and businessmen. The Jewish tradition, expressed for them in simple faith, ritual and Talmud study, is absorbing and comforting. It is abstract, even escapist; yet it is also 'practical', conveying a certainty that transcends the confusions of ordinary life in which they are involved.

In various ways, then, the wholly Jewish background of Israel encourages orthodoxy. It is the setting, too, which allows this to exist side-by-side with what appears to be a fierce kind of secularism. To begin with, coalition politics works through giving way to the dogmatic. There is usually no need to draw a sharp line between sentiments which are pro- or anti-traditional in the religious sense. Even the most pronounced secularists are usually quite happy (as are the non-religious in Christian countries) to go along with traditional forms and rituals to avoid giving offence to those for whom they are important. But this blurring of distinctions has a deeper aspect among Jews. Even if the great majority – as it seems – have no use whatever for any worship of a personal Being in whose hands their fate is supposed to lie, the mystique attached to their concept of the Jewish people is far more religious in expression than occurs in most western nationalisms.

The clue lies in their attitude to the Bible, and it can be seen clearly – if also with some piquancy – in the ideas of David Ben-Gurion, the military leader and first Prime Minister of the new State. In religious terms, Ben-Gurion was undoubtedly agnostic. He was prepared to talk vaguely about 'spirit', but no more. Certainly, materialism by itself got one nowhere: one couldn't believe that man originated 'only from dust'. Geniuses like Plato and Einstein

> are not the products of a blind game of atoms and electrons running to and fro, but a living expression of something great and mysterious called spirit.

Beyond this, however, one can say nothing:

> We stand before a great and awesome mystery which no one is able to solve. There are those who call it by the name 'God'. I do not believe that by giving something a name we clarify and explain what does not lend itself to clarification and explanation.[5]

He was, in other words, unable to make the leap into faith that the concept of a personal God requires. But when it came to faith in his people, his imagination was prepared for any kind of leap. The basis was the Bible story. It was incomplete and included legends: but basically it was 'simple historical fact', and if one looked deeply enough, one found 'hints' that gave a totally new validity to the links of the Hebrew people to the Holy Land.

In the religious view, the Land was promised to the Hebrews by

God, and secured by His direct intervention. Ben-Gurion offered a scenario in *human* terms. At its heart was his conviction – with no proof whatsoever – that Canaan was a Hebrew country long before Abraham arrived on the scene. When he left his birthplace in Mesopotamia, he was joining kinsmen already settled there. Their chief city was Shechem, which was really Jerusalem. Egyptian slavery affected only a small section of the Hebrew people. The conquest under Joshua was a unification of the Egyptian Hebrews with their long-settled kinsmen in their national home.

As it happens, this last part of his thesis is supported, to some degree, by quite a few modern scholars: but on Canaan as originally a Hebrew land, he was on his own. Illustrating this, there is a delightful book recording the arguments at a Bible class that he used to conduct when Prime Minister.[6] One outstanding scholar, Yeheskel Kaufmann, made a tart response when Ben-Gurion kept insisting that 'the land to which Abraham came was the land of the Hebrews'. 'We have only one testimony to that fact,' Kaufmann told the class, 'that of Ben-Gurion.'

Theology and history came sharply into conflict when the Declaration of Independence was being drafted in 1948. It was intolerable to secularists that the name of God should be invoked, but one could refer to the 'Rock of Israel', a phrase used poetically in the liturgy. It avoided explicit theism, but united traditional faith with the national will.

The Jews are not unique in this kind of ambivalence, and there is an interesting parallel to the secularist Jewish attitude in a remark made by Bulent Ecevit, Prime Minister of Turkey, in the course of an interview on British radio. Like Ben-Gurion, Ecevit is a humanist, with a passionate faith in his people. To a question: 'How much do you yourself draw from the Islamic faith?', he replied:

As much as I draw, I would say, from the psychology of my people. Islamic inclination and a sense of values are inherent in the psychology of the Turkish people, and as much as I draw on the Turkish people, I can say I draw from the Islamic religion.

.   .   .   .   .

When one transposes the debate on religious values from Israel to the Diaspora, it takes on a different character. On the one hand, Jews outside Israel do not have to react to the control of their daily social lives by traditionalists armed with State authority. They can therefore be more relaxed, taking what they like from dogmatic religion to express their feelings. On the other hand, the absence of a formal Jewish framework to society can lead some Jews into a deliberately extreme *conceptual* position, as if they feel the need to create a Jewish world around themselves which is consistent and watertight precisely because there is no 'natural' political base to express it.

This approach, it must be said, is that of a small minority. By and large, the Jews of the Diaspora have subsumed religious faith into a faith for their people, exemplified mostly in their extreme concern for Israel. Yet if this is a dominant feature of the scene, it by no means conveys its full character. Underlying the concentration on Israel is the compelling memory of the Holocaust. As a result, Jews who may not take the prayers and rituals literally are led willy-nilly into theological speculation. Why did the Holocaust happen? What kind of God allows it? Is there some way in which the horrors of Jewish experience are annealed into love and worship of a Creator?

Diaspora Jews, especially in America, listen eagerly to those who are moved to address themselves to these questions, at a distance from the practicalities of life. They are shy of answers framed in a conventional mode. What they seem to respond to is the speculative, poetical musing which was a mark of the Midrash, or of the populist preaching of later days, which opened the heart to an accommodation with mystery and looked no further. Two writers in America today who evoke this chord of feeling – though in very different ways – are Elie Wiesel and Bernard Malamud.

There is another tradition – a tougher one intellectually – to which Jews also respond as in the past. In the days of the Vilna Gaon in eighteenth-century Lithuania, Jacob Kranz, the Maggid (preacher) of Dubno, was famed for a compelling eloquence that drew on scholarship equally with folklore. When he grappled with the deep questions of man's fate and the love of God, he spoke intimately to huge audiences, but at a high intellectual level and without a trace of vulgarization. The Gaon would listen to him spellbound. Perhaps his heir today is Saul Bellow.

One can pick a name here and there, but it would be hopeless to try and sum up the general character of the huge flow of writings that try to tackle this underlying theme of Jewish existence. There is one aspect of the subject, however, which illustrates why Israel alone cannot be the focus of religious thought.

Until the emergence of the State in 1948, the abiding concept of the Jews was of a people in exile, not accidentally but essentially. Certainly one had to assume that one day the *Galuth* would end. One dreamed of this day and prayed for it, but it was always unreal. The reality for a Jew was to make sense of the unique character of the *Galuth* situation. We saw earlier how this was expressed for Kabbalists in the metaphysics of the universe: God was Himself in exile. But even for those not involved in these doctrines, a Jew was a man who drew a special meaning out of a life which was always bifurcated. It was the role of the Jew to carry his God with him everywhere in the world not in a missionary sense, as a light unto the nations, but as a light to himself. Accepting this, there was always a give-and-take in Jewish existence. Faith enriched, and was enriched by, the surrounding world.

In this sense, the outpouring of writing among Jews in the Diaspora expresses a response that can reach deeper into the continuum than is possible in the single-focused Israel scene. It is as if life in the ancient homeland is not enough: Jewish history has an extra dimension that continues to demand expression.

One element in this extra dimension is diversity. The common feature of Diaspora writing is the acceptance that the writer is going to continue to live, voluntarily, in the *Galuth*. But beyond this, the drive of the Diaspora Jew to construct a rationale – or a mystique – for his faith is personal and highly varied.

One might take two examples, almost at random, to show how wide is the spectrum of thought and feeling. At one end are those who write without much Jewish erudition but with deep emotion.

One such writer, the novelist Herbert Gold, published an essay recently entitled, 'On Becoming a Jew',[8] in which he tried to give shape to an American-Jewish existence transformed by a mystical identification with the past. In the suburban America he came from, being a Jew had been a meaningless routine, empty of content. 'My isolation as a Jew was a kind of starvation.' Through the dramas of the Holocaust and Israel, he had begun to find his 'obscured allegiances'. The problem was how to relate the dominant elements in Jewish history – the suffering of the masses, the visions of the Kabbalah – to the soft comforts of his own life. A leap into religious faith was beyond him: 'union with God . . . is neither in my nature nor in the possibility of the times.' The answer for him was to leap 'mystically' into a union with those for whom Jewish experience was authentic: 'I am ready to ride with ecstasies which I have not earned, sacrifices I have not shared.'

Ultimately, this is not much more than sheer sentiment, but it shades into the view of a widely-read novelist-theologian, Arthur A. Cohen, who sees Judaism not just for himself, but for all Jews, in terms of an apocalyptic transfiguration. In a work called *The Natural and the Supernatural Jew*,[9] he argues that the Jewish people have to be restored to their historic role as God's witnesses on earth. 'The rediscovery of the supernatural vocation of the Jew is the turning point of modern Jewish history, . . . for the Jewish people is not a fact of history but an article of faith.' The 'natural' Jew is defined by the ordinary categories of history and society, but he has always carried within him the supernatural role. Judaism can fulfil its proper end only so long as it functions in an intimate relation with world history. 'The Jew can no longer afford the luxury of isolated sanctity . . . The truth of Judaism has relevance and bearing upon the destiny of mankind.'

It is all grist to the mill for modern theologians: but in some ways the Diaspora voice is heard more clearly by most Jews when there is an evocation of the old-fashioned preaching of Eastern Europe, with its unique amalgam of the virtues of intellect and conduct. A beloved scholar who saw the moral imperative expressed this way was Abraham Joshua Heschell, a German refugee who had settled in America and who died in 1972. In the Introduction to his last book,[10] he described two forces in the tradition which 'carry on a struggle' within him, personified in two numinous figures – the Baal Shem (d. 1760), revered as the gentle founder of Hasidism, and a tortured, aggressive scholar of the following century, Menahem Mendel of Kotzk (d. 1859) – known as 'the Kotzker'. In the Baal Shem he found love and compassion, in the Kotzker a struggle for intellectual integrity which brought perplexity and contradiction. The Baal Shem was a lamp; the Kotzker was lightning. The truth lay in both. Integrity without love leads to ruin; fervour alone 'may seduce us into living in a fool's paradise'.

This might seem less the language of a traditional rabbi than of John Donne in St. Paul's Cathedral; but it speaks to the heart of many a Diaspora Jew.

V: THREE JEWS AT LARGE

Akiba Recovered
Born in Berlin
An Englishman Forever

AKIBA RECOVERED

I CONFRONTED, in the last section, the problem of adding things up, but with a certain reserve that may have been all too obvious. I am never wholly satisfied with generalizations. One comes closer to what is significant, it seems to me, by looking at individuals, despite all the limitations that this involves.

With this in mind, I propose in this section to talk briefly of three very different Jews, to see what will emerge. 'What I tell you three times is true,' it says in *The Hunting of the Snark*, which is at least encouraging.

I have picked my characters from the two ends of the Diaspora. The first of the three, the great Rabbi Akiba, is separated from us by more than 1800 years. The other two both belong to the twentieth century but are separated from each other by a gap that can seem even greater, since one – now of venerable age – is deeply and solemnly German, while the other was typically – almost comically – English. There is nothing, it might be said, to unite these three men except their common concern with Jewish scholarship: yet one sees them testifying to the timelessness of Jewish experience as uniformly as do any three Jews called up to the age-old ceremony of the Reading of the Torah.

I have been involved with all three, but must write of them in different ways. With Akiba, I want to get rid of a romantic but false view that has invaded the history books. With my German scholar, I am bound to say something of the German experience. How not to? With my Englishman, I can be more relaxed. He was *sui generis*, and we have to look at him this way.

First, then, to the great Akiba, the leading scholar of his day, and probably the most important single influence in the formation of the rabbinic tradition. His life spanned the two great dramas of Jewish history in that era – the destruction of Jerusalem by the Romans (A.D. 70) and the doomed revolt of Bar Kokhbah (A.D.

132–5). It was between these two focal points that the rabbis laid the foundations for the profound study of the Torah that was to eventuate in the Talmud.   There are endless reminiscences of Akiba in the Talmud, telling of his leadership, his travels to many countries, his personal kindness and modesty, and the devotion to study that was to cost him his life.   In all these respects he has come to occupy a legendary pre-eminence in Jewish tradition. The trouble is that the history books have now enveloped this in a further story that distorts everything.

The drama that the historians have developed starts from the well-established fact that Akiba met his death, at the hands of the Romans, at some point during the Bar Kokhbah revolt.   Building on this, the history books tell us that Akiba was not merely a rabbinic teacher, but a kind of freedom-fighter, inspiring the rebellion, proclaiming Bar Kokhbah as the Messiah, and executed for these reasons.   It is a picture that is, I believe, without foundation, as I will try to show.

Having done this, I want to consider what Akiba really means to us in our tradition.   If we put him back into his time as a rabbi who fought a battle of faith, rather than arms, he offers us an authentic insight into the force that shaped Jewish life in all the centuries which followed.   It may be less exciting to see him as a pacifist rather than as a fighter, but we get nowhere through anachronism.   There is a more assured pride in living with Akiba as he was, and not as a cardboard figure in an adventure story.

I have to admit that there is a certain pleasure for me in breaking a lance with all the historians.   One doesn't often get a chance to upset a view as entrenched as this one is.

The romantic view has taken over. With rare exceptions, every book one reads presents Akiba as a leader of the Bar Kokhbah revolt.   To quote just two examples from standard works: in one book, he is 'the soul of the uprising', in another – 'Akiba was the intellectual and Bar Kokhbah the military and political leader'.[1]

This central 'fact' is spelt out in many books with elaborate supporting detail. For years before the revolt broke out, we are told, Akiba had travelled tirelessly to Jewish communities everywhere to lay the groundwork, collecting funds and support. To quote one account: 'his travels extended through Parthia, Asia Minor, Cappadocia, Phrygia, and perhaps even to Europe and Africa . . . with the intention of interesting the Jews of the most remote countries in the coming struggle.' When the moment came to fight, he raised the status of the rebel leader immeasurably by proclaiming him as the Messiah. This proclamation is, of course, the central element in the story, despite the fact that there is virtually nothing to support it.

Factually, all that exists in the whole of rabbinic literature linking Akiba to Bar Kokhbah in any positive way is a sentence of three words he is supposed to have applied to the rebel leader: *zeh melekh ha-mashiah* – 'this is the king-messiah'. But even this apparently clear statement is flimsy in the extreme. For before we build it into a picture of Akiba as 'the soul of the uprising' we have to consider the circumstances in which it was made and recalled. If we transport ourselves to the setting of the time, we find the rabbis concerned not with nationalism, still less with warfare, but with the unravelling of biblical verses.

Akiba's famous three words were not, so to speak, embedded in a *communiqué* from the battlefront. The rabbis of a much later date were discussing stories of a rebel, by now semi-mythical, whom they knew as Bar Koziba, with a messianic pun-name 'Bar Kokhbah'. In the course of the discussion, one rabbi mentions that Akiba, when he saw Bar Koziba, said: 'This is the king-messiah.' Another recalls the mythical feats of strength ascribed to Bar Koziba. In fighting the Romans, he used to catch the stones of the *ballistae* with one of his knees and hurl them back, 'killing any number of men'. *That*, he says, is why Akiba hailed him as the Messiah.

It hardly seems, as it stands, much of a support for Akiba as 'the soul of the uprising'. Did he say these words in Bar Kokhbah's presence? Very doubtful. To get the flavour of Messiah-talk in those days, one has to see it embedded not in hard politics but in speculation. The rabbis of that time – and later – loved talking dreamily about the day the Messiah would come, turning to biblical verses which might be applied, given sufficient ingenuity, to fix, or rule out, an actual date. Some saw the Messiah in apocalyptic terms, symbol of the divine refounding of the Universe. After desperate travail, there would be the War of the Great Sea Monsters, followed by the War of Gog and Magog, and only then by the dawn of the Messianic Age. In one calculation of this kind, it was said that God would 'renew His world' after 7,000 years. This concept of 'the world to come' could still allow for a short-term saviour, who might rule, like David, for a lifespan of forty years. Akiba is thought to have held this view, the closest one can get to linking him, at least in theory, with support for a rebellion.

But was Bar Kosiba (his true name, as we know from the newly discovered 'Bar Kokhbah' letters) the kind of military leader who could possibly have led the rabbis, with Akiba's blessing, to endorse him as Messiah even in this limited sense? All we know from the rabbinic literature is that in later years, when the stories were being collected, the rabbis had grown to detest his memory. They projected him as strong and brave (which the letters confirm) but also as ruthless and sacrilegious. They told that he had ordered every one of his soldiers to cut off a finger as a test of courage, which had led the rabbis to cry: 'How long will you continue to maim the men of Israel?' When he suspected his uncle, the famed scholar Eleazar of Modi'in of treachery, 'he gave him a kick which killed him'. When he went into battle, he would address God with a bravado that the rabbis clearly thought deplorable: 'We pray to Thee, do not give help to the enemy: us Thou needst not help.' Perhaps the most significant of the various scattered references to him is a story in the Talmud that Bar Koziba, 'after he had ruled for two and a half years', said to the rabbis: 'I am the Messiah.' The rabbis, we are told, 'tested' this by a very fanciful criterion they had devised, decided that his claim was false, 'and killed him'.

What are we to make, then, of Akiba's famous three words? The anecdote of the *ballistae* catches the tone perfectly. Akiba, hearing the tale of this mighty deed and other Paul Bunyan type

stories of his superhuman strength, observes – surely with a touch
of irony – 'he must be the king-messiah'. His colleague Rabbi
Jonathan ben Torta rejoins in the same spirit: 'Akiba: grass will
be sprouting out of your cheeks, and the Messiah will still not
have come.' The whole picture is one of scholarly talk, alternately serious and earthy, sacred and secular, but always essentially
abstracted from the world of fighting and politics. It hardly
corresponds to the notion of a nation in arms, with the most
respected rabbi of the time standing side-by-side with the rebel
leader.

The one thing that mattered to the rabbis was their freedom to
study the Torah. Resistance by arms was alien to them. They
were willing to find ways of accommodation with the Roman
authorities on everything if study was permitted. Rabbi
Yohanan ben Zaccai had led the way on this during the 'Great
War' ending in A.D. 70 by making a deal with the Romans
which allowed him to found a rabbinical academy at Yavneh.
The rabbis followed this line during the scattered uprisings which
followed. One modern scholar, Louis Finkelstein, hovers over
my own view on this. He calls the rabbis 'rationalist-pacifists',
and seems to extend this to include Akiba, for whom fighting
against Rome was 'an insane adventure'.[2]

What about Akiba's alleged travels to raise funds for the revolt?
There are certainly plenty of stories of Akiba travelling, but the
motivation had no relation to armed resistance. His real purpose
– much more prosaic – can be gleaned from a picture of rabbinic
activity presented by Salo Baron in his *Social and Religious History
of the Jews*.[3] With the Temple destroyed, there was a danger that
the Holy Land would lose its hold over Jews in other countries.
One way to keep them in line was to unify a code of law, emerging in the *Mishnah*, on which Akiba's role was decisive. But
there was also a practical issue: it was essential that Jews everywhere accepted the authority of the Holy Land sages in fixing the
calendar according to observation of the moon there, so that the
timing of fasts and feasts would be uniform everywhere. Akiba
was in great demand abroad to help the local people on this.
So much for fund-raising as a motivation.

Finally, what about his martyrdom? It was as a teacher, not as an ally of Bar Kokhbah, that he was arrested. The crisis had come for him and his colleagues when the Romans outlawed the study of the Torah. In this situation one didn't take to arms: one went on teaching. The scholars, with enormous courage, pursued their work, knowing that it would mean imprisonment, and probably death.

Akiba's arrest is reflected in many stories, factual and imaginative, as is the arrest of his equally fearless colleagues, brought together in legend as 'the ten martyrs'. One of these colleagues, Rabbi Judah ben Baba, was found ordaining five young men as rabbis in the mountains of Galilee. He was slain on the spot – 'three hundred spears were driven into his body'. In Akiba's case, there is a similarly graphic account:

> When the wicked Government issued a decree forbidding the Jews to study the Torah, Pappus ben Judah came and found Rabbi Akiba publicly bringing gatherings together and occupying himself with the Torah. He said to him: Akiba, are you not afraid of the Government?

Akiba replied with the parable of the fishes, cajoled by the fox to seek safety on dry land from the fisherman. The fish reply: 'If we are at risk in the element in which we live, how much more in the element in which we would die.'

He was arrested, and there are many stories of his preoccupation with Torah questions during his long stay in prison. The account of his torture and death, with the words of the *Shema* lingering on his lips and a Heavenly Voice ringing out to bless him, has found an undying place in Jewish legend. At this level, we are no longer called upon to test history by facts. We are dealing with myth, which exerts its power over us in a quite different way. When we hear of the Heavenly Voice ringing out, it is as vivid to us as Moses on Sinai. We have lived with this memory through the centuries. We are at home in it.

What moves us, with Akiba, is the concept of an ancestor who left behind him a faith in the Torah which became a constant in Jewish life. In every story told of him he is a symbol of the subjection of material satisfaction, pride, and certainly armed resistance, to the joy of mystic union with God. And it is here, moving beyond the facts to myth, that one begins to approach the true meaning of Akiba to Jewish consciousness.

The myth envisages a continuum of which the Jews of all ages are a part. It is as if one can reach out, beyond the variety of experience, to an abiding constancy. Of all the rabbis, it is Akiba who seems to stand above all for this inspiriting feeling.

The late Yaacov Herzog, who was both a rabbi and an Ambassador of Israel, expressed this thought movingly in an essay which spoke of Akiba as a symbol of 'the timeless identity of the Jew'. If Akiba rose from his grave and came to life again, he wrote, 'it would be as if he had never died, because we could talk to him as if all that had occurred in the meantime had never been, as if Jewish experience had been uninterrupted until this day'.[4]

Here, with time disappearing, is myth in action. It brings to mind, in fact, an almost parallel story in the Talmud in which the continuum of Jewish history is moved back, and the rabbis of *Akiba's* time ask themselves, in effect: what would Moses feel if he came to life today and heard Akiba expounding the Five Books of Moses?

In the story they tell, Moses is receiving the Torah from God on Sinai, and sees him adding 'coronets' to certain letters, which is how the Torah scrolls have always been written. He asks God for the reason. God tells him that at the end of many generations a man will be born, Akiba ben Joseph by name, who will derive many laws from each of these little decorations. Moses pleads to hear this exposition, and is immediately transported to Akiba's study-class at B'nei B'rak. He sits down at the back of the class, and is dismayed to find that he can't understand the logic of the argument at all. How is Akiba deriving all these detailed laws from the relatively simple words of the text? At this point a pupil, equally puzzled, asks Akiba: what is your authority for this law? Akiba replies: it was given to Moses at Sinai. Poor

Moses was still baffled. There was certainly nothing like this in the Torah he had written down at God's dictation. All the same, the story says, he was comforted.

It is hard to resist this story as a paradigm of Jewish history. Moses, in Akiba's classroom, is out of his depth. The argument, the situation, the history of Israel has moved beyond him. Yet he is there, listening to the words of Akiba, just as Akiba is listening to what he feels is an interior communication from Moses. We, in turn, are never surprised to hear echoes of Jewish experience moving back and forth, affecting us most powerfully when they defy explanation.

The latest example of this timeless process is the survival – or is it the rebirth – of Soviet Jewry; and this leads me to end with what I might call a personal Midrash.

It was when I was writing *The Walls of Jerusalem* that I began to feel that the alleged role of Akiba in the Bar Kokhbah revolt was out of key. I continued to think about this later, but felt on my own. I would have liked at least *somebody* to take the same view.

It occurred to me one day, when I was visiting Professor Jacob Neusner at Brown University in America, that he might offer a clue, as he has written a great deal about the biographies of the rabbis. I mentioned the issue to him, asking if he knew of anybody who agreed with me. He reached to a bookshelf, took down a book, and asked me to look at the Appendix.

The Appendix contained a translation of an article by a Russian scholar, Hillel Aleksandrov, entitled: 'The Role of Akiba in the Bar Kokhbah Revolt.' The article had appeared in a recent issue of a Russian journal on Asian studies,[5] and set out to prove, through a careful examination of rabbinic sources, that the widespread view of Akiba's role was all wrong. There was no evidence, Aleksandrov showed, that Akiba was in any way involved in a military rebellion. His importance lay elsewhere.

We know of the revival of Jewish sentiment in Russia, particularly in relation to Israel: but to find someone writing there in the full context of Jewish studies and coming to my own conclusions was like a benediction. It was a good moment of kinship, and I shall remember it always as a tribute to the real Akiba.

BORN IN BERLIN

M Y second hero is Gershom Scholem. I talked of him earlier for his monumental studies of Jewish mysticism, but here I would like to consider him from a more personal angle.

One can never tire of discussing this marvellous man, now more than eighty years old. Single-handed, he has given us a new way of looking at our past;[1] but one is also impelled, reading him, to think about his own background, for if ever time and place were significant in forging the consciousness of a writer, it must be the Germany into which he was born. I met this Germany at various removes as my Jewish experience unfolded. The subject is inexhaustible. Here, I will be very brief in recalling the forces at work there, not only for Scholem but for other important writers who were his friends.[2]

To talk of Germany, after all that has happened, is painful to most of us. But German culture has always exercised a dominant influence over Jewish consciousness. If we shut our eyes to the legacy of the German-Jewish involvement, the story of our time is left with a great hole in the middle – a sequence of events, stunning in its tragedy, that simply tears Jewish history apart, as the pages of an old calendar are torn off and discarded.

One needs to understand Germany, not to soften the unspeakable tragedy, but to identify the extraordinary power that Germany exercised over Jewish feeling, to examine the forms of Jewish thought that burgeoned under that influence, to see the fatal flaws, but at the same time to recognize what was true, revolutionary, and lasting. The historical picture – a story of attraction, conflict, tension and paradox – must be absorbed in appropriately dialectical terms.

There could hardly be a better guide on this than Gershom Scholem. One has always wanted to know what lay behind the intense drive he brought to the study of mysticism, and how his work is related to the German background in general. It may be that an intellectual autobiography will emerge one day, but

in the meantime some of the clues can be pursued in a book by
him called *On Jews and Judaism in Crisis*.[3] Although it is, in form,
only a collection of scattered pieces, we see, behind them, the man
himself, looking back reflectively on the two themes which have
been paramount in his life – Germany and Kabbalah.

The first piece is a long interview in which Scholem talks freely of
his youth, his first involvement with the study of Jewish mysticism, his friendship with other German-Jewish writers, his
Zionist hopes (fulfilled and frustrated), and the underlying question that still baffles him – how Judaism as a religion can establish
living values in a secularist age.   In the essays which follow he
takes up particular aspects of the German involvement, illustrating his approach with a critique of other writers of the same
background as his own.

Scholem – a fourth-generation Berliner – was born in 1897 into
a fully assimilated family.   To his father and his father's generation, German culture was the highest form of civilization.
Although no 'true' German ever set foot in the Scholem household, Gershom's father remained convinced that he himself was a
complete German.   For such a man to have explored his Jewish
heritage in any serious way, would have been to risk diluting
his precious Germanism.

The problem for young Scholem was that in many ways he
agreed with this formulation.   For him too, he says here, the
German language 'bestowed the gift of unforgettable experiences:
it defined and gave expression to the landscape of our youth'.
The appeal of Germany to German Jews was unique in its power,
and there were good historical reasons for this.   When emancipation began,

> it was German culture the Jews first encountered in their road to the
> West.   Moreover – and this is decisive – the encounter occurred
> precisely at the moment when that culture had reached one of its
> most fruitful turning points.   It was the zenith of Germany's
> bourgeois era.   One can say that it was a happy hour when the
> newly awakened creativity of the Jews ... impinged precisely on

the zenith of a great creative period of the German people, a period producing an image of things German that, up to 1940, and among very broad classes of people, was to remain unshaken, even by many bitter and later most bitter experiences.

It was not simply that the Jews admired German culture in its own right.   It seemed to them that it had been fashioned, almost by Providence, to meet their deepest feelings *as Jews*.   Schiller was a 'spokesman for pure humanity' – the interior message of the Jewish Bible.   Goethe echoed the lyricism of the Psalms and the majesty of the Prophets.   Responding to German culture with dazzling speed, the Jews did not merely adopt what lay before them but deepened it incalculably in every field of industry, science, and the arts.   'A list of . . . astonishing Jewish talents and accomplishments (was) offered up to the Germans.'   Symbolically, 'almost all the most important critical interpretations of Goethe were written by Jews'.

With all this, the Jews remained ineradicably alien to the Germans.   The 'bourgeois' Jews (like Scholem's father) were content to love without being loved in return; but to the younger generation of intellectuals, alienness posed a problem that they had somehow to tackle – with, of course, every tool of the German intellectual tradition that they could fashion to their purpose.   Many – including one of Scholem's brothers – fled into Marxist politics.   To Scholem, this was just as misguided as his father's pretence that they were really all Germans.   'You're deluding yourself,' Scholem recollects telling his brother, 'the same way Papa is deluding himself.   You are deluding yourself by imagining that you represent Germany's exploited industrial workers.   That's a lie: you don't represent a thing.   You're the son of a middle-class German Jew.   That makes you furious, so you go off wandering into other fields.   You don't want to be what you are.'

What was Scholem himself?   He saw with admirable clarity that it was morally debasing – and self-defeating – to water down Jewish feeling; it was an expression of self-surrender.   But how did a modern Jew give that feeling a positive content?   A first step was to immerse himself in Jewish literature: but this had to be more than a passive exercise in meticulous scholarship – German style. It had, somehow, to express a breakaway from the Enlightenment outlook which was clearly running to seed as a touchstone of Jewish values. Jewish life, he began to feel, had a dynamic within it that drew on sources outside the ken of rabbinism and a belief in progressive liberalism. This, it seems, is how he began to get involved in Kabbalah.

Kabbalah is a set of cosmic teachings, developed and elaborated over the centuries, that linked the ineffable magic in the letters of God's Names to a philosophy of emanations and the ultimate restoration, through a purified mankind, of God's primordial perfection. A secret lore, it seemed to contain some inner force which had led it to burgeon repeatedly in Jewish history. What lay behind it? To assess intellectually what the kabbalists had been after could be the work of a lifetime. One didn't have to *believe* in these mysterious doctrines – how could one? – but approaching it as a historian, one could illuminate the workings of the kabbalist mind, show the parallels to other mystical faiths, and thus pay tribute to a vitality that drew on sources beyond ordinary reason. 'They knew something we don't know,' Scholem told himself; and this was to be the theme, repeated endlessly, of the magisterial historical works he went on to produce in sixty years of study and scholarship.

I spoke earlier, in discussing the Vilna Gaon, of some of the paradoxes involved. In rebellion against a dead formalism, Scholem had set out to reconstruct the most intricate edifice of absolute doctrine, totally remote from the temper of the present age. From another angle, his project represented a proud and independent assertion of Jewishness in which everything most *German* in him was brought into play – the high standards of German scholarship, the central role of linguistic analysis, the use of Hegelian dialectic. But this, perhaps, was where the true bonus lay. To break away and yet continue fully to express his background was, for him, a resolution of the underlying German-Jewish problem. The proper relationship to Germany, he said, drawing on a phrase of Max Brod, had to be one of 'distant love'. The concept was dialectical. 'Distance is meant to prevent an all too-coarse intimacy, but at the same time a desire to bridge the gap.'

There was a dialectical principle at work, too, behind his decision at an early age to move to the land of Israel and centre his studies there.   If religion was to have any meaning for a secular age, it had to break through the rationalist barrier and draw meaning from the idea of the Kabbalah that the universe itself, and not merely the individual man, had to return from 'exile'. In the kabbalist conception, the Kingdom of God is not just the realization of good on earth – 'a state in which the good would be done by natural impulse' – but 'the actualization of this reign in all the infinite spheres of creation'.   Scholem sees 'a vehement appeal' in this notion, and relates it to what he calls 'secular messianism'.   It is no accident for him that modern philosophers who have expressed apocalyptic ideas are often Jewish in origin and from his own background.   With formal religion abandoned, there had to be a new approach to the redemption of man:

> This is the attitude behind the writings of the most important ideologists of revolutionary messianism, such as Ernst Bloch, Walter Benjamin, Theodor Adorno, and Herbert Marcuse, whose acknowledged or unacknowledged ties to their Jewish heritage are evident.

If this broad philosophical – or theological – framework sounds daunting, and too German in flavour for some, one has to remember that Scholem is not himself a dogmatic ideologue but an expounder.   Ideas appeal to him; he loves defining them with care, but instinct warns him that speculation run riot has dangers as well as joys.   The effect of Germany on Jewish writers is central to this question.   One sees it reflected in the essays included in this book on three outstanding writers of the twentieth century – his friends Walter Benjamin, Samuel Joseph Agnon and Martin Buber – each of whom struggled as he did with the German involvement but to different effect.

The factor common to these friends of Scholem was their resolve, as young men, to do something that would transform the

sterile heritage of the past.   For Walter Benjamin, who is recognized now, after an obscure life and tragic death, as a literary
Marxist of genius, it was for some time an open question whether
he would follow Scholem's encouragement and give his attention
to serious *Jewish* studies; but his absorption with European literary
criticism proved too strong.   The tribute to him in this book is an
elegy of the deepest friendship, made all the more poignant by
Scholem's still keenly-felt disappointment and irritation at the
Marxist 'aberrations' in Benjamin's thought.

Agnon, who won the Nobel Prize in 1966 for his novels (in
Hebrew) on Jewish life, seems much closer to Russia than to
Germany, and this is how I spoke of him earlier in this book.
But I now see from Scholem that he spent twelve years in Germany (1912–24) that were formative to his vision, forcing a
reconsideration of the culture he had inherited.   Scholem knew
Agnon for fifty years, and with the guidance he offers in a loving
essay, the reader can begin to come to terms with the old Jewish
tensions that lie behind Agnon's calm, almost noble style.   This
elegist of Russian Jewry, bound to that community with every
fibre of his being, was torn between the acceptance and rejection
of tradition in a way that was utterly familiar to Scholem, even
though he himself had had no direct experience of Agnon's
Russian-Jewish world.   Scholem sees Agnon as the supreme
expositor of 'the *Verlorenheit* and alienation of the modern Jew
who must – or fails to – come to terms with himself without the
guiding lights of a tradition that has ceased to be meaningful'.   If
Agnon's dilemma as a Jew, uprooted and left without faith, was
universal in its implication, it is appropriate that Germany – arch-
symbol of secularism to Russian Jews – should have been the
generative focus of his vision.

But it is Martin Buber – perhaps surprisingly – who emerges as
offering the deepest tribute to the German involvement.   To the
young Scholem and his friends, Buber – an older man – had
seemed the true prophet of a Judaism restored.   Rejecting the
stifling rabbinic background in which he had been nurtured,
Buber expressed a truly Nietzschean resolve to create new values,
leaping over the sterility of exile to the true spirituality of pri-

mordial biblical feeling. By reinterpreting history as self-perpetuating myth, he seemed to be rescuing Jewish life from a dead historicism. In collecting and publishing Hasidic tales of quiet mysterious power, he was revealing the insight that lies in simplicity, in paradox, in personal involvement. *Erlebnis* – the living experience – was the locus of truth. The here-and-now, however humdrum and fleeting, could come to express eternal significance.

As the years passed, however, the German windiness in Buber's approach became more pronounced, and it was probably this, more than anything else, that gradually made Scholem suspicious of what Buber was doing to resolve the Jewish problem they had all inherited. Scholem is impish with Buber, full of admiration for the power and originality of his mind, but gently satirical over the fact that, as time went on, the man whom the non-Jewish world came to regard as the apostle of a new Judaism, 'spoke a language that was more comprehensible to everybody else than to the Jews themselves'. On the proper interpretation of Hasidism the two were straight rivals. It annoyed Scholem that Buber refused to produce the sources for his Hasidic tales, and he took this as support for his contention that in turning his back on the kabbalist theology from which Hasidism sprang, Buber was being false to history.[4]

The real trouble lay deeper. Buber was essentially a poet, though a cloudy one, in a high-flown style redolent of the German *Geist*. '*German* mysticism attracted him even before he sought and came to know *Jewish* mysticism.' Scholem says, with a certain impatience. 'He wrote not as an observer but as one deeply affected.' And from the inside, rather than as an observer, Buber's language had taken off into a realm beyond ordinary Jewish experience. For Scholem, such an approach 'could not bear the scrutiny of historical observation'. Yet in expressing his own growing sense of distance from Buber's ideas he saw the 'considerable magic' they exuded, emerging from a depth of direct mystical feeling that was, perhaps, beyond his own grasp. He concedes, in tribute to their lifelong friendship, that 'Buber's capacity to grasp nuances of the inexpressible in words was extraordinary', even though – he quickly adds – 'it makes his writings well-nigh untranslatable'.

If, for Scholem, the trouble with Buber is that 'he wrote not as an observer but as one deeply affected', what, one is tempted to ask, is Scholem's own relation to Kabbalah, the body of thought he has devoted a lifetime to analysing and explaining?　An anecdote in this book is very much to the point.　It seems that on his arrival in Jerusalem as a young man of twenty-two, Scholem sought out a community of kabbalists.　He asked the leader – a man of about seventy – if he could be instructed.　The man look-ed at Scholem for a long time, checked his forehead lines, and said: 'I am prepared to teach you, but only on condition that you do not ask any questions.'　Scholem thought about it, and then said, 'I can't.'　The historian, with centuries of European enlightenment behind him, could never stop asking questions.　He was never going to become a 'believer', even though he could identify himself with the movement as a scholar.

But if in this sense Scholem has remained outside Kabbalah, magic has surfaced nevertheless in the extraordinary impact his books have had on the Israeli reading public, especially the young. A generation overwhelmingly secular has found in his work a marvellous historical illumination – almost an annealment.　In a quite unexpected way, his work has enriched the Israeli present by bringing it into tune with the past.　Scholem must feel this, and perhaps it serves to soften the sadness he expresses when he looks back, after his long identification with Israel, at the spiritual con-dition of the Jewish community there.　That the tone of Israeli society is secular does not in itself disturb him; secularism is a phase that man has now to pass through.　'The barbarism of the so-called new culture' would be tolerable if one could see some fructifying seed for the future.　But 'I see something today that I didn't see fifty years ago: the threat of death, of oblivion . . .'

This is Scholem at an uncharacteristically sombre and apocalyp-tic moment.　Scholem the historian, however, has shown repeatedly and emphatically that history works in unpredictable ways. In what may be an unconscious kabbalistic metaphor, he says at one point that we cannot explain to ourselves 'what sparks functioned and sustained whatever remained alive' in the successive crises of Jewish history. Even Germany, with all its horror, has left a positive force in Jewish life. In kabbalistic terms, the readers of Scholem's books are collecting divine sparks from the *klipot*, or husks, in which God's original perfection lies scattered, awaiting restoration through faith.

AN ENGLISHMAN FOREVER

I PROMISED that the third member of my trio would offer a sharp contrast, for since he was an *English* scholar, the reader is safe from any high-blown theories of politics or history in his work. The Germans and French go in for that sort of thing, and look where it's led them. The English prefer to be pragmatic, coping with each situation as it arises. Of course, one is free to say: and look where *that's* led them!

All one can say in their defence is that it seems to offer a view of history as enjoyment: and the most English writer I can think of in this sense was the Jewish historian Cecil Roth, who died in 1970. I knew him well, and never ceased to be astonished at the paradox that he expressed.

His knowledge was certainly encyclopaedic. As the author of a vast array of works on Jewish history, he seemed to have been lifted out of his little English world of origin into an intimacy with the Jewish past in every country and every age. Yet by his own admission it was the byways, the oddities, the minutiae of Jewish life which really interested him. He could evince pride or sorrow at the great events like everybody else. But ultimately history came to life for him in terms of individual Jews whom he came across in odd books or manuscripts and then pursued, as a detective might, to see where their story led, fitting things together not by some abstract theory but like a jigsaw puzzle. In this sense, a great Jewish historian remained, *in style*, an Englishman who never left home.

What surfaced from fifty years of working and writing in this vein was an approach to Jewish history with its own delight, precisely because it was so idiosyncratic. If we go in search of Roth himself to get its flavour, we have to come down from the great heights and follow some of his personal – and occasionally quixotic – wanderings in the field, exactly in his own spirit.

·   ·   ·   ·   ·

First, we need to find out what kind of background he had in England, and what kind of Jew this made him. There is an oddity in Anglo-Jewish life which, in the period of his childhood, produced strong *parochial* Jewish feeling without the separation from general society that was the experience of the Jews of Central and Eastern Europe. In the English way, nothing had to be forced into a logically consistent pattern. Roth could feel as English as Scholem felt German, but without worrying about how to reconcile this with his Jewish loyalties. The two went together. His fervour for things Jewish could be fully indulged, yet he expressed it in a manner that was heavily, almost excruciatingly, English. I am thinking particularly of his style as a human being and the kind of subjects outside Jewish history that attracted his interest. On his style, the thousands who heard him lecture on his many tours abroad must have wondered sometimes if they were looking at a renowned Jewish scholar or at a character from one of Evelyn Waugh's novels. His careless lock of hair, his lackadaisical elegance, his air of effortless superiority carried unmistakable overtones of the young men who would wander off to Europe in the eighteenth century on the Grand Tour, returning laden with antiques and other marvels from Italy and Greece; and it was no accident that his most beloved area of interest was, in fact, Italy, and that he amassed, over time, a quite unusual art collection reflecting this interest.

As he had no Yeshivah studies behind him, one wondered, sometimes, where he had acquired the rabbinic knowledge that a Jewish historian is bound to draw on. It seems that his father procured a *melamed* (tutor) for him in London, which must have started him off: but the part of the story which is most thoroughly in keeping with his style is that he was nursed along, while a student at Oxford, by the then Reader in Rabbinics at the university, an orthodox but very much Anglicized scholar called Herbert Loewe, whose grandfather had been Orientalist to the Duke of Sussex and then secretary to Sir Moses Montefiore. Everything that followed was somehow true to these colourful beginnings and the tone they must have inculcated.

One has to spell this out in order to prepare the setting for a drama, highly significant – alas – to our time, in which this devout but sophisticated Jew ran head-on into the devious obscurantism of some of the orthodox rabbis of Bar-Ilan University in Tel Aviv. One has to emphasize that in all Roth's writings there was nothing but the greatest respect for the tradition. He had made a special point of tapping obscure rabbinic works for source material, and had documented the inter-communications of Jewish scholars through the ages as a living chain of the faith. This still leaves, of course, a *theological* problem, which he tackled in the first chapter of his famous work *A Short History of the Jews*. As an ardent traditionalist, he argued there that the archaic picture of Jewish origins as presented in the Bible comes to life for a Jew in the force of his faith, even though the Higher Critics have thrown doubt on the literal story of Jewish origins. Whatever 'really' happened, a Jew can safely take refuge in the living force of the tradition as received.

To fundamentalist rabbis, the sting lay in daring even to *raise* the question of what 'really' happened in the days of Abraham, Isaac and Jacob. Roth was confronted by the rabbis because, after teaching at Oxford for twenty-five years, he had become Professor of History at Bar-Ilan. Within a month of his arrival, an agitated rabbi on the staff circulated a document quoting some isolated phrases *out of context* from the first chapter of the *Short History* to prove that Roth was a heretic whose teaching at the University would corrupt the young. To their credit, the University authorities stood firmly behind Roth in the ensuing witch-hunt: but he had fallen ill, and soon retired from his post. One understands, given these forces in Jewish public life, why Roth felt it pleasanter to plough his own furrow during his long working life. Certainly, it was more entertaining to us as readers, if only for the variety of writings which resulted.

In place of the Yeshivah, which might perhaps have turned him into a fundamentalist, Roth cut his teeth, as a young man, on the study of Italian history. One can see, with hindsight, that this was the real clue to all his later writing, not simply because it led him quickly into Italian *Jewish* history, but because a feeling for colour and excitement that Italy symbolizes permeated his writing forever afterwards.

It became visible immediately in his first book, a product of his graduate research, called *The Last Florentine Republic, 1527–30*. It is a young man's book, immensely romantic for the glories of Florence, in language that the rabbi of Bar-Ilan might not have approved – 'the Campanile, in its ethereal beauty . . . the whole surmounted as with a crown by the majestic cupola of the Duomo'. At this stage, Roth thought to continue as a 'normal' historian. He never tired of telling how it was that he was diverted, by accident (or Providence) into the specialized area he made so much his own.

One of these diversions occurred in Italy itself when, as he described it, some papers fell into his hands, leading back, through typical detective work, to the documentation of the life and times of a hitherto obscure worthy of the eighteenth century – Rabbi Menahem Navarra of Verona. The more obscure, the more Roth loved to dig the person up. As he put it himself in opening this early essay (1925):

> Jewish history . . . has tended to restrict its attention exclusively to the greater personalities . . . Lesser characters have perforce been neglected and with them we have lost that intimate glimpse into the life of ordinary men and women which is one of the most fascinating and certainly not the least important among the multitudinous branches of historical study.

What he could have added later was that studies of this kind – he published scores of them – repaid themselves by a kind of geometric progression in furnishing bits and pieces of all shapes and colours for his historical jigsaw puzzle. It was out of this growing jigsaw that he created his monumental knowledge of the Marranos – the secret Jews of Spain and Portugal. The subject overlapped with two other major works – *The Jews in Italy* and *The Jews in the Renaissance*.

·   ·   ·   ·   ·   ·

But a more entertaining diversion from general history had come even before Rabbi Menahem hove into sight. Roth telling the story frequently, always allowed it to illustrate both his own acumen as a young prodigy (he never suffered from false modesty) and also how, for the first but not the last time, he was ultimately able to prove his theory against the built-in opposition of all the experts. It was a favourite story with him, too, because its ramifications brought in an English king and a pretender to the throne. He always delighted in throwaway observations about how the Royal Family, the aristocracy, the Church, and many others believing themselves beyond range were in fact heavily involved in Jewish connections. And, finally, it was a favourite because the central Jewish character, far from being the good man of Jewish tales, was without doubt a scamp – or adventurer – who had the *chutzpah* of the devil and got away with it.[1]

As Roth told it, the story began for him in 1920 when, as a history student at Oxford, he was struck by the coincidence of names between 'Edward Brandon', a young Portuguese Jew who was an inmate of the *Domus Conversorum* (Converts' Home) in London from 1466 to 1472, and 'Sir Edward Brampton', godson of the king (Edward IV), who held various commands under the Crown from 1472 onward, became Governor of the island of Guernsey, and was somehow involved in the career of Perkin Warbeck, pretender to the English crown in 1497. Roth published a paper in 1922 – his first on Anglo-Jewish history – exploring the possibilities of this identity: but his ideas were received with scepticism by 'the specialist historians'.

Twenty-five years later, with a wealth of expertise now in his hands, new discoveries led him to Portuguese documents which established beyond doubt that he had been right – and much more. The story now emerged that Brandon/Brampton, having started as a penniless Jewish boy from Portugal with the name (assumed) of Duarte Brandao, was welcomed back in 1490 by the King of Portugal, to whom he had in the meantime given many services, as 'a gentleman of the household of the king of England', after which he turned up with one name or the other in England, the Low Countries, and Portugal, expanding his trading franchises, encouraging PerkinWarbeck with reminiscences of his supposed father Edward IV, but ultimately gravitating towards the establishment of an aristocratic base in Portugal, where he died and was entombed with all Christian honours and much flourishing of imaginary coats of arms.

The story had rumbled on through the documents because the descendants of Brandao, in an attempt to get rid of at least *some* of the taint of Jewish blood, had claimed that their noble ancestor was illegitimate! His mother was Jewish, but his father was a Portuguese nobleman. We have learnt to smile at these little ironies, especially when we find the same theme used in reverse by some Spanish historians to prove that Christopher Columbus was not a Genovese Christian but – at least in origin – a Spanish Jew. The idea is that his family had lived in Spain as Marranos and found their way to Genoa in the fifteenth century with other kinsmen. Roth, as the expert on Marranos, wrote an amusing essay to prove that the idea was nonsense.[2] He was always ready to unearth the Jewish origin of famous people, but this was one example he was prepared to forego. He had already shown elsewhere how many *authentic* 'Jewish Contributions' there were to the voyage of the *Santa Maria*.

There was nothing that he liked better than flourishing his technique to startle or titillate the reader. He has an essay on the socio-economic background of sixteenth-century Venice to show that if Shylock was real, he was not a Sephardi, as one might have expected, but an Ashkenazi. In all these essays his implicit approach seems to be: throughout history, most Jews, living quietly within their communities (as in tenth-century Cordova, sixteenth-century Venice or twentieth-century London) led decent, unremarkable lives, which is what the Jewish religion stands for; but at the same time, there was always, at the margin, a fascinating creativity which slots into general history in a host of unpredictable, interesting, and often funny ways. The historian's first object is to document all this. Philosophies of history can be left to other people.

There is, therefore, very little moral fervour in most of Roth's work. Sometimes, it is true, he would launch into a violent attack – *à la* Savonarola – on the low standards of contemporary Jewish life. He saw the decencies he loved—loyalty to tradition, respect for scholarship – neglected or even despised, and it offended him. On the major issues of our time, his response was predictable. Hitlerism outraged him, and when Mussolini joined in it was like a personal blow. He returned all the decorations he had received for his historical work on Italy, though they were given back to him after the war.

In his regular work, however, there is no sense of a grand theme or even much drawing of lessons. He would occasionally try to justify what might seem mere antiquarianism – such as his researches into the tiny field of Anglo-Jewish history – by claiming that it would end up by removing damaging ideas about Jews. It could now be established, for example, that the Jews of mediaeval England, far from being merely 'urban usurers', were very widely settled, with a host of 'ordinary' occupations. One day, perhaps, it would be shown that they constituted 'a large Anglo-Jewish proletariat'! But if he fell into this sometimes, he was more usually content to urge study *lishmah* (for its own sake). It was not the proletariat but the scholars whom he loved, as he showed in a masterly British Academy Paper: 'The Intellectual Activities of Medieval English Jewry' (1949). It could be argued, of course, that in this paper he was not really exulting in the Jewish scholars whom he had tracked down but rather proving that his beloved England was not the intellectual backwater in mediaeval times that 'foreign' Jewish scholars had assumed it to be.

In what must have been one of his last lectures in England – delivered in 1968 – Roth has a disarming passage on his role:

> When people speak of me as a Jewish historian, I know in my heart of hearts that I can speak without fear of contradiction only on the history of the handful of Jews in Oxford (never, I suppose, exceeding if they approached, 200) between approximately 1150 and 1290 A.D. Yet I cannot say that I can speak with confidence. I wish that I knew – really knew – the details of a single day in the life of a single

one of the Jews in Oxford at this period of which I have written so
volubly.   In that case, I would know far more than I do about
social history, legal history, religious history, constitutional history,
administrative history.   Indeed I would know quite a lot and would
perhaps qualify for some of the encomia I have received.   But alas,
I do not.

He was being unduly modest.   It was, in fact, precisely in this
kind of knowledge that he excelled.   One sees it particularly in
the graphic detail he gives, in his book *The Jews in the Renaissance*,
of the activities of Jews in the Renaissance theatre, especially in
Mantua in the sixteenth century.   The whole subject comes alive
not only by his explaining the origins and character of Jewish
theatre in the detailed setting of Mantua, but in the full account he
gives of the actor-producer Leone de Somni, a true Renaissance
man, 'the Max Reinhardt of his time' but so much more – a
Hebrew scholar and poet who could share and intensify the broad
culture into which he had been born.   It is, of course, true that
anything Italian seemed to add an extra dimension to Roth's
writing and enthusiasm.

It is the infectious enthusiasm in Roth's work that is his lasting
contribution to any of us who feel drawn to the study of the
Jewish experience.   Early in life he had ruled out the 'lachrymose' conception of Jewish history.   If one writes (he said in the
lecture mentioned above), 'it is frankly for the pleasure of the
thing ... the pure detective work ... the discovery of historical
byways hitherto unexpected or unexplored, the revealing of
unknown characters and personalities – heroes, scholars, saints,
charlatans, adventurers, scoundrels'.   There are Jewish historians
whose involvement carries with it a would-be sense of destiny.
Roth could say, perhaps tongue in cheek, to explain why he
ploughed this field: 'I commend to the young in heart among you
my ultimate answer: *because it is fun.*'

VI: ENVOI

Joseph

JOSEPH

I HAVE to leave the reader now; but one cannot end a discussion, according to the rabbis, without bringing in something directly related to the Bible: 'if two sit together and do not exchange any words of Torah, it is a meeting of scoffers.'

I must follow instructions, but the prospect need not be too daunting. Torah-talk for the rabbis did not have to be pompous. It could be a combative exchange of verses, a dreamed-up version of a familiar story, or the exploration of a Bible character. Their free-wheeling style was always entertaining, taking in legend, folklore and popular psychology, with no holds barred. They could be brusque in analysing Bible heroes, though they often spoke with tongue in cheek. They needed some light relief, and they had a sense of humour.

In this spirit, let us take a Bible character ourselves, Joseph, since we have already borrowed his coat for our title. We shall try to see what the rabbis made of him, and how some of their rather wry ideas may match our own. We must certainly end with a word of Torah: no scoffers we.

Joseph, in rabbinic hands, was a fertile subject. There are so many twists and turns in his adventures, as described in the Bible, that the opportunities for speculation on what really happened were endless. Nor were the moral problems all that easy.

The rabbis, living with the story, fastened on one fact, as given in the Bible, which they saw as the key to everything – that Joseph, as a young man, was stunningly beautiful. They never forgot this in their embellishment of the story, nor, indeed, did the Arabs, in their version in the Koran and in the romantic fantasies of their story-tellers.

But it seems more surprising for the rabbis. They speculate at one point on the feelings of the brothers, arriving in Egypt hungry and friendless. Their brother Joseph, whom they had sold as a

slave, might be there – to forgive, perhaps to help.   Where to find
him?   And the rabbis tell how the brothers split up to search
among the male brothels, to which his beauty would have con-
signed him.

We are explicitly told of his beauty only once in the Bible,
immediately before the scene in which Potiphar's wife tries to
seduce him.   The Authorized Version describes him as 'a goodly
person and well-favoured'.   The Catholic *Jerusalem Bible* is
better: 'well-built and handsome'.   In the original Hebrew, the
words applied to Joseph – *yepheh to'ar vipheh mareh* – ring a bell
instantly: they are identical with those applied to Rachel, the
mother of Joseph, when Jacob first met her and fell hopelessly in
love.   The *Jerusalem Bible* gives the phrase there in a feminine
version: 'shapely and beautiful'.

It is skilful, but of course the verbal echo has been lost.   However, the idea of the parallel survives.   We have never forgotten
Jacob's passion for the beauty of Rachel.   Joseph had this same
elegance and beauty.   What did it do to him?

For a large part of the story, some of us are not very happy with
the character of Joseph.   At the beginning, as his father's favourite, he is a tale-bearer and prig, boasting to his brothers.   We are
prepared to admire him later for rising to high position so brilliantly in Egypt, but even here there is something dislikeable in the
way he always succeeds.

Even the rabbinical glosses convey it.   How did he manage it,
they ask?   By anticipating every wish of his master.   If Potiphar
wanted a hot drink, Joseph had it ready; a cold drink – it was at
hand.   The perfect servant, but also the perfect Uriah Heep.

The next place disturbs us still more – the tricks he plays on
his brothers, the anguish that he inflicts on them when they are at
his mercy.   It is not really, as he later claims, out of a desire to see
his brother Benjamin: he is just revengeful and spiteful.   Only
at the end does he grow into a character we can fully accept –
benign, rich, generous, bringing his old father and all his family
from *der haim* to settle amid the comfort and plenty of Egypt.

It is surely our ambivalent feeling about Joseph that gives the
story its appeal.   If it were simply a moralist's tale we might think

of him as an innocent overtaken by a malign fate – his brothers'
enmity, the false accusations of Potiphar's wife – and rising above
it all to triumph.

But because it is a truly imaginative story, we never think of
Joseph this way.   He is no innocent: there is a twist of character
in him that attracts punishment.   His supreme self-confidence is
a pose that keeps him going, but, as with the boy in Shakespeare's
sonnet, 'the lovely gaze where every eye doth dwell' can spell a
torment within and around him.

Some of the rabbis of Talmud times – though of course not all–
knew this.   The orthodox view, then as now, was to exclaim at
the perfection of his character.   Like his father Jacob, he was
held to have been a kind of pre-ordained rabbi.   Jacob, it was
said, had managed to transmit to him all the rabbinical ordinances
– about 1500 years before they were framed, of course – and
he practised them faithfully.   His rejection of Potiphar's wife
was the natural action of a man too pure in spirit to hesitate.   His
teasing antics when his brothers arrived in Egypt were simply a
way of ensuring that they were saintly enough to reach his own
high level.

But not all the rabbis thought that Joseph – or even Jacob – was
perfect, and neither do we.   Rabbi Simon ben Lakish put the
blame on Jacob for making one son a favourite.   Rabbi Judah ben
Simon said that it was precisely because of Joseph's tale-bearing
that God had punished him with so many misfortunes, in each
case making the punishment fit the particular slander in which he
had indulged.   Rabbi Levi had the same idea, applying to Joseph
the verse from *Proverbs*: 'I discerned among the youths a young
man void of understanding.'   'How stupid of him to slander his
brothers,' said Rabbi Levi.   'Is there any greater lack of understanding than this!'

Nor were they all so sure, as we were usually taught to be, that
Joseph was cold to the advances of Madame Potiphar.   The
Midrash discusses this rather engagingly, though in a style of
pas devant les enfants.   The tone is set by the *matrona* who asks one

rabbi: 'Is it possible that Joseph, at seventeen, with all the hot blood of youth, could act thus?' The rabbi gives her a pious reply, but his colleague Rabbi Abbahu is not so sure.

It seems to him that one verse of the narrative (*Genesis* 39:19) indicates that they actually went to bed, despite all Joseph's protestations. Rabbi Samuel ben Nahman, commenting: 'The bow was drawn but it relaxed', is impishly graphic. Where guilt, and a fear of discovery, are operating, what was more natural than that Joseph was not equal to the occasion? Rabbi Samuel, however, read the meaning a little differently. For him, Joseph's virtue was saved at the crucial moment only by the direct intervention of Providence.

On this and other incidents the rabbis offer many different interpretations. However, they seem to agree in dwelling on the vanity – and perhaps something more – that flowed from Joseph's beauty. A passage is repeated more than once describing him as 'pencilling his eyes, curling his hair and walking with mincing step'. It is an aspect of the story that Thomas Mann draws on in his own relentless Midrash: *Joseph and His Brethren*. In the opening chapter of the first volume of this novel, one of the brothers – the outspoken Gad – turns on Joseph with a cry that is clearly meant to provide a clue: 'Away with thee, little fop and harlot.'

Almost immediately we are invited to consider the feminizing influence of this unique beauty. To Mann, it was linked for Joseph with his feeling about his circumcision, which, though common enough at the time, had 'a peculiar mystic significance' for their tribe:

> The bond of faith with God was sexual in its nature . . . It inflicted upon the human male a kind of civilising weakening with the female.

And this was especially powerful for a young man whose beauty already embraced 'a consciousness of femininity'.

It is one approach. One might find it more significant if one could believe that Mann's whole attitude to Joseph – an archaic figure drenched in an archaic background – had any chance of coming to life. To most people, the appeal of Joseph is precisely the opposite. For though some of the patriarchs and their wayward children do carry archaic overtones – as in the story of Judah and Tamar, or the massacre of the men of Shechem – Joseph is a completely modern figure. One has seen his story acted out repeatedly in Jewish experience – the boy coming from the ghetto or some other primitive background, rising to immense success in a new world, and leaving clouds of questions as to how it all happened.

Inevitably, I think of America. I seem to have met Joseph a hundred times there – a settled man, secure, apparently untroubled, but harking back in memory to the magic of a childhood where the sense of promise was of an entirely different order. The child was a dreamer, perhaps in a Yeshivah, with ringlets and big brown eyes, or perhaps some other kind of *Wunderkind*, the offspring of some wildly beautiful or intelligent parents. One hears the faint nostalgic story when they reminisce; there is a photograph somewhere.

One knows the beginning; one sees the end. It is the middle period which is mysterious – the years (as one might say) in Potiphar's household, the breaking through to high posts in Pharaoh's government. One assumes a spur of ambition, and can relate it, perhaps, to a sense of selection in childhood. Fate showered some special gift; the recipient feels driven – when it works this way – to prove a continued excellence, overcoming every obstacle.

In such a situation, one cannot take a steady progress up the ladder for granted. Some might accomplish it honourably and peacefully; for others, the conflicts, now over, may have been searing. Externally, the world resents while it admires. Internally, ambition corrupts, calls for guile, leads to guilt. Most particularly this can be so when the early excellence is a wasting asset – as beauty may have been for Joseph. Many a sonnet of Shakespeare hammers away at this, and one has seen its effects in life, turning in some cases into a desperate attempt to compensate, in others – as with Steerforth in *David Copperfield* – into an almost wilful corruption.

Not that a troubled middle period is to be despised: the human spirit is more creative when it is restive. And even if there is a price to pay, the survivor can emerge as the benign patriarch of Goshen, Egypt – or Miami, Florida.

From the resting-point of old age, the childhood traumas can yield to a golden glow, with nostalgia and romance taking over.

In the hands of the old story-tellers, romance seemed, in fact the way to explain the whole story. Not, of course, for the rabbis. As ancestors of Freud, they felt no obligation to soft-pedal the disturbances of growing into manhood. But the Arab and Persian story-tellers had a more comforting touch. If there is to be a happy ending, it has to be through Potiphar's wife, whom they call Zuleika.

For them, she is never simply a temptress, nor Joseph a puritan. After he has risen to power, Joseph (in their story) sees a distraught beggar-woman in the street and is drawn to her. It is Zuleika, fallen on evil days, but still burning with passion for him, as he for her. He rescues her, and they live happily ever after.

I'm sure that the *kinder* and *einiklach* will like this version best, and as this book has been written for them, I had better stop right here.

Perhaps I should just add a word of apology for having detained them so long with my ideas about being a Jew. If they feel that I have still left many questions unanswered, I offer in justification an oft-quoted rabbinic saying from *Ethics of the Fathers*: 'It's not up to you to finish the job, but you are not free to give it up.'

ACKNOWLEDGEMENTS

The approach of this book has taken shape in my mind over a period of years: and I am grateful to the editors of various publications in which some of the ideas received expression, albeit in different form. In particular, I would thank *Commentary* (U.S.A.) for permission to draw on material which has surfaced here to some degree in 'An Englishman Forever', 'Seventy Years On', 'England in Style', 'The Gaon of Vilna', 'Born in Berlin', and 'The Zeppelin' (© 1970, 1972, 1973, 1976, 1977, 1978 by the American Jewish Committee); *Midstream* (U.S.A.) for material in 'A Jew from Pinsk', 'Akiba Recovered' and 'The Raphaels of Vilkomir' (© 1974, 1977, 1978 by the Theodor Herzl Foundation Inc.); *Encounter* (U.K.) and *Commentary* (U.S.A.) for material in 'Jesus'; *Jewish Chronicle* (U.K.) for material in 'Joseph'. I am grateful also for permission to quote from the work of other writers: to Nigel Dennis for lines from his poem 'The Jewish Graveyard in Malta' (*Encounter*, September 1968); to Nathaniel Tarn for lines from his poem 'Simon ben Yohai to the Columns of Light' in *Old Savage/Young City* (© 1964 by Nathaniel Tarn); to Saul Bellow and his British and U.S. publishers for the quotations on page 58 from *Herzog* (© 1961, 1963, 1964 by Saul Bellow) and on pp. 126–7 from *Humboldt's Gift* (© 1973, 1974, 1975 by Saul Bellow); to Chaim Bermant and his British and U.S. publishers for the quotation on page 139 from *The Cousinhood* (© 1971 by Chaim Bermant); to Hamish Hamilton Ltd (U.K.) and Atheneum Press Inc (U.S.A.) for the quotation on page 105 from *A Nation Reborn* by Richard Crossman (London and New York 1960); to the Israel Universities Press and the Oxford University Press for numerous quotations in 'A Jew from Pinsk' from *The Letters and Papers of Chaim Weizmann, Vols. I–VII* (© 1968, 1971, 1972, 1973, 1974, 1975 by Yad Chaim Weizmann); to *Encyclopaedia Judaica* for a number of quotations in 'Seventy Years On' (© 1972 by Keter Publishing House Ltd, Jerusalem); to Gershom Scholem and Schocken Books for the quotations on pp. 200–1 and 203 from *On Jews and Judaism in Crisis* (© 1976 by Schocken Books); I must add a special word of thanks, for encouragement and advice, to Norah Smallwood and Christopher MacLehose of Chatto & Windus, and in New York to Jacob Behrman and Neal Kozodoy.

C.R.

NOTES

The Ancient Memory

1. Yigael Yadin: *Bar-Kokhbah*. London and New York, 1971, p. 15.
2. *The Walls of Jerusalem: An Excursion into Jewish History*, was published in New York and London in 1968. It is currently out of print. Some parts of the Introduction ("A Personal Word") have been drawn on here.

The Gaon of Vilna

1. Shalom Spiegel: *Hebrew Reborn*. New York, 1930, pp. 165–7.
2. Jacob Neusner: *There We Sat Down*. New York, 1972, pp. 72–86.
3. Bernard Weinryb: *The Jews of Poland*. Philadelphia, 1973, p. 264.
4. Gershom Scholem: *Major Trends in Jewish Mysticism*. New York, 1961, p. 344.
5. Gershom Scholem: *The Messianic Idea in Judaism*. New York, 1971, p. 238.
6. See "The Mystic Life of the Vilna Gaon", reference in note 10 below.
7. *Major Trends*, p. 338.
8. *ib.* pp. 325–50 for references to this and the next paragraphs.
9. R. J. Zwi Werblowsky: *Joseph Karo: Lawyer and Mystic*. Oxford, 1962, p. 48.
10. *ib.* Appendix: "The Mystic Life of the Vilna Gaon", p. 307.
11. Jacob Katz: *Out of the Ghetto*. Cambridge, Mass. 1973.
12. *ib.*, p. 124. See whole chapter: "Profile of Emancipated Jewry", pp. 191–219.
13. "Personality of the Gaon and his Historical Influence", in *Zion* (Hebrew), XXXI (1966), pp. 39–86.

A Jew from Pinsk

1. *The Letters and Papers of Chaim Weizmann*. General Editor: Meyer W. Weisgal. Series A, Letters, Vols. I–VII. Israel Universities Press and Oxford University Press, 1968 to 1977.
2. *Encounter*, Nov. 1972, pp. 51–7.
3. Ed: Meyer W. Weisgal and Joel Carmichael: *Chaim Weizmann: A Biography by Several Hands*. London, 1962, p. 6.

4. In conversation with the author, June 1974.

5. "Scientific Research and Social Consciousness" by Ernst Bergmann, in *Chaim Weizmann: Statesman and Scientist*, edited by Meyer W. Weisgal. New York, 1944, pp. 257–64.

6. "Vision and Fantasy" by Aharon Katzir-Katchalsky, in *Chaim Weizmann: A Biography by Several Hands* (see Note 3 above), pp. 126–40.

7. *ib.*

8. The letter (May 6, 1903) begins on p. 301 in Vol. II, and runs for 22 pages.

9. Isaiah Berlin: *Chaim Weizmann*. London, 1958, p. 59.

10. Walter Laqueur: *A History of Zionism*. London and New York, 1973, p. 203.

11. Richard Crossman: *A Nation Reborn*. London, 1960, p. 45.

12. See Note 9 above.

13. Full text in Yiddish and English is given as an Appendix to *A Nation Reborn*. See Note 11 above.

14. Shmarya Levin: *Forward from Exile*. Philadelphia, 1967, p. 264.

Jerusalem U.S.A.

1. The title in the U.K. is *The Immigrant Jews of New York*. London, 1976.

2. Judd Teller: *Strangers and Natives*. New York, 1968, p. 166.

England in Style

1. Stephen Birmingham: *Our Crowd*. New York, 1966.

2. Chaim Bermant: *The Cousinhood*. London and New York, 1971.

3. Many of the Rothschilds had foreign "Baron" titles, but this really didn't count for much in England.

4. *The Memoirs of Israel Sieff*. London, 1970, p. 2.

Seventy Years On

1. *Encyclopaedia Judaica*. Keter Publishing House, Jerusalem, 1972, 16 vols.

Jesus

1. C. H. Dodd: *The Founder of Christianity*. London, 1971.

2. An English version, translated by Herbert Danby, was published in London in 1925.

3. See also his *Jesus and the Zealots* (Manchester, 1967) and *The Trial of Jesus of Nazareth* (London, 1968).
4. Paul Winter: *On the Trial of Jesus*. Berlin, 1961. See also: Joel Carmichael: *The Death of Jesus*, New York, 1966. The trial is examined in great detail in a work by an Israeli Judge who is also an authority on Roman and Rabbinic law: Haim Cohn: *The Trial and Death of Jesus*, London, 1972.
5. Hyam Maccoby: *Revolution in Judaea: Jesus and the Jewish Resistance*. London, 1973. See also a wider-ranging article by Mr Maccoby: "Is the Political Jesus Dead?" in *Encounter*, Feb. 1976.
6. Geza Vermes: *Jesus the Jew – A Historian's Reading of the Gospels*. London, 1973. Dr Vermes mentions in his Preface (p. 10) that he is hoping to publish soon "an enquiry into the genuine teaching of the Master from Galilee – *The Gospel of Jesus the Jew*."
7. David Flusser: *Jesus*. New York, 1969.
8. *Mekhilta*, ed Lauterbach, III, p. 197.

How Faithful?

1. Of the many scholars who criticized the Thirteen Principles, two may be mentioned as substantiating points made in this chapter of the book. Hasdai ibn Crescas (c. 1340–c. 1410) argued in his *Light of God* (1405) that this credo confounds underlying teachings with dogmas, the denial of which does not offend Judaism. Moses Mendelssohn (1729–86) emphasized that the Mosaic law never says 'thou shalt believe' but 'thou shalt do' or 'thou shalt not do'. The subject is discussed conveniently in *Companion to the Prayer Book* by Israel Abrahams, London, Eyre and Spottiswoode, 3rd ed. 1932. Abrahams says (p. civ): 'Judaism, as we should now put it, is a discipline of life rather than a creed.'
2. Arthur Herzberg: *Judaism*. New York, 1962, pp. xiv–xv.
3. Louis Jacobs: *Principles of the Jewish Faith*, London, 1964. See also his later work: *A Jewish Theology*. London, 1973.
4. Introduction to *Studies in Judaism* (First Series), now available in Meridian Books (New York), 1958.
5. David Ben-Gurion: *Ben-Gurion Looks at the Bible*. London, 1972. Chapter One: "Uniqueness and Destiny".
6. *ib.*, pp. 138–164: "The Early History of the Hebrews in Canaan."
7. *The Listener* (BBC). August 26, 1975.
8. "On Becoming a Jew" by Herbert Gold. *Commentary*, March 1972.

9. Arthur A. Cohen: *The Natural and the Supernatural Jew*. New York, 1963.

10. Abraham Heschell: *Kotzker – a Struggle in Integrity*. New York, 1973.

Akiba Recovered

1. Cecil Roth: *A Short History of the Jewish People*. London, 1969 ed., p. 113. Salo W. Baron: *Social and Religious History of the Jews*. New York, 2nd ed. 1952, Vol. II, p. 90.

2. Louis Finkelstein: *Akiba – Scholar, Saint and Martyr*. Philadelphia, 1936, p. 257.

3. S. W. Baron, *op. cit.* II, p. 100.

4. Yaacov Herzog: *A People that Dwells Alone*. London, 1975, p. 170.

5. *Kratkie soobscheniia Narodov Azii*. No. 86, pp. 79–89.

Born in Berlin

1. See above, pp. 78–81. Among Scholem's chief works are *Major Trends in Jewish Mysticism*, *The Messianic Idea in Judaism*, and *Sabbatai Sevi – Mystical Messiah*.

2. For an illuminating discussion of Scholem's friends and the German–Jewish background see "Modernism, the Germans and the Jews" by Robert Alter in *Commentary*, March 1978.

3. Gershom Scholem: *On Jews and Judaism in Crisis*. Edited by Werner J. Dannhauser. New York, 1975.

4. See "Martin Buber's Hasidism" in *Commentary*, Oct. 1961. Reprinted in *The Messianic Idea in Judaism*.

An Englishman Forever

1. Roth told the story in *Essays and Portraits in Anglo-Jewish History*, Philadelphia, 1962, pp. 68–75: "Sir Edward Brampton, alias Duarte Brandao."

2. "Who was Columbus?" in *Personalities and Events in Jewish History*, Philadelphia, 1961, pp. 192–211.

GLOSSARY

Derivations: *Heb.* – Hebrew; *Aram.* – Aramaic; *Yidd.* – Yiddish

Agudah: *Heb.* Federation *(Agudat Israel)* of extremely orthodox Jews, originally anti-Zionist.

Allevei!: 'If only!' *Aram*, carried into *Yidd.*, from a root meaning 'woe'.

Ashkenazi: Jew of N. or E. European origin. *Ashkenaz*, a foreign land in the Bible, was applied to Germany from the 9th c.

Baal-Shem: *Heb.* 'Master of the (Divine) Name'. A man with quasi-magic powers.

Bar-Mitzvah: *Aram./Heb.*: 'Son of (i.e. subject to) the Commandments.' A boy from 13 years on.

Beit-Midrash: *Heb./Aram.* 'Study house' and informal synagogue.

Borsht: *Russian:* Beetroot soup. Favourite Jewish dish.

Bundist: 'The Bund' (founded 1897) was a Yiddishist and anti-Zionist federation of Jewish socialists in E. Europe.

Chazan: 'Synagogue cantor': Talmud word, 'supervisor', from *Heb.* root: 'to see'.

Cholent: *Yidd.* 'stew', kept hot over the Sabbath. Derivation unknown.

Chutzpah: *Yidd.* 'insolence': from *Aram.*, Chatzif, 'impudent'.

Cossack: *Yidd.* slang for any mounted police or soldiers, assumed hostile.

Der Haim: *Yidd.* 'Home'; nostalgic term for E. Europe.

D'rash: *Aram.* 'exposition' of Bible verse; as in *Midrash*.

Einiklach: *Yidd.* 'grandchildren'. From German, 'enkel'.

Galuth: *Heb.* 'exile', 'dispersion' (Diaspora).

Gaon: Title of honour. *Heb.* 'pride', 'excellence'.

Gefillte fish: Fish cakes, traditionally from lake or river fish as found in E. Europe.

Ger Zedek: *Heb.* Righteous non-Jew.

Ghetto: Jewish quarter of town. Name derived from area around a foundry *(ghetto)* in Venice in which Jews were segregated in 1517.

Goy: *Heb.* 'Non-Jew'.

Haggadah: *Heb.* Moralistic or anecdotal interpretation of Holy Writ. Specifically, the *Passover H.*, recited at home. *See* Seder.

Halakhah: *Heb.* Legal interpretation of HolyWrit.

Hasidism: From *Heb. hasid*, 'pious one'. Movement expressing ecstatic form of worship.

Haskalah: Jewish Enlightenment movement. From *Heb. sekhel*, 'mind'.

In shul arein!: *Yidd.* 'Come to synagogue'.

Kabbalah: Mystical lore, studied by initiates: *Heb.:* 'tradition'.

Kaddish: From *Heb.* word for 'holy'. Magnificat recited in synagogue, usually in pious memory of a parent.

Kahal: *Heb.* 'community'. Specifically, autonomous communities in E. Europe.

Kavanah: *Heb.* Intense devotion during prayer.

Kedushah: *Heb.* (see Kaddish): an invocation of God's holiness during prayers.

Kinder: *Germ./Yidd.:* 'children'.

K'lal Yisrael: *Heb.* The Jewish people as a whole.

Kosher: *Heb.* 'fitting, correct'. Specifically, food meeting dietary laws.

Landsman: *Germ./Yidd.* 'Home-towner'.

Le-chaim!: *Heb.* 'To life!' (toast).

Litvak: Jew from Lithuania.

Ma'ariv: Evening service (*Heb. erev*, 'evening').

Maggid: *Heb.* 'preacher'.

Melamid: *Heb.* 'teacher'.

Midrash: *Heb.* Homiletical exposition of HolyWrit.

Minchah: *Heb.* 'gift', 'sacrifice'. Afternoon prayers, recalling Temple ritual.

Minyan: *Heb.* 'number'. Quorum of ten for full synagogue service.

Miqveh: A bath for ritual immersion. *Heb.* 'reservoir'.

Mitnagged: *Heb.* neologism: 'opposer', specifically of Hasidism.

Mizrahi: Religious Zionists. From *Heb. mizrah*, 'East', i.e. looking towards Jerusalem.

N'div: *Heb./Yidd.* 'prince' – rich man.

Pale, The: Provinces of Czarist Russia (Poland, Lithuania, etc.) to which Jews were normally restricted, from 1791.

Pe'os: *Yidd.* Ringlets worn by pious Jews. From *Heb.* 'corners', as in *Lev.* 19:27: 'thou shalt not mar the corners of thy beard'.

P'gam: *Aram.* 'fault', e.g. a nick on knife-blade.

Pilpul: *Aram.* 'dialectic argument'.

Polack: Jew from Poland.

P'shat: *Aram*. 'straight explanation' (of HolyWrit).

Rashi: Commentary on Bible and Talmud by 11th c. French rabbi; acronym of name: Rabbi Shlomo Yitzhaki.

Responsa:Written replies by distinguished rabbis during last thousand years to questions on legal, social and moral issues. A vast historical archive.

Rosh Hashanah: *Heb*. 'New Year'.

Schlemiel: *Yidd*. 'simpleton': derivation unknown.

Schmaltz: *Yidd*. oily style, from Germ. 'grease'.

Seder: Service at home on Passover Eve. *Heb*. 'order' (of service).

Sephardi: *Sepharad*, area outside Palestine in Bible, applied to Spain in Middle Ages. Hence *Sephardi* – Jew from Iberian Peninsula.

Shabbos: *Heb*. 'sabbath'.

Shammus: *Yidd*. 'beadle', from *Aram. shammash*, 'administrator'.

Shechinah: *Aram*. 'Divine Presence'. Cf. *Heb. mishcan* – 'tabernacle'.

Sheheheyanu: *Heb*. '(God) who has kept us alive': key word of familiar blessing.

Shema: First word of famed Hebrew doxology: 'Hear O Israel' (*Deut*. 5:1).

Shtetl: *Yidd*. (from Germ.): small town or settlement in E. Europe.

Shochet: *Heb*. 'slaughterer' of animal in prescribed form.

Shul: *Yidd*. 'synagogue', *lit*. 'school', where children taught Bible.

Shulhan Arukh: Name of famed Jewish Code, 1564, *lit*. 'prepared table'.

Talmud: Compendium of Jewish law and argument, compiled over first 5 centuries A.D.

Torah: *Heb*. 'teaching'. The Bible, or more specifically the Pentateuch.

Tzaddik: *Heb*. 'righteous man'. Specifically, a Hasidic master.

Tzimmas: *Yidd*. stew of vegetables and fruit.

Yeshivah: 'academy' (Talm. word from *Heb*. 'settlement').

Yeshivah bochur: 'young student' (*Heb*. 'lad') at Yeshivah.

Yichuss: *Aram./Yidd*. 'genealogy'.

Yidden: 'Jews'. Term used affectionately.

Yiddishkeit: *Yidd*. Informal code of Jewish faith and behaviour.

Yigdal: Name (first word) of Sabbath hymn (*Heb*.).

Yishuv: *Heb*. 'settlement': specifically, colonization of Holy Land.

Zohar: Mystical work, composed or edited in Spain, 13th c.

INDEX

[*Dates are included only when they may be of special interest as points of reference*]